A Collection of

RANTER WRITINGS
from the 17th Century

A Collection of

RANTER WRITINGS
from the 17th Century

Edited by Nigel Smith
Foreword by John Carey

JUNCTION BOOKS LONDON

First published in Great Britain by
Junction Books Ltd
15 St John's Hill
London SW11

ISBN 0 86245 100 0 (hard)
    0 86245 101 9 (paper)

Printed and bound in Great Britain by
Biddles Ltd, Guildford and King's Lynn

Contents

Foreword

Why read the Ranters? Two different kinds of answer could be given to that question, depending on whether your main interest is in English history or English literature. (A third kind of answer would apply if your main concern were the development of English Christianity – but then you would inevitably be interested in both literature and history as well.)

The historian's answers are the most obvious. The surviving Ranter writings tell us things we could not otherwise know about how the English imagination – or some English imaginations – structured the world, politically and metaphysically, in the critical years of the mid seventeenth century, about the extremes of English Antinomianism and millenarianism, and about their possible connections with the reaction to social injustice (specifically in the period following the suppression of the Levellers, when the hopes of those capable of advanced social thinking seemed finally to be deprived of any practical outcome).

The historian is also likely to be intrigued by authority's antagonism to the Ranters, and by the persecution to which, with the convenient warrant of religious orthodoxy, they were subjected. Are we to read this as an index of the danger the Ranters were believed to represent, and hence as an intimation that their ideas and attitudes were not, as the governing class successfully made it appear, monstrous and eccentric, but typical of a fairly widespread scepticism among the common people?

That we do not know more about such issues, and about the Ranters themselves, testifies to the success of official censorship and intimidation. One of the most difficult and challenging aspects of Ranter study is the disentangling of what these remarkable individuals actually thought and felt, not only from the misrepresentations of their enemies, but also from the confusion of their own writing. This confusion can probably be attributed at times to hopes of evading the attention of the censor. But at a deeper level it sprang from the newness and strangeness of their intellectual and spiritual enterprise, which (though certainly some parallels can be found in the writings of earlier visionaries) lacked any conventional forms and any inherited language that could adequately encompass it.

This brings us to the literary significance of the Ranters – or rather to the question of whether they have any at all; for a certain kind of literary sensibility would find it hard to concede that they have. From traditional histories of English literature, and even from more specialised accounts of seventeenth-century English prose, they have been wholly excluded. No mention will be found of Coppe, of Clarkson, of Salmon, or of Bauthumley in Douglas Bush's *Oxford History of English Literature in the Earlier Seventeenth Century*, even in its revised edition (1962); nor do they appear in the *Cambridge History of English Literature*. Their rediscovery has been the work of historians, notably Christopher Hill, who has the advantage of being a historian who understands literature and has earned the confidence of literary critics. Hill's *The World Turned Upside Down* (1972), and most recently his 1982 Bateson Lecture (printed in *Essays in Criticism*, Vol. XXXII, April 1982), have made it clear that assessments of seventeenth-century literature can no longer ignore the Ranters.

But what kind of literature did the Ranters produce? How can we accommodate their writings within our notions of what literature constitutes, and the pleasures it provides? Sometimes, of course, this presents no difficulty: a work such as Bauthumley's *The Light and Dark Sides of God* is immediately recognisable as a neglected masterpiece of seventeenth-century devotional prose. But more often it is the very difficulty of answering these questions that forces us to acknowledge the importance of the Ranters. Their failure to fit into our accepted categories confirms our need to revise those categories. For it is clear that Ranter writing is more serious, engaged and impassioned and, from the viewpoint of expression, more adventurous, than any of the conventionally accredited 'literature' that emanated from the Civil War years (than, say, the Cavalier lyrics, which students are still encouraged to think of as one of the war's chief cultural achievements). Intensity is the vital factor in Ranter prose, and this intensity not only precludes routine modes of expression, it also impels the Ranters towards, or beyond, the limits of coherence. Yet paradoxically, though it is destructive in this sense of literary effect, it obliges us to widen our concept of literature in order to embrace it – for an idea of literature that could not find a place for such intensity would be unduly shrunken and enfeebled.

The charge of madness, which some critics have used as an expedient for dismissing the Ranters, cannot be taken seriously. For even if insanity and literary significance were obviously incompatible, which they are not, it would still remain true that what the modern mind diagnoses as mental unbalance in the Ranters was common among seventeenth-century Christians. In the tradition of the spiritual autobiography, to which Ranter prose partly belongs, accounts of visions and paranormal revelations are frequent, as Owen Watkins's survey of the genre, *The Puritan Experience* (1972), shows. When Bunyan in *Grace Abounding* tells us how he fled from a church steeple, lest God should topple it upon his head as a punishment for his delight in bell-ringing, we may find it painfully deluded, but only ignorance of history will allow us to pronounce it mad.

Besides, though Ranter beliefs may seem initially surprising, we can identify features in them that relate them to other and potent areas of our literary experience. The godhead of man, as promulgated by the Ranters, is one of the dynamic ideas behind Traherne's *Centuries of Meditation*, though Traherne derived it from the writings of Alexandrian neo-Platonists. The question of God's putative responsibility for evil exercised many minds in the seventeenth century, including Milton's, and is the central issue in *Paradise Lost*. As a historical phenomenon Ranterism seems to have notable affinities with Romanticism. Both coincided with revolutionary political upheavals; both replace authority, and outmoded academicism, with personal illumination; both develop pantheism; both demand a new and compassionate attention to the outcast and oppressed – beggars, rogues, thieves – and both couple this with antagonism towards the great ones of the earth. Both are combatively irrational and anti-intellectual movements, and seek unorthodox means of expression – so that, for example, Blake's prophetic books are, like Ranter utterances, difficult to contain within usual notions of the literary or the intelligible.

Reading the Ranters also brings vividly to mind the pronouncements of a late Romantic, D.H. Lawrence. The sense of a new age, released from old bondages, the shameless celebration of sexuality, the trust in impulse and instinct, and the belief that any act may be good if it is done with passion and conviction, however it may square with the moral codes of the tame and the law-abiding – these are common properties in Lawrence and the Ranters, and in the twentieth century, as in the seventeenth, they have seemed life-affirming to some and hideous to others, and have attracted persecution and censorship.

Some aspects of Ranter thought, such as the rejection of the literal truth of the Bible, disbelief in the actuality of heaven and hell, and incredulity about personal immortality, may strike us as singularly modern. But ultimately the justification for reading Ranter literature (as for reading any literature from the past) must be that it can widen our understanding of human potential by showing us what it was like to be alive in another age. At times Ranter literature can do this more fully, and more startlingly, than any other literary artefacts that have survived from the mid seventeenth century. As an example, we might cite Abiezer Coppe's encounter with the beggar in his *A Fiery Flying Roll* (see pp. 101–3). Christopher Hill calls this 'experimental prose', which is surely right, in that Coppe has found a medium that conveys with unprecedented dramatic force the simultaneous pressure of internal and external stimuli. The raw poetic power of the passage derives from the way in which it brings the ungainly splendour of its Biblical echoes into conjunction with the mundane (as in 'And behold, the plague of God fell into my pocket'). This conjunction is not, as it at first seems, merely artless and intemperate. Rather, it is a stylistic correlative to the situation which the Ranters postulate. For it is Coppe's contention that you are in heaven, or hell, on earth. This apparently squalid little encounter is a focus for mighty influences. It is not a moral incident, nor a psychological one (a conflict, as a post-Freudian might see it, between the ego and the superego): rather it is, in Coppe's eyes, as spiritual as a Bible narrative, and his style signals this. Where else, we may ask, in mid-seventeenth-century literature could we find a piece of writing which so aggressively conveys the dominance of the inner world over the outer, which simultaneously enacts and analyses a vivid and recognisable psychological situation, and which also exhibits such practical compassion?

A knowledge of Ranter literature which, for these various reasons, seems desirable, is difficult to acquire. Ranter tracts are among the rarest of rare books. Even a great library like the Bodleian lacks copies of several of the texts Nigel Smith presents here. In these circumstances his collection is extremely opportune.

John Carey

Preface

Many books on seventeenth-century literature, culture and society mention the Ranters, often as the absolute end to which liberty of belief could go, but often in elusive, ill-defined terms. This edition makes available, for the first time, all of the major Ranter pamphlets and several other relevant writings by Ranters. A sizeable appendix, containing extracts from Ranter tracts, was attached to Norman Cohn's very successful *The Pursuit of the Millennium* (1957), while The Rota, at the University of Exeter, has published facsimile reprints of Coppe's *A Fiery Flying Roll* and Clarkson's *The Lost Sheep Found*. I hope that this edition enables the Ranters to speak for themselves, with their characteristic variety of expression, in one accessible volume.

Ranterism was usually one phase which religious radicals passed through during a career embracing many different opinions. There simply has not been room to include all of the works written by each Ranter. Only those works which display Ranter tenets, or are closely associated with them, or which were published during the height of Ranter activity, have been included. All of Coppe's writings between 1648 and 1651 are here, as they show the complex continuity and rapid development of his version of Ranterism. From *The Lost Sheep Found*, the section dealing with Clarkson's career as a Ranter and the important changes of direction which he made just before and afterwards, are printed. The Introduction includes accounts of and quotations from those works not included, as well as attempting to provide a pertinent critical and historical context for the reader. The notes are intended to identify individuals, events and places mentioned in the text, and to locate citations. The doctrines and ideas in the pamphlets are explained in the Introduction.

No Ranter pamphlets went beyond a first edition, except for *A Rout, A Rout*, which ran to a second edition in the year of its publication, 1649. This, however, did not differ substantively from the first. I have used square brackets for editorial emendations. Since Ranter language is so heavily dependent upon the Bible, there is insufficient space to identify every source. Italicised citations are identified, where the author has not done so. Where Biblical references inside square brackets have threatened to break up the continuity of a passage, the references appear in the notes. Otherwise the original spelling, italicisation and punctuation remain, and it should be remembered that 'then' was used for 'than' in the seventeenth century.

Three historical studies concerned with the Ranters have been published in the last fifteen years. Two of these, by A.L. Morton and Christopher Hill, are readily available. This edition is intended as a complement to them, and to the expanding literature on dissent and nonconformity. I make absolutely no claim to originality for most of the first part of the Introduction: it is indebted to the work of Hill, Morton and Frank MacGregor. My own interest is with language, and my conviction is that Ranter pamphlets constitute a peculiar stylistic performance, based upon a type of rewriting of the Bible, certain types of allegorisation, and a unique awareness of the politics of their own writing. They represent a mystical strain of writing which, though related to, is quite distinct from the main Platonic tradition.

The Ranters, along with the other radical sects, were rediscovered by historians in the late nineteenth and early twentieth centuries, and they have gained much popularity by being acclaimed as prototypes of the socialist movement. Critics of this view assert that it is anachronistic, and elevates the sects above their contemporary importance. However, the danger of this response is that the sects may be forgotten altogether. History, in any form, is a continuing debate, in which truths are established only through the constant resurveying, recomparison, and reinterpretation of evidence. The literary qualities of sectarian discourse are only coming to light now, and I hope that this edition encourages the modern editing of more sectarian literature.

The transcripts for this edition were made in the Bodleian Library, Oxford, and the British Library, and I would like to acknowledge the facilities of these libraries. Coppe's letter appears by permission of the Librarian and Provost of Worcester College, Oxford, and I would like to thank Leslie Montgomery and Mr L.E. Weeks at Worcester for their attention. Gratitude should also go to Christopher Hill and John Carey for advice, kind help and encouragement. I am very grateful to John Barton for translating Hebrew vocabulary. Michael Mason and Judy Bennett have proved sympathetic and perceptive editors, and Sally Mapstone has helped with transcriptions, as well as providing many editorial and general suggestions.

Introduction

I

The Ranters were a group of religious libertarians who flourished in the three years following the execution of Charles I in January 1649. They represented one extreme response to the religious and social problems which had come to a head in the conflict between King and Parliament in the 1640s. Ranters believed that God dwelt inside them, as an inner light whose authority was above all laws. Salvation existed here on earth, and any act was justifiable so long as it was performed under the working of the spirit. Sin was thus made to disappear. The consequence was, for some Ranters, sexual licence, and for others, blasphemy and swearing. The Ranters did not call themselves so, and the term itself, in its variant forms, 'Rantipoler', 'Rantizer', 'Rantism', was loosely applied to anyone of extreme opinions. There is further confusion in that some of the Ranters' expectations and expressions were shared by other radical and religious groups of the period. Nevertheless, it seems that there was an identifiable body of individuals between 1649 and 1651 which was subject to a thorough persecution by the government. The breakdown of royal authority at the start of the 1640s, especially the collapse of the censorship, resulted in an enormous intensification of radical Puritan activity, and it has become customary to think of the Civil War and Interregnum years giving rise to a milieu in which a heightened popular consciousness became aware of many different religious and political ideas and practices. It was this milieu which spawned Ranterism, and through which the Ranter spokesmen, Coppe, Clarkson, Salmon and Bauthumley passed, on their way to their own millennial and egalitarian solutions.

The victory which the Parliamentary forces had secured by 1648 did not satisfy all of its supporters. No small degree of religious toleration was established, and the continuity of all but the most extreme Puritan sects seemed assured in the early years of the Commonwealth. However, in London and the New Model Army in particular, interests arose demanding more than the Parliamentary gentry were prepared to give. The Levellers called for legal reforms and a considerable extension of the franchise, while Gerrard Winstanley and his True Levellers, or Diggers, cultivated common land in Surrey as a commune so that all might share God's bounty equally. It was in the aftermath of the brutal defeat of the Leveller movement that the Ranters acquired their notoriety. This was also a period of some economic hardship, and it appears that Ranterism appealed to a distressed, subjected urban artisan class. Their use of ritual and narcotics might therefore be seen as a form of social escape. Indeed, the Ranters possessed no organisation or programme as such, and a careful distinction must be made between the many people who were arrested in taverns as Ranters, then released immediately on a promise of good behaviour, and the Ranter prophets who published and were felt to be far more dangerous, as well as more sophisticated. For the Ranter, Christ had returned to inspire man directly through the spirit within. This attitude did lead to striking social outrage, but its spiritual aspect afforded the potential for quietism. Many Ranters turned to the spiritual withdrawal offered by some Quakers and other groups as the 1650s progressed.

To read the Ranter pamphlets is a very exciting experience. Ranter style, different for each writer, is continuous with the ideas and practices of the movement. The pamphlets reveal a deeply expressive language, a performance which attempts to render the inner light in words. Here, words become not only the means of representing a divine truth, but the initial key to that understanding, and more pressingly, a tool in the struggle to maintain a separatist identity. The result is an imagistic panorama, which, though rooted heavily in the Bible, elevates the experiential above the horizon of the scriptures. This is one form of the personalised discourse with which we associate Bunyan. There is also a mystical strain in Ranter writings akin to the sublime style and sources of other extreme Puritans, and it is here that the experiential, the social and the theological meet. The peculiar development of the Ranter prophetic voice is typified not only by its enunciation of a form of divine poetry, but also by its sensitivity to the threat of severe and violent repression which threatened the Ranters. The Ranters had distinct ideas upon the nature and proper use of language, and they attempted to escape from verbal forms and rhetorical conventions which they identified with the unenlightened. Since this escape was necessarily compromised, the inspired quality of Ranter discourse is finally coupled with an embarrassment concerning formal aspects of its expression, for these are associated with the hierarchy reacted against. It is in such frustration that the anti-rationalism of the Ranters becomes located, in the most complex and residual manner.

II

The Ranters believed that Christ's atonement on behalf of mankind, as witnessed in the Gospels, was sufficient to save all, so that man lived on earth in a state of grace. This is known as the Antinomian heresy, where such 'free grace' is asserted over and against the Law of Moses embodied in the Ten Commandments. There were many Antinomians during the middle years of seventeenth-century England, and the heresy's assurance of election acted as an antidote to the harsh strictures of Calvinism, which emphasised salvation through predestination, making eventual grace beyond the control of the individual. Nevertheless, Antinomianism was an ultimate extension of Luther's justification by faith, and the first modern Antinomian was Luther's follower, Johannes Agricola.

English Puritanism itself came to place an emphasis upon the immanence of Christ in the hearts of all believers. This was so in the enormously popular sermons of the Puritan patriarch, Richard Sibbes. The first Antinomian statement in England, though, came with John Eaton's distinction between Gospel and Law in *The Honey-Combe of Free Justification* (1643). Tobias Crisp went somewhat further, and though anxious to avoid the charge of Antinomianism because he foresaw the claims it made against the social order, his insistence upon free grace is unremitting,

> So, beloved, your hearts are dry things, there is no sap, no moisture, no life in them. Christ must first be poured in, before you can get any thing out. Wherefore then stand you labouring and lugging in vain? Oh stay no longer, goe to Christ; It is he that must break thy rocky heart before the plough can come over it, or at least enter into it. As I told you before, so I tell you again, you must consider Christ as freely given unto you by the Father, even before you can believe.[1]

Significantly, both Eaton and Crisp were published posthumously, while Archbishop Laud's inquisition clamped down hard on cases of popular Antinomianism in the 1630s. Other Antinomians included Roger Brarley, the 'Grindletonian', and John Webster. The tendency passed into the army to John Saltmarsh, William Dell and Henry Denne. The great majority of Antinomians did not take the doctrine to its extreme. Most were Independents, more interested in questioning church covenants and ordinances, as well as universal salvationists, like Paul Hobson and Thomas Lamb, and Seekers, like William Erbury, who concentrated upon experiencing the inner revelation. It was in the Ranters that critics of Antinomianism were able to see their fears of individual licentiousness, of moral and social anarchy, fulfilled, 'in our outward dancing and sporting, there thou kissest us and there thou dandlest us on thy knees. When we go in to a Whore-house we meet thee'.[2]

The Ranters were millenarians in the sense that they believed that Christ would return to earth to rule a kingdom of perfect saints, and they held that this would occur in a violent apocalypse in which all would be reduced to a 'base' material and spiritual level. The prediction of the second coming of Christ had been appropriated for the Reformation by several divines in the sixteenth century including John Alsted and Henry Mede. Precise dates were given, as opposed to Augustine's metaphorical interpretation of Revelation, which had indefinitely postponed the return. In the seventeenth century, millenarianism intensified as the events of the 1640s and the upheavals in Europe convinced many that the millennium was imminent. Many shared Joseph Salmon's view that the New Model was God's first instrument in bringing on the Last Days (p. 193). Generally millenarians, like the Fifth Monarchist Sect of the later 1650s, assumed that Christ would appear again in his bodily form, but the Ranters believed that Christ would return in the spirit, and that the inspiration which they felt was the first manifestation of the new age. Eventually, the spirit would return to live in all mankind, destroying all earthly institutions and material possessions, so that man would live by direct inspiration of God.

Most millenarians believed that Christ's kingdom would last for one thousand years, after which the Last Judgement would be made. Again, the final day of reckoning was denied by the Ranters. Instead their eschatology was rooted in the projection of the twelfth-century thinker, Joachim of Fiore, who saw history in three stages. Firstly, there was the Age or Dispensation of the Father, recorded in the Old Testament, which was succeeded by the Age of the Son, related in the New Testament, and finally the third Age of the Spirit, in which perfection would be reached on earth by man. Joachism occurred in the thought of many Puritan sectarians, including the army chaplain John Saltmarsh, Erbury, Winstanley and Laurence Muggleton, who founded his own clandestine sect dedicated to experiencing and prophesying the dawning of the third and final Dispensation. It was in the Ranters, however, that the claims for inspiration were most flamboyantly presented. There were other prophet figures working under divine inspiration, the most akin to Ranter expression being the Welsh poet, Morgan Llwyd. There were also those who claimed to be the risen Christ, like John Robins and William Franklin with his Mary Magdalene, Mary Gadbury. However, these latter two men did not articulate their beliefs in writing, and made no attempt to explore the ramifications of their ecstasy beyond a simple assertion of their privileged status.

III

Separatist religious activity, that is, activity outside the Established Church, had been known in England since the Lollards of the fourteenth century, and commentators in the late sixteenth and early seventeenth centuries warned of the threat to order posed by pre-Civil War sects like the Brownists and Familists. The onset of toleration permitted what had previously been underground to flourish in the open. Apart from the staunch Calvinism exhibited in the Presbyterian Church, there lay to the 'left' of this mainstream several alternatives. Independency was the next stop, followed by the Baptist congregations, featuring rebaptism, 'dipping', for members. It was from the Baptist movement that most of the Ranters came, though they had usually experienced every form of religion, including Anglicanism, genuinely seeking the most personally satisfying belief. The extent and variety of sectarian opinion is most famously recorded in Thomas Edwards's *Gangraena* (1646), which, if exaggerated, provides much evidence for the 1640s. Separatism may be associated with particular areas, and the continuity between Lollard and later sectarian occurrence is remarkable in Coventry, Kent and East Anglia. Coventry happened to be where the Ranters made their greatest mark, though it was only events in London which stirred the Rump Parliament into action, and reports of Ranters came from East Anglia, the Midlands, Wiltshire and, more dubiously, Yorkshire.

Edwards detected the first man to engage in Ranter activity at least three years before the main outbreak. Thomas Webbe, a Baptist preacher, appeared before the Westminster Assembly on the charge of professing Christ to be formed inside man, and that the deity was limited with humanity.[3] He toured Sussex and Essex, to be ejected eventually from a living at Milton, Kent for seditious preaching. Then Webbe acquired the living of Langley Burrell in Wiltshire, where he gathered together a community which practised sexually licentious rites, featuring music and dancing, under the alleged dictum 'there's no heaven but women, nor no hell save marriage'.[4] Webbe defended himself against *Gangraena* in his *Mr. Edwards Pen No Slander* (1646), which reveals little about his activities, but Webbe, who was pro-Leveller, was tried in 1650 under the Adultery Act of May that year. He was acquitted, but was finally ejected by the Committee for Plundered Ministers in September.

Abiezer Coppe, perhaps the most notorious Ranter, was born at Warwick in 1619. He went up to Oxford, where he showed Presbyterian leanings, and left without a degree at the beginning of the war. Anthony Wood provides some colourful anecdotes concerning Coppe's career as a seducer, but the first reliable account we have of Coppe after Oxford is provided by Richard Baxter.[5] By 1646, Coppe had turned Baptist and was preacher to an army garrison at Compton House in Warwickshire. It seems that Coppe had a sizeable following with many converts in Warwickshire, Oxfordshire and Berkshire. He was capable of 'admirable good oratory', and recommended the necessity of rebaptism and of reproaching the ministry in defiance of ordinances. During the next two years he met Richard Coppin, whose influence set Coppe on the road to his eventual Antinomian stance. Coppin was often confused with the Ranters because he knew many of them, and because his Antinomianism was of the egalitarian variety. Though he was imprisoned in 1655, he took no part in the most demonstrative Ranter activities.

In 1648, Coppe provided the preface to the anti-clerical *John the Divine's Divinity*, and a year later, another preface for Coppin's *Divine Teachings*. The latter is important for its 'hieroglyphical' representation of the Trinity as a unity, which establishes the symbolic code elaborated in Coppe's later works. 1649 also saw the publication of *Some Sweet Sips, of some Spiritual Wine*, as fiercely critical of formalised religion as the two prefaces, and excitedly Antinomian, but also stressing the sublimity of God in man and in nature. It is Coppe's first deeply pantheistic statement. The pamphlet seems to have circulated mainly in the Midlands: George Thomason did not acquire it for the collection he was building up in London, while John Osborn, an Oxfordshire minister, cited it in 1651 as one of the most dangerous exponents of 'sensual liberty'.[6]

Some time towards the end of 1649, Coppe experienced his true awakening (p. 82) when, in Baxter's words, 'God gave him over to a spirit of delusion that he fell into a Trance, and professeth himself that he contrived it three or four dayes, *that he fell into it*, and that he was in Hell'.[7] This was an extreme form of melancholy which Baxter felt was 'worse than mad in his delusion'. But Coppe's subsequent recourse to swearing, the claimed language of God in him, attracted some support, and received printed expression in late 1649 with the publication of *A Fiery Flying Roll*, bound together with *A Second Fiery Flying Roule*, so adding a crushing denunciation of the rich to Coppe's apocalyptic hopes. Parliament was sufficiently worried to respond with an order condemning the *Roll's* 'horrid blasphemies, and damnable and detestable opinions', and authorising the collection and burning of all the copies of the tract, while those responsible for it were to be investigated. The broadsheet carrying the order is dated 1 February 1650, but Coppe himself had already been arrested in Warwick early in January, and transferred to Coventry gaol on the 10th.[8]

During the second week of March, Joseph Salmon arrived in Coventry with the intention of visiting the imprisoned Coppe. Salmon had been in the army and had preached in London. His first pamphlet, *Anti-Christ in Man* (1647), was written from a Seeker position though it looks forward to the birth of the spirit in man,

This Mother of Harlots, thy fleshly wisdom wil propose herself to be all to thee, that so She may draw thy affections after her; Shee will tell thee that she can supply all thy wants and relieve all thy necessities, and therefore thou needst not to be beholden to God for any thing, She will tell thee with Adam, that She can give thee the knowledge of good and evill; and she can open thy eyes, and She it is that gives thee any thing.[9]

This type of allegory, structured around the Three Dispensations, and applied to the events of the 1640s, the war and the execution of the King, formed Salmon's next work, *A Rout, A Rout*, of February 1649. Soon after this Salmon embraced Ranterism fully, 'His Hour spent with us to the admiration of Honest Men, ... but soone after found a disciple in Coppe ... and heard him swear many sad oaths'.[10] Salmon seems to have known most of the figures in the Ranter milieu, not only Coppe and Wyke, but also Coppin, possibly Bauthumley, and certainly Webbe, with whom he corresponded (p. 20). Salmon began to preach in Coventry, and Bulstrode Whitelock reports of his 'wicked Swearing, and uncleaness, which he justified and others of his way, *That it was God which did swear in them, and that it was their Liberty to keep company with Women, for their Lust*'.[11] Arrest for Salmon followed quickly.

Nevertheless, another Ranter arrived to preach. This was Andrew Wyke, who had come with his mistress, Mrs Wallis. Wyke came from Colchester, where he had been active, according to *Gangraena*, as a preacher and a dipper, refusing to answer questions put by the Assembly of Divines in 1646. Wyke was held in custody, during which time he is reported to have written his first work, *The Innocent in Prison Complaining*, though this does not seem to have survived.[12] Wyke's behaviour in Coventry was as astonishing as Salmon's, as he 'kissed a Souldier three times, and said, *I breath the Spirit of God into thee*, and many the like abominable Blasphemies'.[13] Wyke was attempting to leave Coventry when he was arrested and imprisoned with the others, though both he and Salmon were able to attract a considerable audience by preaching through the grates of the prison on Sundays.[14]

Salmon and Wyke were originally fined two shillings each for common blasphemy by Coventry Corporation, but their connection with Coppe caused their cases to be referred to London. In goal, Wyke wrote letters protesting against his imprisonment. Salmon also wrote to friends outside, and he later claimed to have produced *Divinity Anatomized*, his most Ranter-like pamphlet, whilst still locked up (p. 218). Like Coppe, he was prepared to make a protest of belief even in captivity.

The government was not particularly worried by the events in a provincial city, but it was concerned when it became apparent that Ranters were active in the capital. Coppe had, in fact, been acquainted with the London Antinomian group which used nakedness in its rituals, My One Flesh, through the publisher and bookseller, Giles Calvert. Calvert was instrumental in the publication of Ranter literature, as well as much other sectarian material, including Winstanley, Saltmarsh, a re-edition of some Familist writings, and later on, many Quaker tracts. Calvert acted as an important link between individuals. He was not unsympathetic to any one group, and it was also through him that Lawrence Clarkson was able to contact My One Flesh, the sexually oriented centre of Ranterism (p. 180).

Clarkson, or Claxton, was born at Preston in 1615, and drifted from Anglicanism to Presbyterianism, Independency and Antinomianism. He served as an army chaplain under Paul Hobson until 1644, when he became an itinerant preacher in East Anglia. In 1645, he was arrested with the Baptist, Hanserd Knollys, and charged in Suffolk with dipping. The following year, he had turned Seeker, and was unofficial preacher to the troop of Cornet Nicholas Lockyer, soon to become a Leveller agitator. This story comes largely from Clarkson's account of his religious career which he published in 1660, *The Lost Sheep Found*. Clarkson goes on to relate how he was paid £14 for penning a Leveller piece, *A Generall Charge or Impeachment of High Treason, in the name of Justice Equity, against the Communality of England*, in 1647. It argued that Parliament derived its power from the people, and crudely imitated the dialogue form developed by Richard Overton. Clarkson at least knew of Winstanley, and accused him of being a self-seeking tithe-gatherer in disguise. It is impossible to tell whether Clarkson was one of the Ranters the Diggers ejected from their commune, and whom Winstanley felt had sacrificed inner Reason to outward lustings.[15] Clarkson then joined the Ranters in London publishing *A Single Eye All Light, no Darkness* in 1650, in which he justified adultery by means of a close extrapolation of the phrase from Isaiah, 'I will make darkness light before them.'

Another pamphlet appeared in the summer of 1650. Thomason dates his acquisition of the anonymous *A Justyfycation of the Mad Crew* as 21 August. Interestingly, the pamphlet condones both swearing and sexual licentiousness, and explicitly attacks the idea of an impersonal God acting *on* rather than *in* man. This it sees as a form of idolatry. The egalitarian impulse is also there, 'money is your God, that all your care, industry, pains, is to get and keep this God money', together with the inversion which we find in Salmon (p. 202), that the righteous shall never be saved, that the Godly shall go to Hell, the wicked to Heaven. The resurrection of the dead is thus reinterpreted according to the Third Dispensation, 'now they are risen from the dead they twain shall be one flesh, one body, one life, one spirit'.[16]

The Rump was more worried by the threat to social order than by shades of theological opinion, and it established a committee on 14 June to investigate the Ranters, and to find a means of dealing with them. John Weaver was nominated chairman, and authorised to interrogate and hold offenders. On 21 June, Weaver reported back to Parliament, having questioned several people.[17] *A Single Eye* had come to his attention, and an order was given for the searching out of its author, while the committee was charged with the responsibility of drawing up a Bill which would quell Ranterism. What emerged was the Blasphemy Act of 9 August 1650. It outlawed the essential opinions held by Ranters, and enforced this with severe penalties.[18] An 'Atheistical, Blasphemous and Execrable' opinion consisted, it was decided, of denying 'the necessity of Civil and Moral Righteousness amongst Men', of affirming that man or any creature was God (which was not a Ranter tenet), and of affirming that God lived inside living beings. To this last was added the qualifier, 'and nowhere else', whereas most of the Ranters who wrote, particularly the moderate ones like Salmon and Bauthumley, believed that God lived everywhere in all of creation.

The Act also outlawed 'Uncleanness, prophane Swearing, Drunkenness, Filthiness, Brutishness, ... Stealing, Cozening and Defrauding others, ... Murther, Adultery, Incest, Fornication, Sodomie', and professing that 'Heaven and Happiness consisteth in the acting of these or such things'.

These later sections meant that the Act compounded the intentions of the Adultery Act of 10 May 1650, as Coppe pointed out (p. 119). Parliament may have aimed at precise terminology, or it may be that some of the blasphemies identified by the committee were too close to beliefs held by members, for the House voted out a clause which made illegal the attribution of sins 'only through the Darkness that is in Men'.[19] The debates over the penalties are equally interesting. The Act finally instituted six months imprisonment for a first offence, with banishment for a second, and death if the offender returned. Parliament voted out clauses which would authorise the punishment of publicans who harboured Ranter meetings, and officers of the law who were lax in their investigations, as well as vetoing the adoption of the army's punishment for blasphemy: being bored through the tongue.

As it turned out, the authorities were content just to keep Ranters locked up until satisfied with their recantations. Many were quickly released on a promise of future good behaviour. One pamphlet, entitled *Strange News from Newgate and the Old-Baily* (1650), described the interrogation and confessions of one J. Collins and one T. Reeve, both of whom were given six months imprisonment. Though the ringleaders and pamphleteers did present a more serious problem, the administration of the Act was again inconsistent. Wyke was released on bail as early as 28 June, giving surety that he would appear before the Council of State when required.[20] Salmon was interrogated by Robert Beak, the officer supervising the captured Ranters in Coventry, and the staunch Puritan soldier and politician, William Purefoy. As he recalls in *Heights in Depths* (p. 205) he was able to satisfy both of his integrity and return to conformity, though he had been held for six months.

At the command of Parliament, Coppe had been transferred from Coventry to Newgate prison in London early in April.[21] Purefoy was ordered to bring Coppe to trial on 19 July, though Parliament was still pressing for the completion of the case of *A Fiery Flying Roll*'s author on 27 September.[22] Coppe actually held up his trial by throwing balls around the court room from the dock. He was returned to Newgate, and remained there for the first half of 1651. Early in January of that year he published his first 'recantation', *A Remonstrance of the Sincere and Zealous Protestation*, which is more of a protest, expressing indignation at being imprisoned for opinions which he had never held, and for acts which he had never committed. In May, Coppe wrote *Copp's Return to the wayes of Truth*, which did deny the tenets levelled at the Ranters in the Act, though Coppe's language is as ambiguous here as Salmon's was in his own recantation. John Dury, the ecumenicist, was impressed by Coppe's apparent reformation (p. 122) but John Tickell was far from convinced when he witnessed one of Coppe's recantation sermons at Burford later in 1651.[23]

The committee had examined *A Single Eye* towards the end of July 1650. Clarkson describes his arrest at a meeting in Bishopsgate soon after this in

The Lost Sheep Found (p. 183); he had displayed his gift of the gab in resisting arrest, for which he became famous,

> he framed an excuse to return back into the house, pretending he had left something of great use behind him, and so escaped away at a back door; but is re-taken, and at this day in prison.[24]

On 27 September, Parliament published a broadsheet condemning *A Single Eye*, and authorising its collection and burning. The same publication announced the outcome of Clarkson's trial. At his interrogation before the committee, we know that Clarkson had stood on his right to refuse to answer questions, as Lilburne had done before him, but his persecutors were convinced of his guilt, and sentenced him to three months imprisonment, with labour, to be followed by banishment. Clarkson's connection with Major William Rainborough, brother of the murdered Leveller Thomas, had interested the committee who suspected that Rainborough had financed the publication of *A Single Eye*. Consequently, Rainborough lost his right to sit as a judge on the Middlesex Bench. As for Clarkson himself, he was released from New Bridewell prison after a month, and returned to see his long suffering wife in East Anglia (p. 185).

Jacob Bauthumley has no connection with either Coppe or Clarkson, though Salmon had heard of him (p. 201). He was born in Leicester in 1613, the son of a separatist shoemaker who was excommunicated and forced to leave the county.[25] Bauthumley was given redress against Laud by the Long Parliament, and joined the army early in the war. He stayed in for a long time, eventually being promoted to Quartermaster in Colonel Cox's regiment. He published *The Light and Dark Sides of God* in 1650, an entirely personal, mystical and pantheistic meditation. It is probably fair to see Bauthumley as the most moderate of the Ranters. His denial of the Trinity is clear, but he did not reach the extreme conclusion regarding sin to which Clarkson came (p. 244). Nevertheless, the pamphlet was published by the Leveller William Larner, emphasising the possibility of a connection between Ranters and disaffected Levellers. Most important though is how Bauthumley was perceived by the authorities. His pamphlet did worry them, and Bauthumley was tried under military law for spreading blasphemous doctrines, cashiered, and pierced through the tongue.[26] Bauthumley was not the only Ranter in the army. Salmon had already left service by the time of Coventry, but there was also the case of Captain Francis Freeman, whose defence, *Light Vanquishing Darkness* (1650), reveals a belief in a pantheistic Antinomianism. God was inside table-boards and candlesticks, and 'every Scripture is a mystery untill it be made known to us, or revealed in us; and so it comes to be above that Scripture without us; for, it is said to be a hidden mystery'.[27] Freeman, a man popular with his troops, was accused of singing bawdy songs on the march and in private meetings, and his superiors tried to be rid of him. His case came before Cromwell before he lost his commission. It seems, then, that the army was marginally more consistent in punishing offenders than were justices, though the force of Bauthumley's pamphlet, and its coincidence with the events in Coventry, singled him out for exemplary punishment.

Ranter gatherings occurred sporadically throughout the 1650s, though without the intensity of the early years of the Commonwealth. The subsequent history of each of the major Ranters shows a return to separatist activity, though with a quietistic emphasis in most cases. Bauthumley guardedly preached at Leicester and managed to become a corporation official after the Restoration,[28] publishing an abridged version of Foxe's *Book of Martyrs* entitled *A Brief Historical Relation*, in 1676. Coppe and Wyke returned to the Baptist community. Wyke eventually took a living in Ireland, while Coppe continued to preach in Baptist conventicles, though he thought it prudent to change his name to Higham, under which he earnt his living as a physician.[29] An anonymous broadsheet of 1657, *Divine Fireworks*, has been attributed to Coppe by Owen Watkins.[30] In stylistic terms this would seem to be just, and the millennial element is still there, but the expectation and prophecies are much quieter, and less violent. Coppe was amongst the Ranters who visited George Fox in prison in 1655, and their behaviour was not compromised. Even so Fox managed to abash them somewhat:

The Ranters began to call for drink and tobacco; but I desired them to forbear it in my room, telling them, if they had such a desire for it, they might go into another room. One of them cried, 'all is ours', and another said, 'all is well'. I replied, 'how is all well, while thou art so peevish, envious and crabbed?', for I saw he was of a peevish nature. I spoke to their conditions, and they were sensible of it, and looked upon one another, wondering.[31]

In 1680, eight years after Coppe's death, there appeared a broadsheet poem called 'The Character of a True Christian', signed A. C., which asserted salvation and blessedness for all on earth in the same ambiguous manner as his second recantation.

Salmon returned to Kent and became popular in the locality of Rochester, there laying the seeds for what became a Quaker community.[32] He preached on Sundays in the Cathedral, and recommended his successor, Richard Coppin. It appears that Salmon then emigrated to Barbados, where he may have been in trouble for organising separatist meetings.

Clarkson obtained a living in Kings Lynn after his release, but left, so he claims, to rant once more in East Anglia (p. 185). Towards the end of the 1650s he met the Muggletonian prophet John Reeve, and was converted. In his Muggletonian affirmation, *Look About You, or the Right Devil Discovered* (1659), he rebuked any who regarded sin, including lying with women, as justifiable as he had done previously. These were 'white ranting devils' who sinned under the pretence of religious liberty. The Muggletonians were Joachites and believed in the Doctrine of the Two Seeds, where all the right and wicked descended from Cain, and all the poor, oppressed and devout, from Abel, so Clarkson retained his egalitarian element. He tried and failed to challenge Muggleton's authority in the movement in 1661, and died a debtor in Ludgate prison in 1667.[33]

IV

The Ranters provoked a mass of hostile pamphlets. The great fear in men's minds was the anarchy and slaughter experienced when the Anabaptist communities controlled Munster in the earlier sixteenth century. Many saw Ranting as simply the antithesis of their idea of any form of proper devotion. Some pamphlets were extremely crude and exaggerated, confusing the Ranters with the underworld of bawdy, libidinous revellers and false prophets, the tavern community of which they were certainly a part. The Blasphemy Act seemed to aim at this world in general.

A few tracts, however, were reasoned and intelligent, like John Holland's *The Smoke of the Bottomless Pit* (1650), which gives a fairly accurate account of what was in Ranter writing itself. Holland accuses Ranters of holding that God is in man and in every creature, and that there is one spirit in the world: good and bad spirits are imaginary, while there is no sin since God has made it. Thus, the Devil is the left hand of God, and there is no heaven and hell but what is in man. The Scriptures and Biblical commandments are rejected as contradictory, and church ordinances are denied. Christ is a form or shadow only of a transcendent truth, and what he did in the flesh is now inside men in the spirit. Marriage is seen as a curse, and there should be a complete liberty for all to choose sexual partners. Holland grasps the characteristic Ranter language, where God is defined as 'Being', 'Fulnesse', a 'Great Notion', 'Reason' and 'Immensity', while 'when men dye their spirits go into God, as the small rivers go into the sea'. There are also some examples of a kind of free-thinking logic at work. For instance, the world must surely pre-date the Biblical creation since Cain went off to build a city, implying that there was more than just Adam's family alive.

Some pamphlets divide Ranterism into several sects, like Shelomites, Clements, Athians and Adamites, though there is no other evidence for this. The important point is that the Ranters are being·identified with earlier forms of heresy, and the words 'Gnostick', 'Donatist' and 'Nicolaitan' are used. Indeed, Coppe attacks the last of these in *Copp's Return* because their beliefs set them against the law, while the Gnostics had a theory of the soul similar to the Ranters, that the body must ascend from its earthly shell into its divine, ecstatic and spiritual truth. Another telling distinction, made by Samuel Fisher, was between 'Rantizers' who were flamboyant sprinklers of water at baptism ceremonies, who were too 'formal', and Ranters, who had dispensed with religion altogether.[34]

Most of the pamphlets which aim to lambast Ranting are obsessed with sexual licence,

> They affirm that all Women ought to be in common, and when they are assembled together (this is a known truth) they first entertaine one another, the men those of their own sex, and the Women their fellow females: with horrid oaths and execrations, then they fall to bowzing and drink deep healths (O cursed Caitiffes) to their Brother God, and their Brother Devill; then being well heated with Liquor, each brother takes his she Other upon his knee, and the word (spoken in derision of the sacred Wit) being given, viz. *Increase and Multiply*, they fall to their lascivious imbraces, with a joynt motion, &C.[35]

This accusation is then linked with the denial of heaven and hell, good and evil,

> They taught that they could neither see Evil, know Evil, nor act Evil, and that whatsoever they did was Good and not Evil, there being no such thing as sin in the world. Whereupon Mistress E.B., striking fire at a tinder-box, lights up a candle, seeks under the bed, tables and stools, and at last coming to one of the men, she offers to unbutton his cod-piece; who demanding of her what she sought for? She answereth, For sin: whereupon he blows out his candle, leads her to bed, where in the sight of all the rest, they commit fornication.[36]

God in man paradoxically results in the levelling of all to the beastly. Nakedness (Adamitism) is familiar, together with the parody of the Christian sacrament in buttock kissing, orgies and even coprophilia. Eating becomes a similar bestial ritual, 'Ranters at dinner – one eating a piece of beef, tearing it asunder, said "This is the flesh of Christ, take and eat"',[37] and the desire for mystical union is seen as an excuse for the physical.

In some accounts of Ranterism, the work of the Devil is detected. Samuel Sheppard's *The Joviall-Crew, or the Devill turn'd Ranter* (1650) is a condensed twelve-page pamphlet drama, probably never intended for performance since it was so short. The play mediates charges of drunkenness and wife-sharing by means of a comic confusion, where the Devil controls Ranters through the 'mask of religion', and where drugs, the ironic agent of illusion, are the means by which licence is obtained. The play shares part of its title with Richard Brome's *The Jovial Crew, or the Merry Beggars* (1652), and it is clearly part of the satiric tradition previously dominated by Ben Jonson. Sheppard's characters are as much roysters as Ranters, with the emphasis on sexual performance,

Wriggle. I thank you fellow creature, I'l serve either of you soul and body.
Robustio. Lovely Mrs All-prate, in this *I celebrate the creature's health*, who is now plowing on the angry main, whose saddle I supply, hel'l thank me for't …
Mrs. All-prate. He were a dead man else: Here's to the dear *Violentus* this will able thee 'gainst next performance, you were faultingly feeble in the last.[38]

However, Sheppard does seem concerned with the danger of the spread of Ranter ideas and their consequences, especially violence. For John Tickell too, Coppe's endorsement of 'Robbers and Spoilers' was a threat to the social order, and exemplified their hypocrisy, their worship of a 'two-faced Janus'.[39] Elsewhere, the Ranters, like the Familists, are alleged to create their own institutions and organisations,[40] a charge which is only appropriate for the groups which met to practise rituals.

V

Few have read Ranter literature without being in the first instance impressed by its obsessive images of violence and carnage. They map distinct, profound experiences which entirely energise the speaking subject in each tract. Coppe's intimation of his awakening to rant is both shocking and compelling,

I was utterly plagued, damned, rammed and sunke into nothing, into the bowels of the still Eternity (my mothers womb) out of which I came naked, and whetherto I returned again naked. And lying a while there, rapt in silence, at length (the body or outward forme being awake all this while) I heard with my outward eare (to my apprehension) a most terrible thunder-clap (p. 82).

Visions were not confined to Ranters, but we have to go to a Fifth Monarchist to find something as visually compressed and intense,

My first call was upon a dream, which I had of a great black terrible dog, which seized upon me, and took hold on my ear fast, which I thought was the devil; at which, I waked with shreeks and cries, and such frights, as for three weeks I thought I should have gone distracted.[41]

But Coppe is persistent with his image: a little later, we learn that the Presbyterian churches died in the womb, never achieving such awareness. The fact that Coppe uses parentheses to indicate the distinction between his inner experience and the outside world paradoxically asserts the vital centrality of the experience. The division of self into inner and outer 'formes' permits an abandonment to the inner universe until there are no distinctions, and the withdrawal inside becomes the prelude to a total reawakening. Norman Cohn suggests that such an 'allegorical fancy' begs a 'psychological explanation' for religious millenarianism. The list of those who have denied rationality to Coppe is not short, from Anthony Wood's accusation of a 'wandering head and filthy lusts' to Alexander Gordon's 'a clearly dis-ordered mind',[42] but his words lack neither clarity nor immediacy. The analogy of being reborn is harsh and painful, the reference to nakedness combining with the reverberative power of the initial four verbs. Coppe evokes the essential and timeless substance of creation, from which all life comes, and equates it with the picture of embyronic security. The appeal is highly somatic, taking the reader to a realm beyond the rational and verbal.

Similarly, in his preface to *Heights in Depths*, Salmon recounts his persecution by the Beast, until 'tumbling in my own vomit', he achieves a catharsis of release,

> Angry flesh being struck at heart with the piercing dart of vengeance, begins to swell, and contracting all the evil humors of the body into one lump, to grapple with this throne of wrath, at last violently breaks out, and lets forth the very heart and coar of its pride and enmity (pp. 212–13).

Again, the image is active and physical, relying upon a conflation of actual mutilation, some medical elaboration and the ethical imperative, to achieve a high degree of integration as the figures slide into one another. For Coppe, the exhilarated enthusiasm of 'the pride of my fleshly glory' is an affirmation of a pantheism, a state of communication between the elements of creation, anterior to language, relying upon harmony, and a realisation of the interconnection between all things and beings. Thus the letter cited from 'Mrs T.P.' reworks Daniel, and looks forward to Coleridge,

> all kinde of creeping wormes, and all kinde of Fishes ... we had so free a correspondence together, and my selfe with them, as I oft-times would take the wildest of them, and put them in my bosom, especially such (which afore) I had exceeding feared (pp. 64–5).

Elsewhere, the process of decay, desolation, destruction and rebirth becomes a warning to others. Those who give themselves to fleshly activity without first realising what they are partaking of, are to be criticised. For Salmon, his fellow soldiers in the New Model would kill with blithe justification, rather than submit to the 'divine dispose', possessed as they are with Anti-Christ and the Whore. This is a state of spiritual bondage and death, which is facilitated by 'appropriating of things to ourselves and for ourselves', and which prevents the mystery of the light breaking upon mankind at large. It is closely associated with the Ranter attack upon greed and privilege. In a broadsheet ballad of 1652, Lionel Lockier ironically posited that if Ranters were to be defined by their licence, then it was the rich who were the real Ranters.[43] For Coppe, the Levellers act out of genuine human empathy and pity, 'out of their own hearts', and Salmon's anger is directed against those who withhold arrears of pay from the soldiers (p. 191). 'Liberty' thus becomes a possession of the privileged, and an extension of their control over the dispossessed (p. 194).

Coppe's is a completely uncompromising illumination, as images of apocalypse grow out of each other by association, with impressions of fire, shouting and chaos (p. 101). This is compounded in every writer by a realisation of cities in Biblical terms, as if they were actually wandering through the squalor and vice of Babylon (p. 97). The climax is reached with the wrathful consumption of the great un-levellers, gold and silver. In Coppe, this occurs as a direct attack upon the rich, and his emotional response seems to bear authentically the burden of the oppressed, instanced in his concern for Maul in Dedington, and the cripple in Southwark (pp. 100, 105). He is indignant at social imbalance, as the crushing imperative to give is accompanied by threats of subversion to the social order,

> Thou has many baggs of money, and behold now I (the Lord) come as a thief in the night, with my sword drawn in my hand, and like a thief as I am – I say deliver your purse, deliver sirrah! deliver or I'l cut thy throat!

It is echoed by another levelling visionary, George Foster,

> I came and will make you howl, howl ye rich men for the rust of your silver and gold will rise up in judgement against you, for I come to destroy all things besides my self, and will suddenly take from man his gods, and pictures of gold and silver, and will make them for fear of me give them away; for I come to take vengeance on those that have afflicted the poor; and give up with speed before I take you and throw you into my wrath, and into my sore displeasure.[44]

Coppe's critique develops as a dialectic, built upon his own highly personalised allegories. At the root is a form of spatial pun. Though he does not condone 'sword-levelling', it is necessary for all men to return to, and appreciate, 'base' things. Likewise, Jacob Bauthumley's entire discourse is devoted to the establishment of a dispersed, benevolent God everywhere and nowhere, 'God is that high and lofty one that inhabits eternity, and not any circumscribed place, and so he is in low spirits'. It is in Bauthumley's spatial metaphors, set within a perspective of limited perceptions, that sin is exonerated. Rather than develop an idealistic vision, like Winstanley, Coppe proceeds to interpret his own envisioning, concentrating upon its ghoulish terror, He focuses upon the connection between gesture, action and morality, achieving a stunning identity between wealth, possession and corruption. The image of the 'WEL-FAVOURED HARLOT' who 'flattereth her lips' suggests a connection between money and illicit seduction, and she exists for the reader as a force of privilege and selfish appropriation (p. 102). She has the potential to own, to possess the speaker. The result is a verbal transference, 'tear it not, for if thou dost, I will tear thee', as if the speaker matches inequity with frustrated anger, word for word. This eventually accelerates into a catalogue of rupture images, so that the speaker's previous powerlessness and pathos is met by a dramatic envisioning of the levelling apocalypse, 'On this day, purses shall be cut, guts let out, men stabbed to the heart, women's bellies ripped up, specially gammer Demases, who have forsaken us' (p. 101).

Ranter language comes almost entirely from the Bible. Coppe and his fellow Ranters possessed an interpretative understanding of the Bible which allowed them to grasp Biblical images as shadows of real truths, perceived with the inner spirit. In an oppressive Calvinist milieu, where sin is taken as a fiercely serious offence, a phrase like Clarkson's 'The cutting of a dog's neck', becomes a fearful (and, in this case ironic) appendage to his insight (p. 165). The effect is completed with a Blakean representation of the impoverished, 'How long shall I heare the sighs and groanes, and see the teares of poore widowes; and here the curses in every corner' (p. 91). There is a concentration upon citation from the prophetic books of the Old Testament. Coppe's eccentricity is marked by his ability to break out into the Lord's prayer, as if it were his hallmark for devotional integrity. Coppe's first three pamphlets are modelled upon the structure of the prophetic books, and both *Rolls* feature preliminaries which imitate printed Bible and sermon forms.

Biblical imagery is sublimated into Ranter discourse so that each recalled phrase, be it protestation, condemnation or an affirmation of Antinomian grace, is personalised and specified by its location in the allegory. Salmon sees a direct connection between the quality of his own vision, and that of his phonic similar, Solomon. So, 'I am the Lord's Lillie amongst thieves' works its way above citation, as if Salmon had said it himself, serving to privilege himself amongst the other soldiers. The potential for emotional response is thus heightened in the sense of mystical becoming, 'be thou as a young Roe, or a young Hart upon the mountains of Bether' (p. 191). *A Fiery Flying Roll* is, in fact, a mesh of recalls, some acknowledged, many not, from Ezekiel. Like him, Coppe has ingested God's Word, hurling it forth now as a frenzied type of 'automatic speech'. Coppe augments the Scripture, expanding upon the concern with bodily function and divine presence. Ezekiel's roll tasted like 'honey in the mouth' whereas Coppe's was 'as bitter as wood; and it lay broiling and brewing in my stomach, till I brought it forth in this form' (p. 83). Obedience is due only to God, the controller of essences, as Coppe sardonically remarks, 'Your breath is in your nostrils'. Here, the Ranter perversion of the Antinomian heresy, as it occurs in Crisp and Eaton, is achieved through a supplement which intensifies the violent and inspirational powers of God, and then couples them with the sublime glory of the illuminated. The distinction from the Puritan mainstream can easily be missed. Both Sibbes and Coppe use the evocative image of the 'reed shaken with wind'. In the former it is taken from a context which advises humble behaviour and patience for the Godly, while the Ranter's usage is a further imperative to prophecy.[45]

What is more important is the elevation of Biblical imagery, filtered through separatist mystical sources, to the status of representations of the universe. There is an affinity between the imagery and typology of Coppe, Clarkson, and Salmon and that of the separatist fringe which was engaged in unifying sectarian, mystical, hermetic and neo-Platonic sources, and which included John Everard, John Pordage, and abroad, Jacob Boehme. Though this has been previously noted (first in Tickell's complaints of obscuring, abstruse and vacuous 'chambers of imagery'),[46] the extent to which these categories control Ranter expression remains unexplored. There is insufficient space here to map these influences precisely. Suffice it to say that there are no more than echoes of neo-Platonic writers, but distinct affinities with sectarian mystics. Coppe knew Pordage, described by Baxter as a 'leading Behmenist', and their language shares some of Boehme's terminology.

Coppe sees the hypocrisy of religious orthodoxy as the 'cloak of fleshly holiness and Religion', the 'shell of Episcopacy', which compares with Boehme's 'and then his Eternal Spirit may enter into that which is within the Vail, and see not only the Literal, but the Moral, Allegorical, and Anagogical meaning of the Wise and their dark sayings.'[47] For the Ranters, this metaphysical concern is generally stated rather than elaborated upon or explored. Here, Coppe, like Pordage, makes the distinction between the inner and outer, or 'huske', disappear, 'A Call, to arise out of the Flesh into the Spirit, out of Form into Power, out of Type into Truth, out of Signes into the Thing signified; and that Call sparkles through these Papers' (p. 43). John Warr, the legal writer, who was also published by Giles Calvert, used the same categories to make the distinction between the idea of the law and its institution, linking them with Equity, the reason that should lie behind the law, and Form, the use and custom of the law.[48] Essentially then, the objective material world is a 'veil of oblique' or 'umbrage' which hides the real world of inner union with God, and it corresponds to the use of the distinction between substance and shadow, taken from Hebrews 10, in *John the Divine's Divinity*.[49] Such a union occurs as a transcendental signified, and, not surprisingly, it is identified and augmented with illumination imagery, dwelling upon the difference between light and darkness, 'in the being is but one appearance because he that is the being of light is the appearance of the light, in what kind or degree whatsoever' (p. 166). It is compounded with a mixed image of milk and fountains: as saffron converts milk to its own colour, so the fountain of light, transferring the image of flowing milk, converts 'sin, hell and devil into its own nature and light as itself' (p. 172).

In 1646, Giles Calvert published a translation (nominally by Giles Randall, but more probably by John Everard) of Nicolas of Cusa's *De Visione Dei*, entitled'Οφθαλμòς 'Απλûα or *The Single Eye*. Cusa was almost as important as the *Theologia Germanica* for these mystical separatists, and it is conceivable, of course, that Clarkson had read the work. The ideas in Cusa were talked about in the sects. There are occasional imagistic similarities, especially concerning light. Also, the almost clumsy logic of the translation resembles that of Clarkson, 'because there to have, is to be, the opposition of opposites, is their opposition without opposition, as the end or bound of things infinite is no end or bound without end or bound'. But Clarkson bases his own pamphlet much more upon his exegesis of Isaiah 42, and aims exclusively at arguing away sin.

Such an explanation of reality functions as a secret code, the holders of which possessed a privileged knowlege of the true nature of the divine reality. In *Some Sweet Sips*, Mrs T.P. is evidenced to possess this knowledge, which Coppe interprets for the reader into the specialised vocabulary (p. 66). The concern with the form of God enabled the Ranters to conceive of the political community in relatively sophisticated terms. In the first instance, Coppe's community is apostolical, and seeks to avoid all accusations of heresy by recourse to its Biblical roots. But also, the divine is 'a naked God, unclothed of flesh and form', and likewise should 'divorce them from Type, marry them to Truth' (p. 53). The opposite for Bauthumley is 'the Egyptian bond of self and flesh', while Coppe's vision of his chest as the ark holding the inner light enables him to depict his misrepresentation in the public eye. Instead, mankind must engage with the riddle of the mystery in 'Signes, Vials, Glasses, Forms, Shaddows'. The equation of formless 'Power' with 'Purity' is made later by Clarkson (p. 169), and in Salmon, it is seen to move through civil bodies, including that 'Glorious shew and Idol', Parliament,

In this form of Monarchy god hath vailed his beautiful presence with a thick cloud of darkness: He hath made darkness his secret place ... Tyranny, persecution, opposition, evil, nature and creature, hath been (as it were) that vail betwixt God and man in this dispensation (p. 193).

For all the Ranters there is this presence in the universe which reduces all to an a-historical centre or origin, and we are 'transported with the sublimity of the notion'.

VI

It would be a mistake to divorce the visionary aspect of Ranter literature from its context in the forum of polemical exchange. After all, the Ranters, like most other pamphleteers of the time, were seeking to impose their vision upon the world, to assert a universal, essential truth over all others. Anyone who published subversive material during the Interregnum was liable to severe and violent censure, and the Ranters' close awareness of the conditions of publication and censorship is revealed in various and complex ways. This has an axiomatic effect upon the way in which the pamphlets would have appealed to readers. They show the inevitable clash between the enunciation of a subversive critique and the necessity of avoiding persecution in order to maintain uninhibited speech. This is the case even when there is no programme for organisation of change. The basis for Coppe's rant at the beginning of *A Second Fiery Flying Roule* is a warning to those in power that they will go the same way as the dead King Charles if they do not give their money to the poor. This is not so much Cohn's alleged 'wary and clandestine propaganda' but rather a blatant confrontation, 'wherein the worst and foulest of villanies are discovered, under the best and fairest of outsides' (p. 80).

Like Milton, Henry Robinson and the other radical sects, the Ranters use the freedom of speech debate as a guise for avoiding the censor.[50] But rather than explore the debate, the Ranters grasp its implications, shaping their discourse to make themselves secure. Such is Salmon's caution that *A Rout A Rout*, published for the army, admits the authority structure in two prefatory epistles. One is addressed to the commanding officers, and one to the soldiers (pp. 201–2). Salmon praises the generals and asks permission to speak to the soldiers. He claims that the generals have really too much important work to perform for Providence, to be interested in a Ranter: after all the divine onslaught is coming and they are partly responsible for it. Presumably, this would appeal to any of the differing versions of millenarianism then prevailing in the New Model, and Salmon is merely trying to make himself too small for the censor's net. Then Salmon immediately identifies himself as one of the soldiers, and places all responsibility for his views upon the divine within him. Having thus bantered on in a suitably friendly and colloquial manner, Salmon is able to confront the soldiers with the deceitfulness of their carnage. Conversational rhythms, as an assurance of honesty, good will and integrity, are of considerable persuasive importance throughout Ranter writings. In Coppe, they feature as the actual representation of dialogue, an index of the fundamental and personal nature of sectarian experience, and a further enhancement of the sense of community.

Salmon's later pamphlet recommends a simple maxim to the reader, 'give it entertainment, – if so, it will return thee satisfaction' (p. 204), which matches William Erbury's apparently incidental concern for the reader, ''tis well if truth rise in them that read'. This reflects the growing quietism of the sects as the 1650s progressed. *Heights in Depths* is, in fact, Salmon's recantatory tract, though it reads more as an assertion of anti-rationalism, by means of a withdrawal into silence. Salmon claims to have gained a new enlightenment from being imprisoned, but ambiguity is fostered in the suggestion that it is 'vanity' to engage in any positive activity whatsoever. Salmon's apparent indifference to the public is as much an incitement to read, since he claims no desire to impose his opinions upon the reader. The rant is therefore merely disengaged, 'I am quite aweary of popular applause, and I little value a vulgar censure; the benefit of the one cannot at all affect me, nor the prejudice of the other much molest me' (p. 217).

The most interesting case of enforced recantation and assumption of quiet conformity is that of Coppe. His first recantation, *A Remonstrance of the Sincere and Zealous Protestation,* is peppered with asides in which he puts himself in the wrong. He is incompetent, 'the Author hath (through Mistake)', but his willingness to repent is not withheld, '(a little) peeping forth' (p. 118). Coppe deals directly with the Blasphemy Act, claiming direct agreement with the gospel, 'the desire of my soul is to propagate the gospel', while presenting himself as powerless: he merely 'takes notice' of his persecution. As becomes evident, Coppe's refutation of his heretical profession is more exculpation than recantation. He only answers those parts of the Act where he can turn hostile accusations into conformity between his doctrine and the orthodoxy, involving the manipulation of logically vague terms (pp. 119–20). Theological controversy is relegated to a level below that of the action of professing. Simply to believe in a god seems to be enough to counter the accusations of immoral behaviour, which are flatly denied with no supporting evidence.

Further imprisonment resulted in *Copp's Return to the wayes of Truth.* Here the author presents himself as a figure even more penitent, with repeated apologies to Parliament, and a panegyric to Marchamont Nedham, the government censor. After a point-by-point admission of his errors under the Blasphemy Act, Coppe bolsters his argument with a favourable character description (p. 146). The effect of the citation of Dury's letter in this passage is thoroughly to occupy the reader's attention, while the pamphlet begins to read like the parody of an apology, as if Coppe is mocking the authorities. The praise of Nedham is fulsome, while the enormous preface still functions as Ranting propaganda: the impetuous tone remains, and Coppe still leaves affirmed his responsibility to publish that which God wills him to. Indeed, he makes himself the subject of a divine command, 'And furthermore, in what way and places soever divine providence shall dispose of me, I shall not cease to publish it, and what God hath wrought in me' (p. 155).

For the Ranters, recantation is, to say the least, ambiguous. They do not pursue dogmatism, of which Coppe accuses the Anabaptists (p. 96). If their truth did not operate as a dogma it would be entirely possible for them to act in conformity with an orthodoxy, but secretly to retain their own principles. As far as theology went, this was certainly what John Tickell thought, and he compares the Ranters with the 'double tongues' of the Familists. Familist and Ranter rhetoric (Tickell does not make a distinction) operates thus, they will first insinuate an interest in your affection, and then corrupt your judgement. They will smile upon you, and cut your throat using melting words, *Honey-Sweet*, smooth as oyle, but full of poyson, since in exalting Christ within, they kill Christ without.

Furthermore,

they will put themselves in all expressions, wayes and writings, to keep themselves from being *known*, but to their *owne*: you shall not know where to find them, so as to fasten on them, but their own shall know their meaning, and so may you when you have once got their *Key*.[51]

If Tickell's indignation is anything to go by, authority was further mocked here.

It is clear that the Ranters were involved in complex modes of address. Unlike the writings of other radical groups, the Levellers and the Diggers, and the pamphlets of Royalists and Parliamentarians, there is no narrator figure of apparent common sense and good will, an impartial observer of events. Neither is there a satirical or jesting 'persona'. There is no sequence of events, or history, which is recounted by a narrator for a persuasive end. Nevertheless, there is a characteristic speaking subject, an 'I' in each pamphlet, who speaks with the vast emotional depth and force of Coppe, or the self-assured enthusiasm of Salmon or Bauthumley. The way in which Salmon tries to wheedle his way into the reader's affections seems to be an admission of the heretical nature of his views. It is not so much a question of flying a colour of political or religious identity, as might a polemicist, but a strategy of driving home the locus and consequence of the Antinomian experience, 'But I tell you ... whilst you are embracing his body of self-safety and outward Liberty, he is dying and departing from it, though you see it not' (p. 195). The repeated 'you's force the reader to confront the presence of God in and around him or her, so that there is an impression of a shared experience between speaker and reader. The reader is then denied fully entering it, and so is enticed onwards by the sheer fervour of the statement. By contrast, the speaker in *The Light and Dark Sides of God* attempts to obliterate the distinction between himself and the reader: the reader is not mentioned but is assumed to be engrossed in following the discourse. Simultaneously, the speaker makes his presence omnipotent by admitting that he has no objection to any opinion, but then couches this inside the governing explanation. The speaker here is an honest 'I', alone with the 'pure Spark of Reason', supported by the 'Return of Understanding'.

Bauthumley is an anomaly amongst the Ranters, the characteristic speaker having much more resemblance to the semi-crazed state of the visionary. Coppe hurls his utterances out and expects their power to communicate itself to the reader. This involves a crude assumption of superiority. Coppe's speaker 'pities' those who mistake and attack him, and demands the 'great ones' not to laugh at him since he is sanctioned by divine authority. The modern reader is amused by the imperative (p. 99), but the desire for seeing spiritual and material equality is coupled with an acute fear of persecution. Further it does seem that the act of 'thundering' is a means of maintaining a connection with the One. Coppe styles himself a 'boanerges', a roaring pulpit-thumping priest, and openly claims his forerunners as Ezekiel, Joshua and Christ. While there were men wandering around Britain claiming to be Christ, like John Robins, Coppe actually identifies with God so much that it is indeed God who speaks. Again, it is not an identity made without distinctions, 'My most Excellent Majesty (in me) hath strangely and variously transformed this forme' (p. 81). In Coppe's view this is a form of possession which runs to God's literal ownership of the man. It is necessary for the speaker to conceive of his own performance in hypostatic and dramatic terms, as a prerequisite to writing. Coppe speaks of the young man on his spiritual journey between Oxford and Coventry, a fictional representation of his own experience (p. 113). Bauthumley disseminates his speaker across the entire network of creation, the 'I' appears to become identified with, and reborn through, the anatomy of the universe.

Even so, the speaker still operates by means of an awareness of the possibility of persecution. Coppe notices that the Blasphemy Act is passed while he is in prison, so making him guilty before trial (p. 119). This insight is compounded with his own self-abnegation: he acts 'not for my own sake', thus reasserting himself, in a manner characteristic of Lilburne. Then Coppe offers a pun on 'enlarge' as his supposed selflessness goes hand in hand with his continued imprisonment. Having created such an omnipotent utterance sustained by the accusatory, large signifiers, 'Weakness', 'Malice', 'Ignorance', 'Mistake', the speaker can, in this case, clear his own slate against the attacks of enemy pamphleteers. So *A Remonstrance* ends with the speaker denying his own involvement in both utterance and action, while drawing a distinction between his opponents and the 'authority' of the Parliamentary imprint (p. 123). Such is Coppe's own persuasive authority by now that he can accuse his enemies of making ridiculous identifications: his supposed she-disciples are none other than the soldiers who are guarding Coppe.

The speaker, or prophet figure, does become obsessed with his own identity. This functions as a central aspect of illumination. Salmon and the frantic Thomas Tany, 'Thereaujohn', both identify themselves with the Hebrews, the latter claiming to be their risen leader for the approaching apocalypse.[52] Early in *Some Sweet Sips*, Coppe becomes the enlightened ' אביעור '. Simply to change the language of one's name is to change the nature of one's perceptions and one's authority. The fact that, for the Ranter, there can be no guarantee of the morality of the outward act focuses all importance upon the intention within the individual. This is reflected in the naming process, 'I might have a new name, with me, upon me, which, I am —' and again, 'I am what I am' (pp. 50, 82). It is a process of self-deification, self-exultation, which passes through a yearning for enunciation, through intense desire, to the climax of knowledge and naming, 'Heart-knowledged by divine inspiration'. The speaker becomes deprived of the surface identity (at least the name on the printed page) and is inscribed throughout the process of illumination. In his preface to *John the Divine's Divinity*, Coppe finds a familiar identity in this shared experience, below the naming convention, 'I know not whose they are, or who writ them, though I know the Authour' (p. 41). Here, speech can degenerate into a Babel, and the destabilized self assumes a pose of frenzy, which could be a convenient guise to hide behind, 'Deare hearts! Where are you, can you tell? Ho! Where be you, ho? are you *within?* what, no body at home? Where are you?', though for Salmon, folly is an irony which places him beyond all reproach, 'but I am now a fool' (p. 53).

VII

The Ranters were concerned with the status assigned to language in its capacity as a bearer of divine truths, and its ability to communicate Ranter ideas to the illuminated and to other people. Special code words were used, which embodied the ideas and intentions of the movement, 'Welcome Fellow Creature!' like the Lollard 'Brother in Christ'. The 'Ranting mood' was certainly anti-Baconian in spirit, as Salmon realised, 'The form, method and language invites not the curious and nice spirit of any man' (p. 200). The essence of Ranter experience is beyond language, 'My great desire (and that wherein I most delight) is to say and see nothing' (p. 216). The naming process becomes hollow, void of meaning, and for Clarkson, even the imagination, when employed, is nothing compared with the infinite state of knowing God within. To 'arise into the Letter of these letters', without realising what is behind them, what is truly signified, is to outstep oneself.

Total illumination would result in the ability to understand all tongues. Babel would be comprehended, while Tany regards Hebrew as the original signifying language, which communicates God. The English, he maintains, are unable to cope with the stupendously powerful intimations of the ancient tongue. John Everard tried to preserve some 'vestigia' of this energy when he produced his translation of Hermes Trismegistus, which had already been translated from Arabic to Latin, and thence to Dutch.[53] Here, Ranterism is in tune with the search of Boehme, Dury and Hartlib, for a language which will exactly describe the divine nature of the objects it names.[54] Coppe seems to realise the problems which his readers face with a solipsistic language. Since each utterance is determined by God dwelling within him, the speaking subject has no control over what he says: it can only be hoped that the statement is eventually understood, 'If I here speake in an unknown tongue, I pray I may interpret when I may' (p. 49). The link with Boehme is evident. For Boehme, his publications are transcriptions of his personal book, his divinely inscribed mind. This authorises the private vocabulary and irregular phrasing, the sense of God's imprint evading linguistic understanding, which is exactly the point of the peculiar repetitions in Coppe.

Robert Browne urged the clergy not only to 'preache' but also to 'teache' the Word to the people, to instil the truth in the flock.[55] At the other extreme, to endow individual utterance with the autonomy of the Ranters is to divorce oneself from the authority of the Scriptures, as well as that fostered by ordinary language. In the Puritan Platonist, Peter Sterry, there is an essential link between accumulated authority and individual experience, 'He that defaceth the Prints and Image of the Eternal Word in his natural Man, crucifies his Saviour in the Flesh a second Time'.[56] Robert Beake, writing of the imprisoned Ranters in his keeping claimed that his captives had 'acute wits and voluble tongues', and regarded the Bible as no more than a ballad.[57] Others were held to refer only to the Bible when it suited them, as if 'it were *Gesta Romanorum*'. However, none of the Ranters explicitly states, despite their opponents' accusations, that the Scriptures are a 'bundle of contradictions'.[58] What happens is that the distinction between individual utterance and Scriptural authority disappears in the Ranter imagination, 'there is nothing in the treatise then the very Language, and the correspondency of Scripture in the Letter of it' (p. 230). The Bible is the 'History' which the 'Mystery' in the spirit comes to bear upon. For the Ranters, there is a link between the Word as it occurs in the Scripture and the divine language in the book of nature, which would seem to disprove the notion that the broad influence of Bacon and Hermeticism increasingly regarded divine speech as only an ancillary to the divine presence in nature.[59] By this argument, if God did not express himself verbally, human speech could not possibly resemble or communicate divine activity. On the contrary for the Ranters divine inspiration goes hand in hand with the stricture that in Biblical time, figures of speech were understood literally. Ranter language is rooted in a divine signifying act in the individual, which has a totally free interpretative value, 'You must take it in these tearmes, for it is infinitely beyond expression' (p. 82). This clearly contradicts the projects of both Hobbes and Wilkins, who were searching for a precise one-to-one relationship between signifer and signified. Coppe's theory of language is closely related to his epistemology of forms. His utterances attempt to preserve the inner within the outer form of language. The inner disrupts the outer form, though Coppe has no final control over his public discourse. As Winstanley sees the connection between language and property, where the Church appropriates 'strange tongues' to rule the masses through doctrine, so Coppe's 'great ones' in 'outward declarations ... professe me'. To have a title is to be someone's property. However, since God owns us all, his propensity to name stands above that of the rich and clergy. Interpreting the Tree of Knowledge of Good and Evil in this way, Coppe shows how appearances switch: angels turn out to be Ranters, for 'what God hath cleansed, call not thou uncleane' (p. 92). If nothing is the Word of God unless it is revealed in the individual as well as in the Scriptures, each Ranter can arguably write them. In this instance language, opaque in its outer form, receives a 'sparkling through' the page, so that 'I write ... as it flows by inspiration or revelation from my Royal Seed spring, otherwise it were none other than reason's imagination'.

The Ranters' propensity for cursing and swearing is well documented. It has been identified as a form of ritual which parallels other Ranter rites. By parodying orthodox social conventions, such as preaching, the Ranters were able to find an escape from oppressive social restraints, as well as bolster their ranks against threats of persecution. But swearing is also a manifestation of a privileged knowledge. After all, it is God who is swearing in the individual. Coppe would rather attend to the angelic knowledge in swearing than to a preacher, and his pamphlets are punctuated by subversive, game-like motives which match inspired utterance with 'posture'. Ezekiel, that 'son of contempt', is admired for his trangressive 'pranks', while Coppe is 'confounding plaguing, tormenting nice, demure, barren *Michal*, with *Davids* unseemly carriage' (p. 107). Riddle also functions as part of the secret key, 'Neither can they understand what pure honour is wrapt up in the Kings motto, *Honi Soit qui Mal y pense:* Evill to him that Evill thinks' (p. 93). Astrological elements are involved here: 'Queene Wisdome' descends to rule Coppe's exposition, and every time the 'dominical letter G' occurs (G being the letter which astrologers calculated to represent each Sunday in 1649), it is seen to have supernatural powers, signifying and assuring the presence of the supreme will (p. 101).[60]

VIII

It would come as a great surprise if Ranter pamphlets were seen to follow the five-part pattern of Aristotelian rhetoric, or the exegetical methods of preaching. Coppe, Clarkson and Salmon deliberately react against the forms of disputative reason, which are seen by them to be the means of the imposition of orthodox uniformity and religious hegemony. There is some influence of the evangelical insistence of John Everard,

> What manner of People are these, that so chump the letter between their Teeth, and troul it on their Tongues (For God's sake) what are they in their lives? have they got any Virtue from Christ, by being so conversant with him? Are they transformed and made *New Creatures?* Do they live *The Inward and Spiritual Life* of the Word? Are they dead to the world, and the world to them? Doth Christ's life shine in them and by them, so that they live not any longer in themselves.[61]

The impulse is anti-rational and non-aesthetic, so that the typical Renaissance figure of Apollo, sitting inside his 'O', the perfect source of knowledge, virtue and grace, is replaced by a circle which is evasive and deceptive, a 'womb of wind ... an airy notion, even while it appears to be something, it proves nothing' (p. 208).

The roots of Puritan preaching style were embedded in William Perkin's *The Art of Prophecying* of 1592, which demanded plain and methodical procedures. The 'grammaticall, rhetorical and logicall Arts' were to be used in analysing the Scriptures 'whereby teaching is used for the reformation of the mind from error'. This reflected the increasing influence of Ramism.[62] Ramus had enhanced the restrictiveness of logic by divorcing it from its traditional connection with stylistic and oral presentation. Hence 'Interpretation is *right division or cutting*. Interpretation is the *Opening* of words and sentences of the Scriptures, that one entire and natural sense may appeare.'[63] Such intense 'division' led to an expression which was precise and tightly enthymemic. Puritanism itself displayed an intense distrust of the imagination, emphasising the Word as pure Logos, devoid of all sacramentalism, and this distrust extended to the use of the imagination in secondary procedures of devotional exploration.

The Ranter monistic impulse does not allow such a distinguishing movement. Each pamphlet attempts to merge reason, logic or 'formality' with the totalising moment of illumination. Since they are using language, semantic categories are necessary for the generation of verbal sense, and the organisation of larger arguments does result in some Ranters relying upon some form of disputative order. This is itself a symbol of conformity, and the successive argument by points, together with Biblical references, occurs in both of Coppe's recantations. There is a sense of acute embarrassment, revealed again in self-parody, when Salmon uses an exordium (p. 191). Bauthumley's meditation dispenses with citation, 'and so I would loose, or let pass what was spiritually discovered inside me, I was willing to omit the outward viewing of them in a chapter or verse'.

The conflict between literalism and freer interpretation is exemplified in a debate between the Presbyterian John Osborn, and Richard Coppin,

Coppin. 'That he shall see God was true but the time and place was not true: he spake not aright according to the time and place, only as to the thing, that he should see God was true, but that it should be after he had laid down his body, that was not true: and accordingly he did see him, but in his natural life, before he died.'

Osborn. 'That the sight expected ch. 19 was accomplished before his death, you only affirm, without one reason of Scripture to demonstrate it; your bare assertion must be of no weight or consideration with me, so long as I have the text so plainly and fully speaking the contrary, let me hear what you say to this, that Job's sight of his Redeemer was not expected to be accomplished until his skin and bones were destroyed by the worms. What say you to this?'[64]

Coppe begins *A Second Fiery Flying Roule* with an attack on the 'Formalists' who would tie religious expression down to such tight forms. Thomas Tany bursts forth from a welter of unregimented Biblical citation and Hebraicisms to 'the glory of the skie that's buried by man's incredulity'. While Salmon does, in *Heights in Depths*, answer his opponents point by point, the arguments themselves are based not upon the Biblical reference but upon the suggestive trigger in the phrase. Analogous meanings rebound off one another as the sense of spiritual death in the outer body grows paradoxically into rebirth and essence with the inner arrival of God (pp. 213–17).

Clarkson's logic seems to collapse under the weight of his own realisations. As opposed to his first works, *A Single Eye* is intensely anti-syllogistic, so that the insistent repetition of 'light' imparts an impression to the reader. And with this strategy it is not so much the nature of the light that matters, but our ability to realise light as the divine origin and engulfer of darkness, 'though but one God diverse lights, and that all made by God; for he said, "*Let there be light, let there be Lights;*" therefore he is called the *Father of Lights*' (p. 164). It is a procedure which relies upon the presence of an 'I', an enunciator, to paper over the cracks of a sometimes contradictory argument. In Coppe, the result is the sense of a deliberate anti-rationalism, fostered by a comic juxtaposition between the Ranting narrator and the ordered etiquette of controversy in the precise page references to both Blasphemy Act and Bible. Curt commands follow, forcibly directing the argument ('But to proceed') while blunt denunciation is paralleled by apparently glaring ambiguity. In *Copp's Return*, 'sinners' could mean anybody, and so Coppe is still able to attack his captors in the moment of his recantation.

Ranter literature has more to do with another tradition in Protestant discourse; the individual meditation upon personal religious experience. Though there are no true examples of what might be termed meditation, with the exception of Bauthumley, the propensity to recount personal experience as part of a doctrine provides a clear link between the Ranters and later dissenting groups, such as the Quakers. Bauthumley claims his work is 'meditational', while the confessional nature of *A Second Fiery Flying Roule* balances the prophetic drive of the first one. For Coppe, existing modes of worship are 'stumbling blocks' to progress, and Salmon talks of the space necessary to 'ponder' his condition. But the intention is not pastoral, as if the Godly writer should provide an example to others. Instead, the recollection of the inner arrival of God, and the consequent change in the individual's perception and behaviour, serves to enhance the authority of the speaking subject. The narrative endows the Ranter with the power of prophecy, rendered in the continuous space of the individual's life.

Moreover, the moment of ranting, the reiteration of the inner light in words, is obviously in opposition to any considered meditation. Here there is no place for the recounting of one's life as a second scripture, a rational whole in which God works. Clarkson could only recount the significance of his life in *The Lost Sheep Found* after he had ceased to be a Ranter. Indeed, Bauthumley's meditation is not concerned with the shape of his life, but with the presence of God in the universe, and in this sense, his concern for the 'innocent' perception of infants matches that in the poetry of Vaughan and Traherne.[65] All the Ranters do refer to states of spiritual desperation which exist as preludes to enlightenment. For Salmon, his awakening itself causes alienation, 'Well, my folly being discovered, I lay as a spectacle of scorn and contempt to every eye; yea, my mother's children were angry with me' (p. 213). Again, the ambiguity increases. Coppe's attraction to the diseased and deformed occurs as an inversion of any concentration upon heaven. Yet Coppe's imagination is emblematic: the image of the hearts being blasted by God (p. 62) perfectly matches Cramer's well known picture in form and intensity, and the Ranter description of the arrival of inner light and grace recalls the emblems prefacing the 1969 translation of the Familist, Hendrik Niclaes.[66] In keeping with Puritan tradition, the Ranters verbalise significant recollections in their own private register, and this accounts for the highly individualised nature of each Ranter's style. But they are using a mode of devotional exploration only when it can accommodate the fierceness and enthusiasm of previous spiritual experience. After all, the Ranters are already elect: there is no search for salvation, no need to interpret events to make them correspond to the Word; there is finally just the will to express God's presence within.

The Puritan emphasis upon plain style is most famously stated in Bunyan's Preface to *Grace Abounding*,

> I could ... have stepped into a stile much higher then this ... but I dare not: God did not play in convincing of me; the Devil did not play in tempting of me: neither did I play when sunk as into a bottomless pit, when the pangs of hell caught hold upon me: wherefore I may not play in my relating of them, but be plain and simple, and lay down the thing as it was.[67]

Ranter prose style follows a similar link between moral impulse and expression, fulfilling St Paul's imperative, 'not with enticing words of man's wisdom, but in demonstration of the spirit and power'. As with the reaction to rhetorical and devotional conventions, the construction of sentences for the Ranter is both an escape from and a dependence upon what already exists. Coppe parodies the staid measure of the spoken sermon, deliberately sprinkling his discourse with the conversational, comic apostrophe, 'Well!'. Coppe's Latin and Hebrew phrases have a part to play in conveying his enthusiasm, but in doing so, they tend to parody themselves, and the liturgical patterns which they represent (pp. 62–3, 69). The ranting speech act does not sustain grammatical organisation in the final instance, and there is a sense of trying to make words say more than they possibly can. The frequent repetition of adjectives, though it has a Biblical root here in Ezekiel, intimates a feeling of frustration with the language, a 'strange new way new new new', while a hurried breathlessness is evoked with the use of parentheses, as if the normal sentence structure cannot hold the full extent of the illumination. Coppe's mind outruns his capacity for expression, as his performance heightens. There is a confused sense of half-hatched ideas (p. 90).

Since no manuscripts of Ranter tracts have yet been discovered, it is impossible to tell just how far this is due to poor compositing. In *A Single Eye* and *Heights in Depths* in particular, the punctuation is in places grammatically nonsensical, 'Nor the Beast (without you) what do you call 'em?' (p. 88), and the normalisation of this leads, in some cases, to a different reading. It may be that the compositors simply misunderstood the copy, or that the copy was punctuated in this way in order to foster ambiguity. This would leave a large measure of flexibility if the pamphlet was to be delivered orally. Sentences often remain unfinished, degenerating into an 'etc.', as if the reader is expected to know what is coming next, and to accept the inevitability of the coming apocalypse. Here the authority of the citation, most of which is omitted, is subjugated to the awareness triggered in the reader by the writer, but the latter is focused upon the unsaid. It is in these brief, aphoristic sentences that the sense of mental imbalance is transmitted, though the meaning is clear; 'My flax, saith the Lord, and the Thiefe and the Robber will steale from me my flax, to cover his nakednesse' (p. 88). In Salmon, colloquial interruptions halt the general fluidity of the discourse, while the exchange of sound between phonic similars in the same sentence serves to confuse meanings, just as Coppe causes extravagant echoes, where the phonetically and semantically similar follow one another, 'Omnipotent', 'Omnipresent'.

If there is a consistent denial of the verbally rational, there seems also to be a considerable degree of ratiocination, and a design to inculcate enlightenment in the reader. Like Biblical poetry, Coppe's poems and poetic organisation stand as the most economic and precise expression of Antinomianism. The result is a dramatic intensity as the wrangling syntax is interrupted by the sparse simplicity of Coppe's renunciation of possession. There is an intimation of an intelligence of impeccable authority in the orderly distribution of vowels, as the hurriedness of 'But we brethren are persuaded better things of you etc./Here's some Gold and Silver' is cut short by the pious 'But that is none of mine/The drosse I owne.' There are rhyming phrases which function as *leitmotifs* of Antinomian experience, of the free grace dwelling in Christ, 'my love, my dove' being repeated throughout Coppe and Salmon, as well as the more ferocious 'Rod of God' in Salmon alone.[68]

There is a sense of playfulness, as the rhymes border on doggerel, which is another familiar characteristic of Familist writing, 'Each Begger that you meet/Fall down before him, kisse him in the street.' Music can also reveal the light of God's grace, the immanence of which is felt in Coppe's ascending grammatic 'scale' towards the optative (p. 62). It is as if, having gone beyond Biblical literalism, the Ranters search for some form of symbolic representation of what is beyond the Word. In Sheppard's satire, dance is also a divine signifier, though the song which accompanies it is quite wrongly Bacchanalian,

> Viole. By Pluto's Crown, *Proserpine's* hair
> Rob. *Cerberus* yell, *Alecto's* chair,
> Pig. By Epicurus' happy life.
> Dose. And *Messalina, Claudius'* Wife.[69]

and the simple rhyming couplets of the poem prefacing *A Single Eye* (p. 162), or the complex imagery of the two poems discovered in the Clarke papers, are much closer to the movement's sentiments.[70] On the other hand, Coppe and Francis Freeman are supposed to have sung blasphemous songs to the tune of metrical psalms in taverns, and one pamphlet cites a Ranter prayer which works upon similar lines. This biting materialist aspect is captured in the Ranter's 'Christmas Carol', despite the extreme pantheism,

> They prate of God! Believe it, fellow-creatures,
> There's no such bug-bear: all was made by Nature.
> We know all came of nothing, and shall pass
> Into the same condition once it was
> By Nature's power and that they grossly lie
> That say there's hope of immortality,
> Let them but tell us what a soul is; then
> We shall adhere to these mad brainsick men.![71]

Elsewhere pauses, for the recuperation of thoughts, are instituted by the elongation of stress patterns, 'patiently, cheerfully, silently'. Salmon shows himself to be a master of the apostrophe, made all the more effective by phrasing his argument around them. The reader is led effortlessly forward, with challenges to realise the importance of the supreme Will, 'It will be a sweet destruction, wait for it', and urgent pleas to pay attention, 'Again, for I draw homewards' (p. 197), a phrase which is repeated near the end of the pamphlet like a musical coda. A measured deliberation is clear in the alternation between the abrupt defining or introductory sentences, and the extended clausal sequences of explanation. The syntax is tight but it does facilitate lucidity, 'I know God acts in you in this cloud, he goes out with you in this darkness, and lets out his presence through this vail of self-preservation amongst you. He hath crowned you with fame, success and victory, while you have lived and acted in this earthly body of outward liberty' (p. 195).

This writing, like Clarkson's and Bauthumley's, displays a high degree of accomplishment, though it has a tendency to become tongue-tied by using a limited vocabulary to handle different concepts. It is a game of verbal definition which makes Bauthumley's justification of sin compromised (p. 246). Apart from Coppe's colloquial and proverbial phrases, Ranter pamphlets do possess a restricted vocabulary, with a particular concentration upon Biblical words connected with the notion of becoming and illumination, as well as the horrors of prophecy. Part of their anti-rational surge is to attack those who have control of the orthodox view of language, the universities,

> But no more of this till I come to (Doctrine magistri) the leaving of the Master, who is teaching me all the parts of speech, ... And ther is a time to be very (to be very in the Lord) and that is the Present Tense with some, to others for Future (p. 62).

Coppe did study for a while at Oxford, first at All Souls, then at Merton, and his final rejection of the institution is made in deliberately vulgar and nonsensical terms, 'It is about time for me to knock off here for the present; because I heare Interjections of Silence (as on, and such others) sounding in mine eares' (p. 63). Only a few Ranters actually expressed themselves in writing and had pamphlets printed, and it is evident that for these few at least the enforcement of Form was most abhorrently present in formal education.

Abiezer Coppe

Preface to
John the Divine's
Divinity

T his (*modicum bonum*) this little pretty piece, was put into my hands to read: but (for the present) I pocketed it; and lodg'd it there all night, but viewing it in the morning; I conceived it was *conceived of the holy Ghost, and born of the Virgin.*[1] The same spirit moved me to transcribe it; and send it abroad to thy view.

I know (by wofull experience) that the Truth as it is in Jesus hath been *spet on, buffeted, railed on, incarcerated, intullianated, pen'd up, and imprisoned.*[2] But *truth* being *strength* hath made *the gates of brasse,*[3] and *bars of iron flie*[4] and is now at *liberty*; and utters her voice in the *streets*, which voice is rending the heavens, *shaking terribly the earth,*[5] *melting the mountains like wax;*[6] *and making the lame man leap like a Hart.*[7] *And the hearts of those that know the Lord to dance for joy,*[8] &C.

Something hereof *sparkles*[9] through these papers. And I only let thee know: that I *know* thers *some sweetnes*[10] in them; and that I durst not turn my back upon them though (seriously) I know not whose they are, or who writ them, though I know the *Authour;*[11] or are rather known of him.

Stranger! use him, me, and these as thou pleasest; or as thou canst. Maist thou be taught *not to blaspheme the way thou knowest not,*[12] least thou *spurt* out *spite* in the *face of the Heir.* Nor to *presse* fore upon the *man,* even *Lot,* least two Angels smite thee with blindnesse.*[13]

Lastly, *Be not forgetfull to entertain strangers, because some in so doing have entertained Angels unawares.*[14] Maist thou entertain them, then thou wilt. *Farewel.*

From London Jan. 13th 1648
   two or three days afore
  the eternal God thundered
    at great S. Ellens.[15]

However, I am thine,

Abiezar Coppe.

SOME

Sweet Sips, of some
Spirituall *Wine*, sweetly and freely
dropping from one cluster of
Grapes, brought between two upon a
Stáffe from *Spirituall Canaan* (the
Land of the *Living;* (the
Living Lord.)

TO

Late *Egyptian*, and now *bewildered Israelites.*

AND TO

אביעזר בף *A late converted JEW.*

Who must (no longer) hunger, or hanker after the *Fleshpots* of
the *Land* of Egypt (which is the house of *Bondage*) where
they durst not minish ought from their bricks of theie *daily
taske*) but look for, and hasten to Spirituall *Canaan* (*the
Living Lord,*) which is a land of large *Liberty*, the house of
Happiness, where, like the *Lords Lilly*, they toile not, but
grow in the *Land* flowing with such wine, milke, and
honey.—

OR,

One of the *Songs* of *Sion*, sung immediately, occasioned
mediatly by a Prophesie and Vision of one of the Lords
Handmaids, and *Youngmen*, Mrs. *T.P.* and expressed by her
in an Epistle to *A.C.* An extract whereof is here inserted,
with a Revelation, and Interpretation thereof, as from the
Lord.

They cut down—a branch with one cluster of grapes,
and they beare it between two upon a staffe, *Num.*13.23.
She that tarried at home devided the spoile *Psal.*68.12.
The Lord is my strength and *Song*—*Exod.*15.2.

London, Printed for *Giles Calvert*, at the signe of the *Black-
Spread-Eagle*, at the West-end of *Pauls*. 1649.

THE
CONTENTS

The Titularity of the severall little parcels, wrapt up in this little Fardle.[1]

OR,

The severall Titles, of the severall ensuing Epistles here inserted, AS,

I. A *Preambular, and cautionall hint to the Reader concerning the ensuing Epistles.*

II. *An Epistolar preparatory to the ensuring Epistles of* אביעזר *a late converted Jew.*

III. *An Apologeticall and additional Word to the Reader, Specially to the Schollars of* Oxford, *concerning the precedent and subsequent Epistles.*

IV. *An extract of an Epistle sent to A.C. from Mrs. T.P.[2] (another late converted* Jew*) mediately occasioning the precedent Epistles, and the last letter.*

V. *An Epistle responsorie, to the late letter of* Mrs. T.P. *wherein there is an opening of her Vision, and an interpretation of her Revelation, as from the Lord; together with an* indiciall *hint of some particular passages infolded, and unfolded in the Letters following, and that as followeth, as the* Contents.——

1. *A call, to arise out of Flesh into Spirit, out of Form into Power, out of Type into Truth, out of Signes into the thing signified; and that call Sparkles throughout these Papers.*

2. *The danger of arising into the Notion of Spirituals afore the Lord awaken a soul, and saies, come up hither.*

3. *Christ in the Spirit, a stumbling stone, and rock of offence to those*

that know him (only) after the Flesh.

4. *They that Walk after the Spirit, and live according to God in the* Spirit, *cannot be offended at any thing, and in them there is none occasion of stumbling.*

5. *Few as yet know the Lords voyes from* Elies, *and they are trudging to the old man at every turne, till the Lord be revealed in them.*

6. *The Trumpet often gives an uncertaine sound—till the last seale be opened.*

7. *Some Saints are* within, *and at* home, *others* without, *and abroad. Who they are.*

8. *And how they are said to be at* home, *and how* abroad.

9. *They that are at* home, *are kept at a higher rate then those that are* abroad.

10. *The former feeding upon the daintiest of dainties.*

11. *The later wishing and woulding³ for a belly full of* huskes.

12. *Wherein is feelingly, and experimentally exprest what* huskes, *and* bran *are. And,*

13. *What the finest wheate flower is.*

14. *The formall, externall, or outward; and the powerful, glorious, and inward Death, and Resurrection of Christ, and how men walke in darkness, and know not at what they stumble, till they attaine to the latter.*

15. *The death of Christ at* Jerusalem, *and the Resurrection out of* Josephs *Tombe without us, is nothing to the dying of the* Lord *in us; and the Resurrection of the Day-star in our hearts.*

16. *The Sabboth, which some are entred into, What it is, and how they do no manner of* work, *but the Lord does all in them, plowes in them, sowes in them—prayes in them, sings in them, &c.*

17. *The dismall darkness, and sore slavery in the land of* Egypt, *&c.*

18. *What the Holy Land, the Land of* Canaan, *is.*

19. *Some of the great and glorious priviledges of the free-denizens of the land of* Canaan.

20. *What* Man *is, and how* Man *is the* Woman, *and the* Lord *the* Man.

21. *The River of water of Life, What.*

22. *The purity, and clarity thereof, all other Rivers muddy, men muddy, profound men muddy, &c.*

23. *All* Formes *are wilde, and why, and how.*

24. *All Elements shall melt away, what,——and how.*

25. *Some men bravely, and sweetly besides themselves, and how.*

26. *One of the* true *Religion, is the* Kings, *and the* Queenes, *and the* Princely *Progenies, and the* Bishops *and the* Priests, *and the* Presbyters, *the* Pastors, Teachers, *&c. and the* Independants, *and the* Anabaptists, *and the* Seekers, *and the* Family of Loves, *and how.*

27. *The* Day-springs *visit, and the* Day-stars *woing.*

28. *A Pathetical call, and a great pounding at the everlasting* doors, *to open to the* King *of* Glory.

29. *The great* glory *of those who have the glory of the* King *of* glory *risen upon, and* in *them.*

30. *The* Kings *Burglary, and the day of the* Lords *plunder; wherein there is declared, how he plunders—as a thiefe in the night—and of what—— together with a Seraphicall Prayer of* אביעזר *upon* Siginoth, &c.

31. *How the* Cœlestiall Fire *of love burnes mens houses over their heads, and that out of huge love to them.*

32. *Doomes Day come already upon some* flesh, *and it is falling upon all* flesh—*and how (ere long) no* flesh *shall have* Peace.

33. *How* Gods Heritage *hath been a speckled, or party-coloured bird, and when it shall be of one colour, and the Saints of one complexion all of them.*

34. *Severall sweet spirituall Songs, and dainty Dances, &c.*

35. *Many Pastors have destroyed Gods vineyard, and how, and what shall become of them.*

36. *The husbandmens, and Vine-keepers hard usage of the* Lords Servants, *who come from a* Strange Countrey; *and their spite against the* Heire.

37. *Who this* Heire *is, who the sonne of the* Free-woman, *and who the sonne of the* Bondwoman.

38. *Every* Forme, *a persecutor, but the spirit free from persecuting any.*

39. *A loving, and Patheticall admonition to the* Husbandmen; *their dismall, and dolefull doome, and downefall foretold; with a word of consolation to them and a prayer for them in the close.*

40. *A word from the* Lord *to* Men-Pastors.

41. *Who is* Gods *peoples true Pastor,* Shepheard, Teacher, &c.

42. *The knowing of men after the* Flesh, *and of* Christ (himselfe) *after the* Flesh, *out of date, and* Christ *in Spirit is comming in request, being the sword of the* Lord Generall, *is devouring from the one end of the Land to the other:—And the point thereof, set at the very heart of* Flesh, *to let out its very heart bloud, and every drop thereof.*

43. *A sweet, gentle, and loving check to poore* Mary, *seeking the* Living *among the* Dead.

With a prayer for, and Prophecie of an unexpected glory fallen upon some already, and flying swiftly to others.

44. *The pure, and powerfull, various, and glorious, the strange, and immediate teachings of God at hand, even at the doores, and come into the houses, and hearts of many already.*

45. *The evill, and danger of limiting the holy one of* Israel.

46. *The green, and glorious, sweet, and pleasant pastures,——those are lead, and fed in, that know no other*

Pastor *but the Lord.*

47. *No small stirre raised by the Silver Smiths about this way,
in that, thereby their craft is in danger to be set at nought.*

48. *Everlasting wisdome is transacting, and doing over those
things in Spirit, power, and glory* in *his Saints, which were in a
more literall, and externall way done for his people formerly.*

49. *Brave schollers, who.*

50. *A Caroll, and Anthem sung to the Organs.*

51. *The eternal God is preaching quick and keene, short and
sweet Sermons; through bed and board, through fire and water,
light and darknesse, heaven and earth, day and night.*

*Through Carols, Organs, Anthems, any things, all things to
some.*

*Yea, through Tanners, Tent-makers, leathern aprons, as well as
through university men, long gownes, cloakes, or cassocks.*

52. *They that have learned all that their Pædagogues can teach
them, shall goe to schoole no longer, shall be under the lash no
longer.*

53. *The strange things that befall them, who are set to the
university (of the universall Assembly) and entred into
Christ-Church; (the Church of the first borne, &c.) where they
fall* besides themselves, *and* burne *theire Bookes before all men.*

54. *Some spirituall touches upon the six Moodes, together with
the* Lunatique *Moode.*

55. *The* Deane of Christ-Church *(the Metropolitan of all
Christendome, and Arch-Bishop of* All-hallowes*) teaching his
pupils the Accidence, a strange new way, new, new, new.*

56. *An admonition——to entertaine* Strangers *joyfully,
because some in so doing have entertained Angels unawares.*

57. *The Message of two Angels.*

Sodom *must be burnt.*

Lot *must be saved.*

*Flesh must be crucified and dye, And the eternall
Spirit——dwell in the Saints everlastingly.*

58. *Mans* Day *almost at an end.*

59. *The day of the Lord at hand.*

60. *Some Prophecies, being in part fulfilled, and the glory of
them in part enjoyed, are here so farre—opened.*

*And many spiritual discoveries (so farre as my hands have
handled them) are here inserted.*

Cum multis aliis, quae nunc perscribere longum est.[4]

EPIST. I.

A

Pre-ambular, and cautionall Hint to the Reader; concerning the ensuing Epistles here inserted.

Deare Friends,

HEer's something (according to the wisdome given to us) written unto you, in all these ensuing Epistles. In which are some things hard to be understood, which they that are *Unlearned*, and unstable, wrest: as they doe also the other Scriptures, unto their own destruction.

But we brethren are perswaded better things of you &c.

Her's some *Gold* and silver.

But that is none of mine.

The drosse I owne.

The fire will fall upon it, and consume it; yet I my selfe am saved: yet so, as by *Fire*.

Here is Scripture language throughout these lines: yet Book, Chapter, and Verse seldome quoted.

The *Father* would have it so; And I partly know his design in it; And heare him secretly whispering in me the reason thereof. Which I must (yet) burie in silence, till——

Here is a reede shaken with the winde, and the voice of one crying in the wildernesse,

Prepare ye the way of the Lord, &c. The day of the Lord is at hand, is dawned to some.

Here is a great cry, and at mid-night too; Behold, *The Bridgroome* commeth.

Here is a great pounding at the doors,——But it is not I, but the voice of my *Beloved*, that knocketh, saying, Open to me, and let me come *In*.

Here is the voyce of one crying: Arise out of *Flesh*, into *Spirit*; out of *Form*, into *Power*; Out of *Type*, into *Truth*; out of the

Shadow, into the *Substance*; out of the *Signe*, into the thing *Signified*, &c.

——Take this cautionall hint.

Arise, but rise not till the *Lord* awaken thee. I could wish he would doe it by himselfe, immediately: But if by these, mediately. His will be done. His is the Kingdome, the power, and the glorie; for ever and ever, Amen.

I would (by no means, neither indeed can I) pull you out of Bed by head and shoulders.

—May the cords of *Love* draw you out.

If through the heat of love, mixt with zeale, and weaknesse (in these) thou shouldst start out of thy bed naked, into the notion of these——I should be very sorry for thee, Fearing thou mightest be starved these cold winter nights.

If thou shouldest arise into the Letter of these Letters, before the Spirit of life enter into thee, Thou wouldst runne before the Lord, and out-runne thy selfe, and runne upon a rock, For it is set on purpose, as one,——And a stumbling-stone to some,—even to those who know Christ after the Flesh (only). But happy they, who are in the *Inside* of them, Nothing can harme them. And in them there is no occasion of stumbling.

To the Lord I leave you all, (Deare hearts) and to the word of his grace, which is able to build you up.

The word of the Lord is precious in these dayes,——There is no open vision to many.

Few know the Lords voyce from *Elies*, as yet: we shall trudge (it may be) to the old man, once, twice, thrice; till the word of the Lord be revealed to us. And,

Then we shall heare, and say, *Speake Lord, for thy servant heareth*, reade I *Sam.* 3.1. to 15.

There are many voyces in the world. And some know the fathers voyce, in all voyces, and understand him in all tongues.

If the *Trumpet* here give an uncertaine sound, I cannot help it for the present. You will understand by that—the last seale is opened. If the Temple be filled with smoake, you shall not be able to enter into it, till the seven plagues of the seven Angels are fulfilled.

The vision is for an appointed season, but at the end it shall speake, and not lie: though it tarrie, waite for it, because it will surely come, it will not tarrie.

If the leaven be hid in three measures of meale, Queen Wisdome (the woman that hid it there) will make dough, and then you shall taste it in the whole lump.

If the graine of mustard seed here, be buried in the earth, wait for it: because it will surely spring up into a tree, and the fowles of the aire shall lodge in the branches thereof.

If I here speake in an unknown tongue, I pray that I may interpret when I may.

Only take one Clavall[5] hint.

That which is here (mostly) spoken, is inside, and mysterie. And so farre as any one hath the mysterie of God opened to him, *In Him*, can plainly reade every word of the same here.

The rest is sealed up from the rest, and it may be the most,——from some.

One touch more upon one string of this instrument. Some are at *Home*, and within; Some *Abroad*, and without. They that are at *Home*, are such as know their union *in* God, and live upon, and *in*, and not upon any thing below, or beside him.

Some are abroad, and without: that is, are at a distance from God, (in their own apprehensions) and are Strangers to a powerfull and glorious manifestation of their union with God. That their being one in God, and God one in them; that Christ and they are not twaine, but *one*, is to them a Riddle.

These are without, *Abroad*, not at *Home*, and they would fill their bellies with *Husks*, the out-sides of Graine.

That is, they cannot live without Shadows, Signs, Representations;

It is death to them, to heare of living upon a pure & naked God, and upon, and in him alone, without the use of externalls.——

But the former reape a thousand fold more *In* their living upon, and in the *Living Lord* alone, then when they saw him through a vaile.

For instance,

They live not (now) in the use of the externall Supper, or outward breaking of bread,

But upon the Lord (whom they have not now by hearesay) but clearly see, know, and powerfully feele *Him in them*;

Who is a continuall feast of *fat* things *in* them, their joy, and chear, being (now) a thousand fold more in the enjoyment of a naked God *in them*, and of Christ *in them*, uncloathed of *flesh* and *forme*, then it was when they saw and knew him otherwise, in and through Signes, Vails, Glasses, Formes, Shaddows, &c.

Thus you have one Claval hint; if the Lord come *in*, it may be an instrumentall key to open the rest. But the Spirit alone is the incorruptible Key. And so I must have done with this Point, and with the Epistle too. Only I must let you know, that I long to be utterly undone, and that the pride of my *fleshly* glory is stained: and that I, either am, or would be nothing, and see the Lord all, in all, in me. I am, or would be nothing. But by the grace of God

I am what I am,
and what I am
in I am,
that I am.
So I am
in the Spirit

The *Kings* and the *Queenes*,
And the *Princely Proge-*
nies, and the *Lords,* and
the *Bishops* & the *Priests,*
and the *Presbyters,* the
Pastors, Teachers, and
the * *Independents,* and
the * *Anabaptists,* and
the *Seekers,* and the *Fa-*
mily of Loves, and all in
the Spirit;

in a
word

Gods

Christs

the
Saints

And yours; all of ye that are the Lords, by what names or
titles soever distingushed, Yours— אביעזר בף

* The *Key.* * *Christ* was Re-baptized.—The Lord is my *King,*
and my Shepheard, or *Pastor, &c.*—The Eternall God, whose *I*
am, is *Independent,*—*&c.*

EPIST. II.

An Epistolar—Preparatory to the ensuing Epistles of— אביעזר *A (late Converted) JEW.*

TO all the Kings party in *England*, and beyond sea; and to all that *Treate* with *the* King: and to all the Saints in *the upper* and *lower House*; and to all the *Strangers* (Protestants, Presbyterians, Brownists, Anabaptists, Sectaries, &c.. so called by Babels builders, whose language is confounded). To all the Strangers scattered throughout *Pontus*, *Asia*, &c. And to all the Saints in *Rome*, *New-England*, *Amsterdam*, *London*, especially *Hook-Norton*, & thereabouts in *Oxfordshire*, and at *Esnill*, *Warwick*, *Coventry*, and thereabouts in *Warwick-shire*. And to all the Saints, (of all sizes, statures, ages, and complexions, kindreds, nations, languages, fellowships, and *Families*,[6] in all the Earth.

Once intended only, and primely for that precious *Princesse* ב. ח[7] another late converted *Jew*, and for the Saints at *Abingdon*.

But it being told in darkness, it must (by commission) be spoke in light, and being heard in the *eare*, it must be published upon the house *tops*; to All——

And let him that hath an eare to heare, heare what the Spirit *saith.*

CHAP. I.

Deare hearts! Where are you, can you tell? Ho! where be you, ho? are you *within*? what, no body at *home*? Where are you? What are you? Are you asleepe? for shame rise, its break aday, the *day* breaks, the *Shaddows* flie away, the *dawning* of the *day* woes you to arise, and let him *into* your *hearts*.

It is the voyce of my beloved that knocketh, saying, Open to me my *Sister*, my *love*, my *dove*, for my head is filled with dew, and my locks with the drops of night. The *day spring* from on high would faine *visit* you, as well as old *Zachary*. Would faine visit you, who sit in *darkness*, and the *shadow* of *death*, as well as those who dwell in the *Hill countrey*.

The day *star* is up, rise up my *love*, my *dove*, my fair one, and *come away*. The day *star* woeth you, it is the voice of my beloved that saith open to me— I am *risen indeed*, rise up my love, open to me my faire one. I would faine *shine more* gloriously *in you*, then I did at a *distance* from you, at *Jerusalem without* you. I am risen *indeed*; I (*the day star*) would faine *arise* in your *hearts* and shine *there*.

Then *arise, shine,* for thy light is come, and the glory of the Lord is risen upon thee, for behold, the darkness shall cover the earth, and gross darkness the *people*; but the Lord shall arise upon thee, and his glory shall be seene upon thee.

And the *Gentiles shall come* to thy *light*, and *Kings* to the brightness of thy *rising, arise, come up hither.*

Then, For brass I will bring gold, and for iron I will bring silver, and for wood brass, and for stones iron. I will also make thine *officers peace*, and thine *exactors righteousness*. Violence shall be no more heard in thy Land; wasting nor destruction within thy borders. The *Sun* shall be *no more* thy *light* by *day*, neither for *brightness* shall the *Moon* give *light* unto thee; but the *Lord* shall be unto thee an *everlasting light*, and thy *God* thy *glory*.—And the days of thy mourning shall be ended, *Isai.* 60.1,2,3,17, *&c.*

Then, Lift up your heads, O ye gates; and be ye lift up ye everlasting doors; and the *King* of *glory* shall come *in*.

Who is the *King of glory?* The *Lord* strong, and mighty, the Lord mighty.

Lift up your heads, O ye gates, even lift them up ye everlasting doors; and the *King of glory* shall come *in*.

Who is the *King of glory?* The *Lord of hosts*, he is the *King of glory*. *Selah*.[8]

O! Open ye doors, Hearts open; let the *King of glory* come *in*. Open dear hearts.

Dear hearts, I should be loath to be arraigned for Burglary—

The *King* himself (whose houses you all are) who can, and will, and well may break open his own houses; throw the doors off the hinges with his powerfull voyce, which rendeth the heavens, shatter these doors to shivers, and break in upon his people.

CHAP. II.

A Prayer of אביעזר upon Siginoth.[9]

Oh day of the Lord! come upon them unawares, while they are *eating* and *drinking, marrying*, and giving in *marriage*, divorce them from all strange *flesh*; give a bill of divorce to all carnall, fleshly fellowships, betroath them to thy self, (O God,) and to one another in the *Spirit*, marry them to the Spirit, to thine own Son, to thine own Self, O our *Maker*, our *Husband*.

Let them be joyned to the Lord, that they may be *one* Spirit, (if there be any fellowship of the Spirit) sweet fellowship! sweet Spirit*!*

Divorce them from *Forme*, marry them to *power*. Divorce them from Type, marry them to *Truth* (O the truth, as it is in *Jesus*!)

Fall upon them while they are *Eating* and *Drinking without*, Let them eate and drink *within*—Bread in the *Kingdom*—And *drink* wine, *new*, in the *Kingdom*. Even *new*, in the Kingdom. New in the Kingdome, not in the *oldness* of the *Letter*, But in the *newness* of the Spirit.

Fall upon them while they are marrying, and giving in marriage.

Thy *Kingdom come*. Thy will be done on earth as it is in heaven.

For thine is the Kingdome, the power and the glory, for ever and ever, Amen.

O Kingdome come! O day of the Lord come, as a thiefe in the night, suddenly, and unexpectedly, and in the night too, that they may not help themselves.

O come! come Lord Jesus, come quickly, as a thiefe in the night.

Come Lord Jesus, come quickly, these long dark nights, come in the night.

Give the word to the *Moone*, that it may be turned into bloud, and be as black as an hairecloath. Then fall upon them in the dark night, and plunder them of all flesh and *Forme*; that they may henceforth know thee no more after the *flesh*, or in the *forme* of a *Servant*, but in *power* and glory in *them*.

O consuming *Fire!* O God our joy! fall upon them in the night, and burne down *their* houses made with hands, that they may live in a house made *without hands*, for ever and ever, Amen.

The Prayer of אביעזר *is ended*

CHAP. III.

Well, once more; Where be you, ho? Are you *within?* Where be you? What*!* sitting upon a *Forme*, without doors, (in the Gentiles *Court*,) as if you had neither life nor soul in you? Rise up, rise up, my Love, my fair one, and *come away*; for lo, the Winter is past, the raine is over and gone, the flowers appear on the earth, the time of the singing of birds is come, and the voice of the Turtle is heard in our land, And (let him that hath an eare to heare, heare what the Spirit saith) the figtree putteth forth her green figges, and the vines with the tender grape give

a good smell: *Arise* my love, my fair one, and *come away*, Cant.
2.10,11,12,13.

The day breaks, the *shadowes* flie *away*. *Rise* up, my Love, and
come away.

Come with me from *Lebanon*, with me from *Lebanon*, from the top
of *Amana*, look from the top of *Shenir*, and *Hermon*, from the Lyons
dens, from the mountains of the Leopards. Come with me, *Rise*, let us
be going.

Awake, awake, put on thy beautifull garments. Awake thou that
sleepest, and arise from the dead, and Christ shall give thee *light*.

Awake, awake, thou that sleepest in security, in the cradles of
carnality. Arise from the dead.

From the *Dead*.

From the *Forme* thou sittest on, it is a dead Forme. From the *dead*.
From *flesh*, flesh is crucified.

The Cryer crieth. And the voyce said, crie, All *flesh* is grass, and all
the goodliness thereof is as the flower of the field; the grass withereth,
the flower fadeth, because the *Spirit* of the Lord bloweth upon it. The
grass withereth, the flower fadeth, and the glory of the Lord is
revealed. *And* (let him that hath an eare to heare, heare what the Spirit
saith.)

Thus saith the Lord, Mine heritage is unto me as a speckled, or
party-coloured bird, * but it shall be of one colour, and my people of
one complexion; all of them.

They shall not walk after the *flesh*, but in the *Spirit*, where they shall
be united, and as a *speckled bird* no longer.

They shall all come in the *unity* of *the faith*, and be party-coloured
no longer.

* Jer.12.

CHAP. IV.

But many *Pastors* have destroyed my Vineyard, *Jer.*12. Thus my
Fathers Vineyard goes to wrack, while it is let out to Husbandmen.
But it is yet but a little while, and behold, the Lord of the Vineyard
cometh, and will miserably destroy (& that very suddenly) the
Husbandmen, who now (because Summer is neer, even at the doors)
lay about them (especially some grounded men) very lustily, and fall
foule upon some of the Lords Servants; (who come from a farr and
strange countrey,) for they caught one, entreated him shamefully, sent
him away empty, and shamefully handled him; at another they cast
stones, and wounded him in the head: another they beate; (at lest)
smote with the tongue, and devised evill devises against him, saying,

report ye, and we will report it. And another they killed, and so they would all, if they could, and the *Heire* too.

And *Isaac* is the heire, (the son of *the freewoman*, not *Ismael* the son of the *bondwoman*[)], for he is cast out, and must be no *longer heire with* the son of the *freewoman*: For *Abraham had two sons*, the one by a *bond maid* (who is persecutor of all that are not *flesh* of his *flesh*, and *forme* of his *forme*;) the other by a *freewoman*, *Jerusalem* which is above, which is free; and the son of the *freewoman* is free indeed, and persecuted of all *flesh* and *forme*, (for * every *forme* is a persecutor) but the son of the *freewoman*, who is free, and very free too—is also free from persecuting any—so, and more then so, the son of the *freewoman* is a Libertine—even he who is of the *freewoman*, who is borne after the Spirit. And (that which is borne of the Spirit, is Spirit,) thats the heire, which is hissed at and hated. And thats the Israel of God, the seed of the Lord, that Spirit, which the whole seede of the flesh, *Ismael* (in the lumpe) and forme (in the bulk) would quench and kill.

And which all those Vine-keepers at *Baall-Haman*, or those (mystically) fleshly husbandmen would slay. But the time is comming, yea now is, that the Lord of the Vineyard will miserably destroy (at least mystically, and that suddenly) these husbandmen.

Take heed then of medling with the *Heire*, Touch not the *Lords anointed*, do his Prophets no harme; Touch not the apple of his eye, His Saints, that are caught up, out of Self, Flesh, Forme and Type, into the Lord, Spirit, Power and Truth. Into the Truth, as it is in Jesus. That are dis-joyned from carnall combinations, and fleshly fellowships, and are joyned to the Lord, that Spirit, and so are one Spirit: that are *one in* the Father, and *in* the Son; and have fellowship with the Father, and with the Son, and with all Saints; yea, with one another *in* the *Spirit*.

For they are standing before the God of the earth, & if any man wil hurt them, fire proceedeth out of their mouth, & devoureth their enemies; & if any man will hurt them, he must in this *maner* be *killed*, *Rev.*12. And those Husbandmen that conspire against them shall be miserably (at least mystically) destroyed, (when they heare it, they will say God forbid, *Luke* 20.) But the *Lord* of the Vineyard will say, my Vineyard, which is mine, is *before me*, *Cant.*8. I will become keeper of it my *Self*,—What will you do for a living then?—He will recover his Vineyard out of your hands, and what will you do in that day? (To *dig* I cannot, and to *beg* I am shamed) will be a hard story, a (*durus sermo*) a hard saying, who can beare it? I could wish this might not be fulfilled (if it might stand with the third Petition)—(*Thy will be done*) in the rigour of the Letter—(for the Letter kills) But in the Spirit, upon, and in you, and then you will be glad of it.

The second Petition—is mine for you, (*Thy kingdome come*) upon

* *Experientia docet;*[10] and though one forme persecute another, yet they can joyn hand in hand to persecute the son of the freewoman, and *Herod* and *Pilat* can shake hands, and joyn together in this, to persecute Christ, and can mutually oppose the Spirit; this I have seen, I have looked upon with mine eyes, and my hands have handled.

them, which will empty you of Self and Flesh, and staine the pride of all externall glory, and make you dance for joy, (before the Lord) with all your might, and sing the conclusion—(*Thine is the kingdome, the power and the glory, for ever and ever, Amen.*)

I wish you hugely well, though you have denied the holy One, and the Just,—and desired a murderer to be granted unto you, and killed the *Prince of Life.*——

Yet brethren, I wot that through ignorance ye did it, as did also your *Rulers.* And therefore pray—that *Antichrist* in you (for he hath been, and is in us when we knew it not) may be dispossessed, & the strong man cast out, and all his goods spoiled, and the *Man of Sin, in* every one of you, may be destroyed, with the brightness of his coming. And that every mans works may be made manifest, and the *day* may declare it, because it shall be revealed by fire, and the fire shall trie every mans work of what sort it is. And that mans works may be burnt, and they suffer loss, but that they themselves may be saved, yet so, as by *fire*, Amen.

Well, to return to my last Theame—Many *Pastors* have destroyed my Vineyard,—*Pastors!* Thus saith the Lord, I will recover my Vineyard out of the hands of all *Husbandmen* and be *Pastor* my Self, and my people shall know no Arch-Bishop, Bishop, &c. but my Self.

This you will believe and assent to (dear hearts, at first dash;) But they shall know no Pastor (neither) *Teacher, Elder,* or *Presbyter,* but the Lord, that Spirit. You shall see the later, as well as the former swallowed up in——

For, though we have known *men*, after the *flesh*, *Bishops, Priests, Pastors, Teachers, Elders,* after the *flesh*; yet henceforth know we *them*, know we *no man, so*, after the *flesh* any more: yea, though we have known *Christ* after the *flesh*, yet now henceforth, know we *Him*, so, no more. For the *Sword* of the *Lord Generall*[11]——the *Lord*, that *Spirit* shall devour from the one end of the *Land*, even to the *other* end of the *Land*, And *no flesh* shall have *Peace, Jer.* 12.

CHAP. V.

Wherefore awake, awake, and shake off thy *filthy fleshly* garments; shake off Self; cast off thy carnall clouts, and put on thy beautifull garments. Awake, awake, and watch; Seeke yee *Seekers*, Seeke ye, *Seeke* ye the *Lord*, and *David* your *King*, your *King*; Seeke him in heaven, he is not in the bowells of the earth, seeke him above, he is not *below*. (*He is not here, he is risen*—) And if you be *risen with Christ,* seeke the things which are *above*, and not the things which are *below:* *He* is not here *below.*

He is not here.—(Behold the place where the *Lord lay*; behold the place where *they laid Him.*

He is not here, but risen) He is not *below*, in *forme*, in the *forme* of a *servant*; He is above in *power:*—the *Lord*, and *David* your *King.*——

Seeke yee——But, whom seek ye? What seeke ye? What?—crucified *flesh*, took down from a *Cross*, and intombed in the earth? What? the *body*, to anoint it with sweet spices, which you have bought, and brought with you to the grave, to that purpose?

What? Is it Love, Sincerity, and Zeale mixt with weakness that sent thee, (*poor Mary*,) to seeke him in the *Sepulcher?*

Why, (sweet *Mary*) why seekest thou the living among the dead? (*He is not here, but risen.*)

O that the love, sincerity, and zeale of true *Maries* indeed might be prevented with unexpected glory, and their weakness swallowed up in strength, death in victory; and their seeking the *living* among the *dead without*, may be prevented with the *power* of the *Resurrection within*, that they being *risen* with *Christ*, may seeke things *above*, may seeke *Spirit* and *Power*, and not *Flesh*, and *Forme*, which was here *below*, while he was here in *our flesh*, and in the *forme* of a servant.

That they may seeke *Truth*. (The *truth* as it is in *Jesus*) That they may seek *Truth*, and not *Type*, which was here *below*, while he was here in the *Vaile*, which is his body. That they may awake, stand upon their legs and walke, and no longer seeke (The *living* among the *dead*.)

—Thine eyes shall see the *King* in his *Glory*, in his *Beauty*.

Yea, they shall behold the *Land* that is very far off——to some as yet, yet neere to others, *Amen, Halelujah.*

EPIST. III.

AN

Apologeticall, and additionall word to the Reader, especially to my Cronies,[12] the Scholars of *Oxford*, Concerning the precedent, and subsequent Epistles.

Deare hearts!

GOD, who at Sundry times hath spoke to his people, in divers manners; hath spoken mostly, mediately, and muchly, by man formerly.

But now in these last dayes, he is speaking to his people more purely, gloriously, powerfully, and immediately; and that variously, and strangely. More purely, and immediately (I say) and if so (as it is, must, and shall be so) then more powerfully and gloriously. More purely and immediately; for thus saith the *Lord*, I will put my Law in their *Inward* parts, and write it *In* their *Hearts*, And they shall teach *No More* every man his Neighbour, and every man his *Brother*, saying, know the Lord: for they shall all know me, from the least of them to the greatest of them, *Jer*. 31.

Oh thou afflicted, tossed with tempest, &c. I will make thy windowes of Agates, and thy gates of Carbuncles, and all thy borders of pleasant stones. And all thy Children shall be taught of the *Lord*, and great shall be the peace of thy people, reade *Isa*. 54.11. to the end the Chapter.

It is written in the Prophets; And they shall be taught of God, *John* 6.45. And,

Ye have an unction from the *Holy One*, and you know all things. And,

The Anoynting which you have received of him, abideth *In You*, And ye need not that any *Man Teach* you; but as the same anoynting teacheth you of all things, and is truth, and is no lie; and even as it hath taught you ye shall abide *In Him*, I *John* 2.20.27.

——I neither received it of *Man*, neither was I *Taught* it, But by the *Revelation* of Jesus Christ.

Neither went I up to *Hierusalem*, to them which were Apostles before me,—*Gal.* 1.12.17. And the Lords hand is not weakned, neither is his arme shortned—

Neither is it good limiting the holy one of Israel; saying, Can God prepare a *Table* in the *Wildernesse?*——

Yea; he can, and will.

Oh God! my God, my *Pastor*, my *Shepheard* can, doth, and will.——

And though I have knowne *Men* after the *Flesh, Pastors, Shepheards* after the *Flesh.* Yet *Now, Henceforth* know I them so no more. I now know, that *The Lord* is my *Pastor*, I shall not want; *He* maketh me to lie downe in *Green Pastures.* He *Leadeth* me beside the *Still Waters; He Restoreth* my soule, he leadeth me in the pathes of Righteousnesse, for his names sake: yea, though I walke through the valley of the *Shadow* of *Death*, I will feare no evill: for *Thou* art *with Me*, &c.

Thou *Anoyntest My* head with *Oyle*, my *Cup* runneth over.

Thou preparest *A Table* before me, in the presence of mine enemies, in despite of my foes; And that in the *Wildernesse* too. *He* hath prepared a *Table* in the wildernesse.

This hath been fulfilled in a more literall, externall way, formerly; Is *Now* fulfilling in a spirituall, glorious, and *Inward* way.

He prepares a *Table*, and disheth out dainties to us *Himselfe*, Teaches us *Himselfe, Leads* us *Himselfe.* Feedeth, and foldeth us with *Himselfe*, and *In Himselfe.* And we lye downe in *Green Pastures.*

Oh Lord, our *Bishop, Pastor*, Shepherd!

Surely *Now*, goodnesse and mercy shall follow me all the days of my life; And I will dwell in the *House* of the Lord for ever, and ever, Amen. Amen say I. Amen, Amen, saith the *Lord.*——

—(*Sic volo, sic jubeo, stat pro ratione voluntas*).[13] even so, *Father*, for so it seemeth good in thy *Sight*; But not in the *Sight* of *Silver Smiths*, Who raise no small stirre about *This Way.* In that, *Hereby*, their *Craft* is in danger to be set at *Nought*; And their great Goddesse *Diana* to be despised, Reade *Acts* 19.23. to the end.

But these things must needs be, but the end shall not be yet.

Yet live according to God *In the Spirit.* The end of all things is at hand, I *Pet.* 4.6,7. For the Lord is teaching his people more gloriously, powerfully, purely, immediately then formerly, and more strangely too.

For everlasting wisdome is doing over those things in Spirit, power, and glory (more invisible to an externall eye) *In Us*: which were in a more literall, externall, and visible way done to, and for his people formerly.

He protected, guided, lead, and lighted his people by a pillar of fire, and cloud formerly. But this glorie and guidance, this light and lustre was a strange one.

It was not Sunne and Moone which *Ægyptians* were acquainted with, and the light they walked by; yea, that mostly, if not altogether that, which Israel was acquainted with, while——in the Land of *Ægypt*——*The House of Bondage*. But when they were prevented with this unexpected glory (I believe) they were glad of it, and entertained this *Stranger*—joyfully, even this *Stranger*, *This New Light*, this *Strange* Light; which was trouble and tribulation; Death, and darknesse to the Hoast of the *Ægyptians*.

This thing is *Now* transacted upon, and *In* the true Israel, *Spiritual* Israel, *Israel* in *Spirit*. Is done over againe (I say) and transacted upon them in *Spirit*, Power and glory (*Within* them:) And they that are prevented with such unexpected glorie, dare not be forgetfull of entertaining *Strangers*: because in so doing, they have entertained *Angels* unawares.

CHAP. II.

(Being a Christmas Caroll, or an Anthem,
sung to the Organs in Christ-Church
at the famous University of——
the melody whereof was made
in the heart, and heard in a
corner of אביעזר *a late*
converted JEW.)

And it is neither Paradox, Hetrodox, Riddle, or ridiculous to good Schollars, who know the *Lord in deed*, (though perhaps they know never a letter in the Book) to affirm that God can speak, & gloriously preach to some through Carols, Anthems, Organs; yea, all things else, &c. Through Fishers, Publicans, Tanners, Tent-makers, Leathern-aprons, as well as through University men,—Long-gowns, Cloakes, or Cassocks; O *Strange!*

But what will this babling *Battologist*[14] say? Why *Paul*, the *Athenians* Babler said in this *wise*, the eternall Power and Godhead may be clearly seene by the things that are made; and the eternall God may be seene, felt, heard, and understood in the Book of the *Creatures*, as in the Book of the *Scriptures, alias Bible.*

Mine eare hast thou opened *indeed*,—may some say; who heare the *Sword*, and him that sent it, even the *Sword* of the *Spirit*, which is quick and powerfull, &c. Who can (I say) heare the *Sword* of the *Spirit* preach plaine and powerfull, quick and keene, sharp, short, and sweete Sermons, through clouds and fire, fire and water, heaven and earth, through light and darkness, day and night.

That can heare (*Verbum Dei, in verbis diei, noctisque sermone*——)

the *Word* in the dayes, and nights report. For if we were not pittifull poor Schollers, dunces, dullards, and dull of hearing, we might heare the Lord preach precious pieces to us through the heavens and firmament day and night. For the heavens (אביעזר)[15] are telling declare the glory of God, and the firmament sheweth his handy worke. Day unto day uttereth speech, and night unto night sheweth knowledge. There is no speech, nor Language, where their voyce is not heard; Their line is gone out thorow all the earth, and their words to the end of the world,——

To the chief Musician, for the Organist of *Christ-Church*.

Brave Schollers,——they that can heare the eternall God silently and secretly whispering secrets, and sweets into their souls, through bed and board, through food and raiment; that can meet him at every turn, and heare him in all things, that can meet him in this Paper, that can meet him here, and rejoyce in him; that can reade their Lesson in this primer; that can reade him within Book: but better schollers they, that have their lessons without book, and can reade God (not by roate) but plainly and perfectly, on the backside, and outside of the book, as well as in the inside: that can take this Primer in their hands; and hold it heeles upward, and then reade him there: that can spell every word backwards, and then tell what it is: that can reade him from the left hand to the right, as if they were reading *English*, or from the right to the left, as if they were reading *Hebrew*: that can read, God as plainly in the *Octavo* of a late converted *JEW*, as in a Church Bible in *Folio*: that can reade him within book, and without book, and as well without book, as within book: that can reade him downwards and upwards, upwards and downwards, from left to right, from right to left: that can reade him in the Sun, and in the Clouds, and as well in the Clouds, as in the Sun.

Well, hie you, learne apace, when you have learned all that your *Pedagogues* can teach you, you shall go to Schole no longer, you shall be (*Sub ferula*) no longer, under the *lash* no longer, but be set to the *University* (of the universall Assembly) and entred into *Christs* Church, (the Church of the first born, which are written in heaven,) and when you once come to know that you are *there*, you will heare no Mechanick Preach; (no, not a *Peter*, if he be a Fisher-man) but the learned Apostle, who speaks with tongues more then *they*—all,—and then you will fall upon your books (as if ye were *besides* your *selves*) and bring your books together, and burne them before all men; so mightily will (ο λογὸζ-) *the word* grow in you, and prevaile upon you,

that men shall say you are not only in a Lunatick —— *(1)* Moode.
but quite *besides* your selves; you burne your Books, that
is the ———————— *Indicative* ———————— *(2)*
and when you are accounted fooles and mad men, and are

besides yourselves (in good earnest) and your father and
mother are troubled at you, grieve for you, and at length
forsake you, then the Lord will take you up into himself,   *Moode.*
and say, Live in me, dwell in me, walk with me; there is
the ——————————————— *Imparative*,
and you will sing an *Hebrew* Song, one of the Songs of
Sion; the Lords Song, when you are lifted up, out of a   3
strange *Land*——your *selves*, when you are
non-entities, walk with God and are not, because the
Lord hath took you, then (I say) you will sing one of the
songs of *Sion*, an *Hebrew* Song, and say (אבי אחה אלי)[16]
thou art my Father, my God, *Psal.* 89.26. Let my
Father, my God dwell with me for ever and ever, Amen.
Let him there dwell, that is still the —— *Imparative.*
And it must be so, For you are no more *twaine* but *one*, He is in the
Imparative Moode, and so are you; For thus saith the Lord, Ask me of
things to come concerning my sons, and—*command ye Me.*
And (*Utinā, si, ô, ô, si, utinam.*)[17] I would to God the
people of God (*now*) knew their interest *in* God, and
union in Him, what they knew they were *one*, in the
Father, and in the Son, there is the ——*Optative*[18] (4)   *Moode.*
Some may, can, might, should, would know it: (if they
could,) theres the ——————————— *Potentiall (5)*
When the Father pleaseth,—there is the — *Subjunct. (6)*   *Moode.*
And by this time I am so far beside my self, as to add an
Interjection unto an *Adverb* in the *Optative* line (*now*)
ha, ha, he,— Thy will be done on earth as it is in heaven,
where we shall live to sing *Halelujah* to him, that is
the———————————————————*Infinitive (7)*

O *infinite Love*! that Family he is of—who is——Sweet Schollers,
Your Moody Servant,—— אביעזר

From *Christ-Church* Colledge——where the *Deane*, his Tutor
(who will be) (I meane, will be known to be) Primate and
Metropolitane of all Christendome, and *Archbishop* of *All-hallows*,
and that by *All-hallow-tide*; and it is now *Christ-tide* (for this very day
was he borne of a *Virgin*) is teaching him his *Accidence*, a new way,
new, new, new; (*Et hoc accidit dum vile fuit:*——)[19] But no more of
this till I come to (*Doctrina magistri*) the learning of the *Master*, who is
teaching me all the parts of Speech, and all the Case of Nounes, and all
the Moodes and Tenses of Verbs. And there be five Tenses or Times:
there is a Time to be merry (*To be merry in the Lord*) and that is the
Present Tense with some, to others the Future.

There is a Tense or Time to Write, and a Time to give over. It is
almost time for me to knock off here for the present; because I heare

Interjections of Silence (as *an*, and such others) sounding in mine eares. Only I must tell my Cronies at *Oxford*, that such schollers who can speake with tongues more then they all–(and can understand, and interpret all Languages) know this to be sound and *Orthodox Divinity*.

But it is not expedient for me doubtless to glory. I will come to Visions and Revelations of the Lord; and these are looked upon as new Lights too, and *Strangers*.

But one more, be not forgetfull of entertaining Strangers, for some in so doing have entertained Angels unawares. Here are two sent to thee, use them as thou pleasest, or as thou canst: all that they speake, is to this purpose, *Sodome* must be burnt, *Lot* must be saved, *flesh* must die & be crucified, and the *Spirit* live and dwell in the Saints. Mans day is almost at an end; and the day of the Lord is at hand; and the day of the Lord shall be upon all mountaines that are high and lifted up—upon all mountaines, upon mountaines *within* (for there are mountaines *in us*; upon all mountaines *without*,—on all mountaines, and upon all the oakes of *Basan*——upon all the Ships of *Tarshish*, and upon all pleasant *Pictures*,——) and the haughtiness of man shall be humbled, and the loftiness of men laid low, and the *Lord alone* shall be exalted in that *day*.

And they speake out thus much in the words following.
From the land of *Canaan*, the land of *Liberty*——
December 25th. 1648.

Valete

א"ב

EPIST. IV.

AN

Extract of an Epistle sent to *A. C.* from Mrs. *T. P.* (another late Converted *Jew*,) mediately occasioning the precedent Epistles of the last Letter.

Deare Brother,

MY true love in the Spirit of one-nesse, presented to your selfe,——with all that call on the name of the Lord; both yours and ours. It hath pleased *The Father* of late, so sweetly to manifest his love to my soule, that I cannot but returne it to you, who are the Image of my *Father*.

I should rejoyce, if the Father pleased also, to see you, and to have some Spirituall communion with you, that I might impart those soul-ravishing consolations, which have flowne from the bosome of the Father, to our mutuall comfort. What though we are weaker vessels, women, &c. yet strength shall abound, and we shall mount up with wings as Eagles; we shall walke, and not be weary, run, and not faint; When the *Man-Child Jesus* is brought forth *In Us.* Oh what a tedious, faint way have we been lead about to finde out our rest, and yet when all was done, we were twice more the sonnes of slavery then——But blessed be our God, who hath brought us by a way that we know not, and we are quickly arrived at our *Rest*.

For my part——I have been at the *Holy Land*, and have tasted of the good fruit; not only seen that fruit which the Spies brought, but surely I have tasted, And therefore can say, that *now* I believe, not for any ones word, but because I have seen, and tasted—I have one thing to acquaint you with in especiall: And that is,

That of late the Father teacheth me by visions of the night—It will be too large to communicate by letter, yet because to one is given a revelation; to another an interpretation. I cannot but repeate one, which was thus——I was in a place, where I saw all kinde of Beasts of the field; wilde, and tame together, and all kinde of creeping wormes, and all kinde of Fishes——in a pleasant river, where the water was exceeding cleere,——not very deep—but very pure——and no mud, or setling at the bottome, as ordinarily is in ponds or rivers. And all these beasts, wormes and Fishes, living, and recreateing themselves together, and my selfe with them; yea, we had so free a correspondence together, as I oft-times would take the wildest of them, and put them in my bosome, especially such (which afore) I had exceedingly feared, such that I would not have toucht, or come nigh: as the Snake, and Toade, &c.—And the wildest kinde, and strangest appearances as ever I saw in my life. At last I tooke one of the wildest, as a Tiger, or such like, and brought it in my bosome away, from all the rest, and put a Collar about him for mine owne, and when I had thus done it, it grew wilde againe, and strove to get from me, And I had great trouble about it. As first; because I had it so neare me, and yet it should strive to get from me, but notwithstanding all my care it ran away. If you can tell the interpretation of it, it might be of great use to the whole body.

Now I must also acquaint you, that I am not altogether without teachings in it. For when I awoke, the vision still remained with me. And I looked up to the Father to know what it should be. And it was shewen me, that my having so free a commerce with all sorts of appearances, was my spirituall libertie,—and certainly, did I know it, it would be a very glorious libertie, and yet a perfect Law too.——There is another Scripture which hath much followed me. And that is, God beheld all things that he made, and loe, they were very good. Now concerning my taking one of them from all the rest (as distinct,) and setting a collar about it——this was my weaknesse, and here comes in all our bondage, and death, by appropriating of things to our selves, and for our selves; for could I have been contented to have enjoyed this little, this one thing in the libertie of the Spirit——I had never been brought to that tedious care in keeping, nor that exceeding griefe in loosing,——waite therefore upon God for a further understanding in this thing, And when you have it, I make no question but I shall partake of it.——

I know you have the *Anoynting*, which sheweth you all things, to which anoynting I now commit you, and rest,

Yours in the Lord, who is that Spirit.

Here (next) followes the *Epistle* Reponsory, to the late precedent Letter of Mrs. *T. P.* lately sent to *A. C.*

Wherein, there is an interpretation of her Revelation (exprest in the Espistle immediately foregoing;) and an opening of her vision, As from the Lord, and that, as followeth.

EPIST. V.

Dear Sister, in the best fellowship, mine intire love, &c.
presupposed——

I Have received your Letter, and the *Fathers* voyce in it, but it came
not into our Coast till the 12. of *November*, which was the Fathers
time, since which time, I have scarce been one whole day at home,
but abroad, at my *Meate* and *Drinke*.——so (that if I durst, yet) I
could not so much as plunder an opportunitie,—but now it is freely
given me to write.——

I know you are a *Vessel* of the *Lords House*, filled with heavenly
liquor, and I see your love,——The *Fathers* love, in the sweet returnes
of your (I meane) his sweets to me. I love the vessell well, but the *Wine*
better, even that Wine, which we are drinking *New*, in the
Kingdome.——

And it is the voyce of my *Beloved*, that saith, drinke oh friends! yea,
drinke abundantly oh Beloved!

Deare friend, why doest in thy letter say, (what. though we be
weaker Vessels, women? &c). I know that Male and Female are all one
in *Christ*, and they are all one to me. I had as live heare a daughter, as a
sonne prophesie. And I know, that women, who *Stay* at *Home*, divide
the spoyle——whilst our younger brethren, who are (as we were)
abroad, and not yet arrived at our *Fathers House*, or are at *Home*, are
spending *Their Substance* in riotous liveing, and would faine fill their
bellies with *Huskes*; the outside of the graine.—But ere long, no man
shall *Give Them* unto them, then shall they be hastened *Home*, to the
Inside, heart, *Graine*. To the finest wheate-flower, and the pure bloud
of the grape; To the fatted calfe, ring, shoes, mirth, and Musicke, &c.
which is the *Lords Supper indeed*.

I am your eccho, in that which followeth in your Letter. (*viz*) that
strength doth abound, and we walke, and are not weary, &c. when the
Man-childe Jesus is brought forth *in Us*. Till then, we walke in
darknesse, and know not at what we stumble, while the *True Light* is at
a *Distance from us*, or we see him not *In Us*, the hope of glory.

For though *The Light* shineth, and shineth alwayes, yet the
darknesse comprehendeth it not, deep darknesse is upon the face of the

Deep, till the *Spirit* of God move upon it.

And though the *Day-Starre* be up, and up alwayes; yet we are in darknesse, till the *Day-Spring* from on high visiteth us.

And when *The day* dawneth in *Us*, and the *Day-Starre* ariseth *In our Hearts*; then we see that transacted in us, which formerly was done, in, and upon him; we see him, not only dying at *Jerusalem*, but beare about *With Us* daily, *The Dying* of *the Lord in Us*, We see, not only his death *Without Us*, but clearly see also his *Death in Us*.

I protest, by your rejoyceing which I have in Christ Jesus our Lord. I dye daily, yet not I, but *Christ*——in *Me*, dying daily to all things below the living God.

I heare a voyce from heaven, saying to me, *write*; *Blessed* are the dead, which thus *die in the Lord*, *&c*. Thrice happy they, who die to *Formes*, and live in *Power*, who die to *Types*, & live in *Truth*. (O the *Truth*, as it is *in Jesus*!) that die to *huskes*, the *outside*, and live upon, and in the graine, the *inside*; who die to the *bran*, and live upon, and *in* the *fine wheat flower*, the *true bread*, not formall, but spirituall—which came down from heaven, *the living Lord*, the strength, stay, and staffe of my life.

Princes live, and the *Kings daughter* lives at a higher rate then he who was higher than all the Prophets: yea, more than a Prophet: his meat was *locusts* and *wilde honey*. Theirs, the fat of *kidnies*, and *honey* out of the *Rock*, Life *honey*: this is their life; Thou art their life, O *living* God!

How sweet art thou, O *Word*, O *God*, to my taste! yea, sweeter then the *honey*, and the *honey combe*, my *God*, *sweet God*! Awake Lute, awake Harpe, awake *Deborah*, awake, it is a song, a song; a song of *loves*; one of the *Songs* of *Sion*, the *Lords* song, I am not in a *strange land* now, though in a strange posture, almost *besides myself*—*in the Lord*—Do I now *walk with God*, and *am not*? hath *God took me*? O it is good to be *here*. Shall we build here a Tabernacle? not *three*—but *one*—one for *thee*, for *thee*, for *thee*, O God, my God, my *song*!

One day *here* is better then a thousand *here*, *here within*, then a thousand *without*, in the *fine wheat flower*; then a thousand in the *huske* and *bran*, here in the *inward* Court, then a thousand in the *outward*.—the *Gentiles Court: Here* in the *Power*; then a thousand in the *Forme: Here* in the *Spirit*, then a thousand in *Flesh: Here* in the *Spirit*, Oh Spirit! O Spirit of burning! O *consuming fire*! O God our joy!

Thou hast burnt up the bullock, his *flesh*, his *hide*, his dung without the *Campe*; the *fat* upon the *inwards*, the caule above the liver, and the two *kidnies* and their *fat* is thine and ours; and thine againe, *Halelujah*.

Deare friend, he laieth his *right hand* upon me, saying, I am he that was *dead*, and behold I am *alive* for ever more, Amen.

Thou art *alive* for evermore, O *living God*! This thing is true in

Him, and in you, the *Lord is risen*,—the third day he rose again—out of *Josephs* Tombe,—so much *Papists* say, and see, and boast of ther Creede. This is but the outward Court,—and it is given to the *Gentiles*—*The Lord is risen indeed*: I see him, not only risen out of *Josephs* Tombe, *without me*, but *risen* out of the bowells of the *earth within me*, and is *alive in me, formed in me, grows in me*: The *Babe springs in my inmost wombe*, leapes for joy *there*, and then I sing, and never but then, O *Lord my song*! to *me a childe is borne, a son is given*, who *lives in me*, O *Immanuel*! O *living Lord*! This *is life eternall*,—its true, both in *him*, and in *you*, because the *darkness* is past, and the *true light* now shineth: thus hath he brought us into a *way* that we *knew not*, and we are arrived at *our rest*——*The Sabboth* of the *Lord thy God*, in which *thou* shalt not do *any work, thou*, nor thy son, *&c. thy* manservant, *&c. thy* cattle, *&c.* Not *thou*,—but the *Lord*—*in thee*: nor *thy* cattle, &c. But the *Lord*—ploweth *in thee*, sowes *in thee*, reapes *in thee, &c.* with *his winde (in thee)* bloweth away the *chaffe* in thee, *&c.* (for *my Father* is the *Husbandman*) grindeth in thee, makes meale of thee, *Searcheth* thee, till thou art the finest wheate flower, doth *all*—*in thee*, till thou art *all in Him*, (—I *in them*, and they *in me*,—that *they* may be *one in us*,—and I *in them.*) And then are we in the *holy Land* (which you mention) *the Land* of the *living*, the *holy Lord*, the *living Lord*. This *land* is far distant from the *land* of *Egypt*, which is the *house of Bondage*.

This, the land of slavery, and sore servitude, *That* a *large land*, a land of large, (not carnall or licentious; but of pure and *spirituall*) *Liberty*, when we are there, then we are *free indeed*. For the *land* whither thou art gone in to possess it, is not as the *land* of *Egypt*, from whence thou camest out; where *thou* sowest *thy* seed, and waterest it with *thy* foot, *&c.* but the *land* whither thou art gone in to possess it, is a *land* of hills and valleys, and drinketh water of the *raine* of *heaven*; a *land* which the Lord thy God careth for, the eyes of the Lord thy God are alwayes upon it, from the beginning of the yeare, to the ending of the yeare, *Deut*. 11.10,11.

While we were in the land of *Egypt*, we did toile, moyle, work, and sweat, and groane, *&c.* while we durst not minish ought from our bricks of our *daily taske*.—But *here*, like the *Lords Lilly*, thou *toilest not*—but growest in the *land*, the *Lord*. Here, *thou* labourest not, art entred into *thy rest*, ceasest from *thy* labour, as the *Lord* did from his.

Here thou hast *Wells*, which *thou* diggedst not, *houses* which *thou* buildest not, Vineyards, and Olive yards which *thou* plantedst not, Corne that thou sowedst not, *&c. All is given, freely given* thee. *Here* thou has wine, and milke, and honey without mony, without *price*. *Here* thou *standest still*, and seest the salvation of God upon thee, *in thee*. *Here* thou diggest not for a *song*, the Lord (*in thee*) puts a *new song* in thy mouth, O *Lord my song*! Here thou diggest not for gold, nor searchest for fine gold, the Lord is *thy gold in thee*, and thy God thy confidence. *Here* thy garment waxeth not old, for thou art invested with the *best Robe* which shall never be moath-eaten, with the best Robe, O Lord our righteousness! *Here* the morning weede is torne off, and all thy *sackcloath*——(for can the children of the *Bride-Chamber* fast?) *Here* thou art clad with the garments of *Praise*, for the spirit of heavinesse; here is given to thee beauty for a hes, the oyle of joy for mourning. *Here* all *Teares* are *wiped away* from thine eyes; thou shalt not see evill any more. For thou art in *the Holy Land*, the *Holy Lord*, and the Lord thy *God* in the *midst* of *Thee*, who rejoyceth over thee with joy; and *joyeth in*, and over thee with *Singing*. Sing oh Daughter, the *Lord* Sings *In Thee*, Shout oh Daughter, the *Shout* of a *King* is in *Thee*. Take a Timbrell, oh Mirian! the Lord *Danceth in Thee*. Oh *God* My joy! Be merry with all the Heart.

Drink off thy *Cup*, the *Cup* of *Salvation*, its the *Kings Health*, (thy Saving health, oh God) my God! Drink oh friends; yea drink abundantly oh beloved! it is lively wine, liquor of life, it will make the lame man leap like a Hart, causing the lips of those that are asleep to speak; for it is the *New Wine* in the *Kingdom*—good wine, the best wine, of the *best Vine*. Not of the Vine of *Sodom*, and of the fields of *Gomorrah*, whose grapes are grapes of gall, whose clusters are bitter, whose wine is the poyson of Dragons, and the cruell venome of Aspes. But of the *True Vine*, the *Vine indeed* of the sweet grapes: *Sweet God*! grapes indeed, of great worth, and weight——*One cluster borne between two upon a staffe, Numb.* 13.23. Grapes of life, of *Bloud* of heart bloud, *Drinke indeed*, The *Pure bloud* of the *Grape*,— ——Thy Bloud, and Heart, and *Life, Pure God*! *Oh God*! *My God*.

Privil.[20]

Oh Lord, our Lord, how excellent is thy Name——Lord! What is man that thou art thus mindfull of him?

What is man?

Man is the *Woman*, and *thou* art the *Man*, the *Saints* are thy *Spouse*, our *Maker* is our *Husband*; *We* are no more *twaine*, but *One. Halelujah*.

For we are in that pure *River* of water of life, cleere as Christall, and that *River in us*, (which *River* you saw,) which is the *Fountaine* of life, the *Living God, the River*, the streames whereof make glad the City of God.

We are (I say) in that *River*, and that *River in us*, when we are *besides* our selves, undone, nothing, and *Christ* all, in *all, in us*.

The *River* is as cleare as Chrystall, nothing but Christ, all Christ, Chrystall—it is as clear as Chrystall, *Christ-all*. Hallelujah.

And all those beasts of all sorts, wilder and tame, Wormes, and all kinde of fishes (which you saw) proceeded out of the *river*, the *Living God*, the *Fountaine* of *Life*. For by him were all things created, that are in heaven, and that are in earth, visible, and invisible, &c. All things were created by *Him*, and for *Him*, and he is before all things, and in *Him (the river) all things* consist.

The enmity within, and without shall be slaine,——Then shall all channels runne into the Ocean, live in the *river*, returne to the *Fountaine*, from whence they came: *recreating* themselves together there: Reade *Rom*. 8.19. to 24. The riddle, that riddle is read to me—Then shall the *shaddow* of *Separation* wholy flye away,——those that have been *wilde* and are *tame*, shall play together. The Wolfe shall play with the Lamb, the Lion shall eate straw like an Oxe, &c. A sucking *Childe* shall leade them, &c.

First, Wolves and Lyons——*within*, Then Wolves and Lions *without*.——

The Enmity, the *Serpent*, in all, which is exceeding bad, shall be slaine.

But all that *He* made, which is *exceeding good*, shall returne to the (*summum bonum*) *the chiefest good* to the *River*, shall live there, recreate themselves together there, &c.——But these things are, and shall be first transacted *in us*, are in part, (but the end is not yet.——)

The *Wormes in us* shall give over gnawing, the Tygers, Dragons, Lions *in us* (for my soule hath long dwelt among *Lions*) shall give over roaring, ramping, ravening, devouring, shall *play* with the *Lamb*; Doe they not? A *sucking Childe* shall leade them; Doth he not? They shall not *hurt*, Doe they? *Serpents* stings shall be pulled out, are they not? We shall *beare* them in our *Bosomes*; Doe we not? And they shall not sting us; Doe they?——*Lions in us*,——but they are as *tame*, as if they were dead; Dead they are, and a honey-combe in their carkasse.

The Prophecie is in part fulfilled, in part your vision is opened, not by me, but by him in *me* (who openeth, and no man shutteth,——) And *Sampsons Riddle* is read——

(——Out of the mouth of the Eater came sweet.——) What? a *Honey-combe* out of the carkasse of a wilde, dead, tamed *Lion*; Oh sweet!——sweet God!—

We exceedingly feared *them*——Bugbeares frighted us, when we were children, but now we doe not,—now they——cannot. *Halelujah*.

It seems you can carry them in your bosome, and you saved harmelesse, I am glad of it.

But perhaps I now speak with a stammering tongue, that may be confest; And I expect prejudiciall hearts, eares, and eyes from some; But rejoyce exceedingly that I know *the Fathers voyce*, though I cannot yet speak plaine enough after him, or write that smoothly, which is written fairely in me, in this particular. My poore, sweet, dearely beloved Brethren in the *Land* of *Aegypt*, the *house* of *Bondage*, will say; (*The Lord* hath not appeared to me——*Exod*. 4.1.)

Oh my Lord, I am not eloquent, neither heretofore, nor since thou hast spoken to thy servant, &c. But *Aaron* my *Brother*, I know he can speake well, he shall be the spokesman, and speake out this plainly in the eares of *Aegyptian Israelites. Halelujah.*

Well, *The River* (which you saw) is exceeding cleare (you say,) no mud, or setling at the bottome,——It is true; All other ponds are usually muddy. Why, then you must not sit by the *Rivers* of *Babylon* (the great, or the lesser, of *Babylon within*, or *Babylon without*) they are muddy men, profound men are Muddy, *Diviners, mad, and muddy.*

The River, the Fountaine of Life, the living God is cleere, *pure God*! It is good to be here, to drinke deep draughts *Here*: To wade *Here* up to the ancles,——(it is not very deep) (you say) Neither is it by the bankes-side.

If we were but 2000. cubits off the *Bank*, (drie ground, *Earth*,) in *the River* we should be up to the knees. 3000. off—is to the loynes——And at 4000.——off the Banke,——it is deep enough to Swimme in. Oh the *Depth, Breadth*, and *Length*,—how unsearchable, &c.——

We shall ere long *swimme* in the *River*, the *River* of *Pleasures*, for evermore, for evermore, Amen. *Halelujah.*

Then we shall not hug appearances, or *Formes* in our bosome any longer.

It seemes you have tooke some of the *Wildest* appearances, formes, or figures into your bosome.

So have I, but most of them are gone, vanisht in a moment. *They* are all *wilds*, and will *runne away*. (—when the *Day* breakes, the *shaddowes* flie away.) *They* will all turne *wilde*, and runne away, and we shall be *besides* our *selves*, and *Caught* up *into* the *Lord*, *the Substance*, which swalloweth up his appearances into *Himselfe*, Into *Himselfe*, Whither our *Fore-runner* is for us entered. *He* was *here*, in *Forme*, or *Flesh*, in *Flesh*, and Forme, (for he took upon him the forme of a servant.)

He is there, (in the bosome of the Father, at the right hand, O my father, *The river of pleasures, pure river, pure God*) in *power* and *glory*, &c.—

So, *this corruptible*—shall put on *incorruption*, this mortall shall put on immortality, than shall be brought to passe the saying that is written—*Death* is swallowed *up* in *victory*.—

O dear hearts! let us look for, and hasten to the comming of the *Day* of *God*, wherein the *Heavens* being on *fire* shall be *dissolved*, and the *Elements*, (*Rudiments, first principles*). (Imagine formall *Prayer*, formall *Baptism*, formall *Supper*——&c.) shall *melt away*, with fervent heate, *into* God; and all *Forms*, appearances, *Types, Signes, Shadows, Flesh*, do, and shall *melt away* (with fervent heate) into *power*, reallity, *Truth, the thing signified, Substance, Spirit.*

This is the *Day, the Lords Day*, the *Sabbath* of the *Lord* thy God, which we look for, and hasten too, and which (in a great measure) some are already entered into.——

O my beloved! Be thou as a Roe, or young Hart——Even so Lord Jesus, Amen, come quickly, Amen.

I see him comming (to some *come*) in the clouds, with great power and glory, Amen, *Halelujah.*

Let us not therefore any longer single out any appearance, and appropriate it to our selves; no—not a *Paul*, an *Apollo*, or a *Cephas*,[21] &c.—all is yours, if you will not set a collar upon the neck of any—distinct—or beare it in your bosome, &c. For, while one saith I am of *Paul*——(and so single him out—) and another, I am of *Apollo*, &c. are ye not carnall?——But whether *Paul*, or *Apollo*, or *Cephas*, or things present, or things to *come*, or *life*, or *death*, &c. *all is* yours (*in the Spirit*) for you are *Christs*, and *Christ* is *Gods*, Amen, Amen, *Hossanna* in the highest.

Blessed is he that commeth in the name of our Lord. Blessed be the *Kingdom* of our Father *David*, that commeth in the name of the *Lord*, *Hosanna* in the *highest*, *Halelujah*, Amen.

Thy *Kingdom* is *come*
to *some*
——their joy:
But to others *doome*
It is come
——they cry.——

FINIS

An Additional and Preambular Hint,— As a general Epistle written by ABC

Thus saith the Lord, I am (*a*) Alpha* and Omega, the beginning and the ending, the first and the last; and now the last is reaching the first, and the end the beginning.

All things are returning to their Original, *b* where all parables, dark sayings, all languages, and all hidden things, are known, unfolded, and interpreted.

c That God of Peace and Love that eternal and everlasting Being, that eternal Unity *d*, who is all, and in all, is *e* reconciling all things into himself.

And in him, who is *f* the Lyon and the Lamb, *g* the Branch and Root, the Root and Offspring, *h* the eternal and everlasting Father, and *i* the Son of man.

The *k* Servant, and the *l* Lord of all, who is *m* the Prince of Peace, and *n* a Man of War.

o A jealous God, *p* and the Father of Mercies; In him (I say) the Lyon and the Lamb, Servant and Lord, Peace and War, Joy and Jealousie, Wrath and Love, &c are reconciled, and all complicated in Unity.

In him, Lyon and Lamb, Branch and Root, Root and Offspring, Father and Son, are all one.

And all those (seemingly cross)

The A. Alpha is triangular.
Wherein the Trinity (so called) is finely and secretly, certainly and truly seen by the immortal eye, the eye of eternity, the figure only (and perhaps) scearse that is seen into by any mortal eye.
The A. Alpha is the Trinity, viz, Father, Son, and Spirit:
Which A or, Trinity is the Effluence or outspreading of Divinity.
Or out-going of God into ALL THINGS
The figure is thus:
A——

Father

Sonne GOD Sprit. Alpha

Now; internally, or in the eye of eternity † which is seated in the soft, undone, contrite, ie, the heart shattered to shivers, grownd down to meal, pounded to dust, and made up a new one, of a humane, a divine one: This A. is a hundred times more clearly seen to be.
Divinity, stepping first out into Rectitude, in figure thus;

a	Revel.
b	Prov. 1
c	Phil. 4. Rom. 15
d	Col. 3.
e	Col. 1,20.
f	Rev. 5.
g	Isai. 11. Rom. 15, Rev. 7.
h	Isai. 19.
i	Matth. Mark Luke John
k	John
l	Gal.
m	Isai. 9.
n	Exod. 15.
o	Exod. 20.
p	1 Cor.

Denominations do finely and secretly declare him to be all in all, and one in all, according to the Scriptures.

But he that hath eyes seeth not this, and he that hath ears heareth not this, he that hath his own hard heart understands not this.

The rain from heaven may fall upon that nether milstone, and doth not soak into it, &c.

But he that hath an EAR to hear (a single ear) heareth this.

q Prov.

He that hath an eye to see (a single eye) (and his *q* evil eye picked out, and eaten up by the Ravens of the Valleys) sees this.

And he that hath a soft heart, and soft place in his head, understands this.

r Isai. 57.

He that hath a soft heart, ie. and a heart *r* pounded to powder, an old stony heart made new, &c. such a heart as in the third column of the first page at this mark†, whither I refer you.

*Admonition given to fools.

s 2 Cor. 5.

t 1 Cor. 3. 18.

And he that hath (a* soft place in's head) thats out of his wits, and *s* besides himself, besides his own will, knowledge, wisdom and understanding; that is *t* become or made a fool, that he might be made wise, can understand this, and this ensuing Treatise.

u Prov.

Wherein are some sweet secrets and secret sweets, And *u* apples of gold in pictures of silver.

w Isai. 49.

x John.

To the (nominal) Author is given *w* the tongue of the learned, though he *x* knoweth not letters.

y 1 Pet. 4, 10, 11

z 1 Cor. 2.

y He speaks as he hath received, and in many things as the Oracles of God, and *z* the Wisdom of God in a mystery.

a 2 Cor. 3, 12.

And therein *a* useth great plainess of speech, which I am hugely taken with, because to him it is given, and so it is many times to me, but now it is not (in all these) but I cannot, and must not, but be content, because Everlasting will have it so; and I know his design in it in many particulars, I must not mention all, but something there's in it, That I must yet be a Sign and a Wonder

---

in name
Father,

2. *Into Obliquity in figure thus*

In name,

Sonne

3. *Into Obliquity again, in figure thus:*

In name

Spirit

(*In which two-fold Obliquity is no pravity, but purity it self.*)

In the middle of the A. (Alpha) *there is overthwart* I, *in figure thus:*

In name,
God.

Which is eternal Unity; all which, in a word, is God making out himself in various Administrations, as Father, Son and Spirit; and this is (Trinity in Unity, and Unity in Trinity).

And thus much for A. *which no man knows, yet poor, proud man would be called Rabbi, and pretends he knows the* ORIGINAL, *when he hath not learned his Primer, nay his ABC, not yet knows great A.*

All that the in-being, outspeaks for the present in this way of Hiroglyphical Divinity is this, only a further hint of the A. in another figure, name and language, (though one and the same is truth, and the inward ground,) which is in the figure thus;

א

In name,
Aleph.

Which is ONE—*in it selfe, and yet compounded,*

in fleshly *Israel*; and in this (as well as formerly in things of the same nature, and otherwise), I must be comfortable to my forerunner and Pattern, *b* being a stumbling stone, and a rock of offence to both the houses of *Israel*; and for a gin, and a snare to the inhabitants of *Jerusalem* that is below, that many among them may stumble and fall and be broken, and be snared and taken.

That they may stumble and fall (I say) as I have done, before I was raised up; and be broken, as I have been, before I was made whole; and be snared and taken, as I have seen, before I was set at liberty, where I sing, and shout, and dance before the Lord, because I was stumbled, and broken and snared:

Which—is none other but the gate of Heaven, as mourning is the gate of mirth, and sorrow is the gate of joy, &c.

My hearts desire for you, is, That the *c* gates of brass may fly open, and the bars of iron be burst asunder, when they must, that you may enter into *d* the secret place of the most High, which you are mostly afraid of, and so *e* withstand your own mercies.

Well! there are some things in these, somewhat (and in mine muchly) *f* hard to be understood, which they that are unlearned and unable wrest as they do also the other Scriptures, &c.

But they are all *g* plain and easie to him that understandeth, though *h* to the Jew a stumbling block, and to the Greek foolishness: To the scribe folly; To the Pharisee blasphemy, who hath (*ad unquem*) at's fingers ends, He blasphemeth, is a friend of Publicans and Harlots, he is a glutten, and wine bibber; and say we not well, that he hath a devil?

Which Pharisee, in man, is the mother of harlots, and being the worst whore, cries whore first: And the grand blasphemer, cries out, Blasphemy, blasphemy, which she *i* is brimfull of.

She is also *k* WITHOUT, i'th streets, abroad, not at HOME.

The Pharisees not at home, but abroad.

or rather branching forth it self into Obliquity, in figure thus; \

And a tripple semicircularity, in figure thus (˧

And here's Unity in Trinity, in figure thus;

א   Aleph, A

The unity is complicated in the whole figure, and clearly seen, and must not (though it might be) clearly decyphered.
This א *Aleph, or A, is (in lingua sancta) an aspiration.*
And in its ORIGINAL, and in truth, is the out-breathing, or emmanation of Divinity, into Father Son, and Spirit.
And its circularity maketh out after, and maketh up the Omega, which is in Figure thus,
o, or thus, O
Which is the eye or globe of eternity, where the end makes towards and meets the beginning, and makes up a heart full of love, and all's swallowed up into Unity:
And this is Alpha and Omega, the beginning and the end:
ONE, and ALL, God blessed for evermore.
Amen.
Hoc Scriptum est, est Scriptura, et in Scriptura.

b Isai. 8.

c Psalm

d Psalm

e Jonah 2.
f 1 Pet. 3. 16.

g Prov. 8.
h 2 Cor.

i Rev. 17
k Prov. 7

l Matt. 23. 13
   to the end

First, He's not at Home in the Lord, but in fleshliness, formality; Abroad, in the streets, in wide huge, outward zeal, devotion, righteousness, holiness and religion.

Secondly, He is ABROAD, not at home, in his own heart, not looking into his own inside into himself.

Who is *l* a painted Sepulchre, and indeed appears beautiful outward, but WITHIN is full of dead mens bones, putrifaction, and of all uncleaness and filthiness.

Being brim full of worse drunkeness, uncleaness, adultery, theft and murder, then the worst he cries out on.

Being himself in the spirit, power and life of those things (and perhaps in the form also of some of them, at least, in some degrees, and in the time of his Publicanism o'er head and ears in them) of which Publicans and Harlots are but in the form and shadow of only; and Christ (whom he most of all hates and traduces) neither in the form or power of what he accuses him of, though he be numbred amongst transgressors, and is indeed a friend of Publicans and Harlots, and open-hearted, and open-handed to them, &c.

m Matth. Mark, Luke, John.

In a word, he is very zealous against *m* the form of ungodliness:

But hugging, embracing, living and delighting in the power thereof.

And he is (only) in the form of godliness, hugging, embracing it, and contending for it, *vi & armis.*[1]

But dis relishing, dis owning, denying, blaspheming, persecuting, and mostly opposing the power thereof, *vi & armis.*

n A True Prophecy.

But the hour is coming, yea now is, *n* That all his carnal, outward, formal Religion, (yea, of Scripturely cognizane, so far as it's fleshly and formal) and all his fleshly holiness, zeal and devotion, shall be, and is, set upon the same account, as outward drunkenness, theft, murther, adultery, &c.

o Isai 66
p Isai 58

And now the time is come, that *o* He that kills an Ox, is as if he slew a man, &c. And all mans Prayers, Psalms, *p* Fasting (for strife and debate, and to smite with the fist of wickedness, though the very soul be afflicted for a day, and the head hung like a bulrush, &c.) And all man's preachings, hearing teachings, learnings, holinesses, righteousnesses, religions, is a Theft, Murder, and Adultery.

The time is now coming, and now is, That no Prayer shall be in request but (Our Father) (*He that hath an ear to hear, let him hear*).

q Exod. 15.

No psalm shall be sung, but *q* the Lord our Song.

No Holiness,—but the Lord our Holinesse.

r Jerem.

No Righteousness—but *r* the Lord our Righteousness.

s Isaiah
t Phil. 2.

s Reprobate silver shall all other be called, as it is; yea, *t* dung, dross, (σχύβαλα) dogs meat

u Isai
w A strange yet true Prophecy

—*u* Menstrous rags,—worse then the filth of a Jakes house.

w Yea, the time is coming, That zealous, holy, devout, righteous, religious men shall (one way) dye, for their Holiness and Religion, as well as Thieves and Murderers—for their Theft and Murder, &c.

And shall be punished, and put to shame, for their holiness and purity—as well as Drunkards and Adulterers, for their Drunkeness and Whoredom.

But all this while, the righteousness, holiness, purity and zeal of the Lord is pure, precious, excellent, most beautiful and glorious; And so is pure Religion and undefiled, as also, the Lords preaching, praying, singing etc. And I had rather have my tongue cut out of my mouth, and be stoned to death, then speak against this which is my life and joy.

But once more, the time is coming, that Thieves and Murtherers shall scape, as well as the most zealous and most formal professors; and men shall be put to death, (or be murthered by men) no more for the one, then for the other. *x* 1 Joh. 2

And if this come to pass, say, the Lord hath not spoken by me; and let me dye the death.

But sure I am, there are some, that know me, shall live to see this, and say *Amen* to it: And shall know, that there hath been a Prophet amongst them. Which Prophet is not *Abiezer Coppe*; but *x* the Prophet in him, who is among you all, though, as yet, manifested to few. *y* 1 Joh.

And let him that hath an ear to hear, hear.

To him (only) I commend these, and the ensuing Treatise, knowing in him *y* there's no occasion of stumbling; and to him, all mine, and these, are plain and easie: And as for others, who cannot but stumble, be offended and censure, They are to be pathetically and most affectionately told, that our heart akes for them; we have them in our bosom: and the everlasting bonds of eternal love, that dwells in us, yearn over them, are a flame towards them, and towards Publicans and Harlots (*z* Considering also our selves) and knowing that they dwell where we did, and in the remaining part of that *a* old house, which hath been fired about our ears, and over our heads, out of which, in infinite and unspeakable mercy, we were frighted into a house made without hands, the beauty whereof dazelleth the eyes of men and Angels; and at this time the glory thereof amazeth me into silence, and strikes my pen out of my hand, that if I would, yet I cannot now write of its sumptuousness, beauty and magnificence; only, as far as we dare, we wish you were there, and you shall be, when you must be. *z* Gal. *a* Obad. *b* Rev.

In the mean time, the charmer cannot charm you thither, charm ne never so wisely.

Its but yet a little while, and the *b* dividing of times will be sent packing after time, times; and then there's that in us, knows what shall be. *c* Joh 8, 32, 33. *d* Isa 10, 16, 17, 18.

In the meanwhile, be not angry if we groan without ourselves, waiting for your deliverance out of the Land of Egypt, the house of bondage (*c* which Land and house, you cannot believe you are in).

Our heart's desire for you is, That *d Jacobs* house (that little spark that lies hid and buried under all your glorious formality) may kindle and flame up from under all your formal prayers, carnal ordinances, fleshly righteousness, holiness, and religion, &c. (which are exceeding glorious in your eyes) and burn them up, that you may be lifted up into pure Religion, and undefiled; into pure Prayer, Psalms, Righteousness, Holiness, &c.

e Obad.

And that this *e* house of *Jacob* may like fire fall upon the house of *Esau*, (which is as stubble, and now as stubble fully dry) upon this house of *Esau* (I say) which is rough, hairy, red, fiery, fierce, rugged flesh, hatred, strife, envy, malice, evil surmizing &c. and utterly consume them, that there be not any remaining of the house of *Esau*.

1 Joh. 4

And the Lord may be exalted in you, and self debased, That the Lord (I say) may be exalted; The Lord, who is love, joy, peace, light, glory, consolation, &c. may be exalted, *ie* lifted up above sorrow, trouble, tribulation, fears, doubts, perplexities, wrath, war, darkness, envy, strife, self-ishness.

f 1 Cor, 13.

That the Lord (who is *f* love, and suffereth long, is kinde, envieth not, vaniteth not it self, is not puffed up, beareth all things, thinketh none evil,) may be exalted, or lifted up, (in you) above revenge, malice, unkindness, swelling pride, evil surmisings in you.

And that he might ride on prosperously, in glory and renown (in you) conquering, and to conquer, trampling all these (in you) under his feet, as mire in the streets.

g Psal.

To him I leave you, whose heart is larger than you are aware of, and in *g* whose hands are all our times, and remove hence into another coast; whither I am set with

h Joh. 6
i 1 Joh. 2,27.
k Christ.
l His Spouse.

> *The Copy of a Letter written in Heaven—(in the heart of those,*
> *whose heart is in the Lord, who are h taught of God, and who*
> *have their i Teacher in them*
> *By the k Elder.*
> *To l the Elect Lady*

Mine own,
I am thine to all eternity: my joy, my glory, my life, is thine; all mine is thine: I'l as soon cease to love thee; for thou wast taken out of me.
I am a jealous God, and that's thy joy.
If thou hast any lovers besides me, I'l not spare——

**Scriptum est.*

for it is the day of my vengeance; and I in thee, and thou in me art glad on't.
If thou hast any delights but my self, I'l crown them all with discontentments; that thou mightest lie in no bosom, but mine own;
Saith thy Maker thy Husband In

His and Thine

ABIEZER COPPE

*The original was sent by * a friend, which is better then a brother,*   *Prov.
To a friend in a corner, with this

POSTSCRIPT

Do not appropriate this to thyself only; its a general Epistle: and let this *modicum* suffice thee. For should all the words, things, and thoughts, which I have, do, and will, speak of thee, to thee, in thee; act for thee, in thee and think towards thee, the whole world would be too narrow to contein them.

Look into a larger volume, thy heart—
where I am, which I am.

An After-Clap, or second Post-script.

This is musique, WITHIN: The father, the younger brother, and all that are within, in this house, are merry; where this is dainty, and where there are dainties, and dancing, mirth and musique.

But* the serving man—the elder brother, knows not what this meaneth, but is angry, and dogged, puffs and pouts, is sullen, snuffs, swells and censures WITHOUT doors.

Serving brother, the zealous formal professor. Luke 1.5.

Alias, Or another of the same, with the former Epistle Thus:

My *a* heart, my blood, my life, is Thine:
It pleases me that *b* thou art mine
I'l *c* curse thy flesh, and *d* swear th'art fine
For *e* ever thine I mean to be,
As *f* I am that I am, within A.C.

a   Script. est.
b   Cant. 2.
      Joh. 17.
c   Nehe. 13
d   Ezek. 16
e   Mat. 3
      Heb. 13
f   Script. est.

POST-SCRIPT

Before God, this is one of the Songs O *Zion*,
Before holy man (whose holiness stinks above ground)
Its at least whimsey, if not Blasphemy;
But wisdom is justified of her Children.

A Fiery Flying Roll:

A

Word from the Lord to all the Great Ones
of the Earth, whom this may concerne: Being the
last WARNING PIECE at the dreadfull day of
JUDGEMENT.
For now the LORD is come

$$\text{to} \begin{cases} 1 \ \textit{Informe} \\ 2 \ \textit{Advise and warne} \\ 3 \ \textit{Charge} \\ 4 \ \textit{Judge and sentence} \end{cases} \text{the Great Ones}$$

As also most compassionately informing, and most
lovingly and pathetically advising and warning
London.

With a terrible Word, and fatal Blow from the LORD,
upon the Gathered CHURCHES.

And all by his Most Excellent MAJESTY, dwelling in,
and shining through
AUXILIUM PATRIS, בדף alias, *Coppe.*

With another FLYING ROLL ensuing (to all the
Inhabitants of the Earth.) The Contents of both
following.

---

*Isa. 23.9, The Lord of Hosts (is) staining the pride of all glory, and
bringing into contempt all the honourable (persons and things) of the
Earth.
O London, London, how would I gather thee, as a hen gathereth her
chickens under her wings, &c.
Know thou (in this thy day) the things that belong to thy Peace—
I know the blasphemy of them which say they are Jewes, and are not,
but are the Synagogue of Satan, Rev. 2.9.*

Imprinted at *London*, in the beginning of that notable day, wherein
the secrets of all hearts are laid open; and wherein the worst and foulest
of villanies, are discovered, under the best and fairest outsides. 1649.

THE
PREFACE

An inlet into the Land of Promise, the new
Hierusalem, and a gate into the ensuing Discourse,
worthy of serious consideration.

My Deare One.
All or None.
Every one under the Sunne.
Mine own.

My most Excellent Majesty (in me) hath strangely and
variously transformed this forme.

And behold, by mine owne Almightinesse (In me) I have been
changed in a moment, in the twinkling of an eye, at the sound of the
Trump.

And now the Lord is descended from Heaven, with a shout, with
the voyce of the Arch-angell, and with the Trump of God.

And the sea, the earth, yea all things are now giving up their dead.
And all things that ever were, are, or shall be visible—are the Grave
wherein the King of Glory (the eternall, invisible Almightinesse, hath
lain as it were) dead and buried.

But behold, behold, he is now risen with a witnesse, to save *Zion*
with vengeance, or to confound and plague all things into himself; who
by his mighty Angell is proclaiming (with a loud voyce) That Sin and
Transgression is finished and ended; and everlasting righteousnesse
brought in; and the everlasting Gospell preaching; Which everlasting
Gospell is brought in with most terrible earth-quakes, and
heaven-quakes, and with signes and wonders following.
Amen.

And it hath pleased my most Excellent Majesty, (who is universall
love, and whose service is perfect freedome) to set this forme (the
Writer of this Roll) as no small signe and wonder in fleshly *Israel*; as
you may partly see in the ensuing Discourse.

And now (my deare ones !) every one under the Sun, I will onely
point at the gate; thorow which I was led into that new City, new

Hierusalem, and to the Spirits of just men, made perfect, and to God the Judge of all.

First, all my strength, my forces were utterly routed, my house I dwelt in fired; my father and mother forsook me, the wife of my bosome loathed me, mine old name was rotted, perished; and I was utterly plagued, consumed, damned, rammed, and sunke into nothing, into the bowels of the still Eternity (my mothers wombe) out of which I came naked, and whetherto I returned again naked. And lying a while there, rapt up in silence, at length (the body or outward forme being awake all this while) I heard with my outward eare (to my apprehension) a most terrible thunder-clap, and after that a second. And upon the second thunder-clap, which was exceeding terrible, I saw a great body of light, like the light of the Sun, and red as fire, in the forme of a drum (as it were) whereupon with exceeding trembling and amazement on the flesh, and with joy unspeakable in the spirit, I clapt my hands, and cryed out, *Amen, Halelujah, Halelujah, Amen.* And so lay trembling, sweating and smoaking (for the space of half an houre) at length with a loud voyce (I inwardly) cryed out, Lord, what wilt thou do with me; my most excellent majesty and eternall glory (in me) answered & sayd, Fear not, I will take thee up into mine everlasting Kingdom. But thou shalt (first) drink a bitter cup, a bitter cup, a bitter cup; whereupon (being filled with exceeding amazement) I was throwne into the belly of hell (and take what you can of it in these expressions, though the matter is beyond expression) I was among all the Devils in hell, even in their most hideous hew.

And under all this terrour, and amazement, there was a little spark of transcendent, transplendent, unspeakable glory, which survived, and sustained it self, triumphing, exulting, and exalting it self above all the Fiends. And confounding the very blacknesse of darknesse (you must take it in these tearmes, for it is infinitely beyond expression.) Upon this the life was taken out of the body (for a season) and it was thus resembled, as if a man with a great brush dipt in whiting, should with one stroke wipe out, or sweep off a picture upon a wall, &c. after a while, breath and life was returned into the form againe; whereupon I saw various streames of light (in the night) which appeared to the outward eye; and immediately I saw three hearts (or three appearances) in the form of hearts, of exceeding brightnesse; and immediately an innumerable company of hearts, filling each corner of the room where I was. And methoughts there was variety and distinction, as if there had been severall hearts, and yet most strangely and unexpressibly complicated or folded up in unity. I clearly saw distinction, diversity, variety, and as clearly saw all swallowed up into unity. And it hath been my song many times since, within and without, unity, universality, universality, unity, Eternall Majesty, &c. And at this vision, a most strong, glorious voyce uttered these words,

The spirits of just men made perfect. The spirits &c, with whom I had as absolut, cleare, full communion, and in a two fold more familiar way, then ever I had outwardly with my dearest friends, and nearest relations. The visions and revelations of God, and the strong hand of eternall invisible almightinesse, was stretched out upon me, within me, for the space of foure dayes and nights, without intermission.

The time would faile if I would tell you all, but it is not the good will and pleasure of my most excellent Majesty in me, to declare any more (as yet) then thus * such further: That amongst those various voyces that were then uttered within, these were some, *Blood, blood, Where, where? upon the hypocriticall holy heart, &c.* Another thus, *Vengeance, vengeance, vengeance, Plagues, plagues, upon the Inhabitants of the earth; Fire, fire, fire, Sword, sword, &c. upon all that bow now down to eternall Majesty, universall love; I'le recover, recover, my wooll, my flax, my money. Declare, declare, feare thou not the faces of any; I am (in thee) a munition of Rocks, &c.* [Hos. 2.9]

Go up to *London,* * to *London,* that great City, write, write, write. And behold I writ, and lo a hand was sent to me, and a roll of a book was therein, which this fleshly hand would have put wings to, before the time. Whereupon it was snatcht out of my hand, & the Roll thrust into my mouth; and I eat it up, and filled my bowels with it, (*Eze.* 2.8. &c. *cha.* 3.1,2,3.) where it was as bitter as worm-wood; and it lay broiling, and burning in my stomack, till I brought it forth in this forme.

And now I send it flying to thee, with my heart, And all
Per AUXILIUM PATRIS כב [1]

*It not being shewen to me, what I should do, more than preach and print something, &c. very little expecting I should be so strangely acted, as to (my exceeding joy and delight) I have been, though to the utter cracking of my credit, and to the rotting of my old name which is damned, and cast out (as a toad to the dunghill) that I might have a new name, with me, upon me, within me, which is, I am——

THE
CONTENTS

CHAP. 1. *Severall strange, yet true and seasonable informations to the great ones, as also an apologeticall hint of the Authors principle, &c.*

CHAP. 2. *Several new, strange, yet seasonable and good advice, and wholsome admonitions, and the last warning to the great ones, as from the Lord.*

CHAP. 3. *Severall dismall, dolefull cryes, & out-cries, which pierce the eares and heart of his excellent Majesty, & how the King of Kings, the King of heaven charges the great ones of the earth.*

CHAP. 4. *How the Judge of heaven and earth, who judgeth righteous judgment, passeth sentence against all those great ones, who like sturdy Oakes & tall Cedars wil not bow, and how hee intends to breake them, and blow them up by the roots.*

CHAP. 5. *A most compassionate information, and a most loving & patheticall warning and advice to* London.

CHAP. 6. *A terrible word and fatall blow from the Lord upon the gathered Churches, who pretend most for God, yet defie the Almighty more than the vilest.*

The Second Flying Roll.

CHAP. 1. *The Authors commission to write. A terrible Woe denounced against those that flight the roll. The Lords claim to all things; Together with a hint of a two-fold recovery, where-through the most hypocriticall heart shall be ripped up, &c.*

CHAP. 2. *How the Lord will recover his outward things (things of this life) as money, corn, wool, flax, &c. and for whom: And how they shal be plagued that detaine them as their owne. Wherein also are some mistical hints concerning St. Michaels days, and the Lords day following it this yeare; as also of the dominicall letter* D, *&c.*

CHAP. 3. *A strange, yet most true storie, under which is couched that lion, whose roaring shall make all the beasts of the field to tremble, and all the kingdomes of the world quake.*

Wherein also (in part) the subtility of the wel favour'd harlot is discovered, and her flesh burnt with that fire which shall burn down all Churches, except that of the first borne, &c.

CHAP. 4. *That the Author hath been set as a sign and wonder, as well as most of the Prophets formerly; as also what strange posturs that divine Majestie (that dwels in his forme) hath set the forme in: with the most strange and various effects thereof upon the spectators. His communion with the spirits of Just men made perfect, and with God the Judg of all hinted at.*

CHAP. 5. *The Authors strange and lofty carriage towards great ones, & his most lowly carriage towards beggars, rogues, prisoners, gypsies, &c. Together with a large Declaration what glory shall arise up from under all these ashes. The most strange & most secret and terrible, yet most glorious designe of God, in choosing base things, to confound things that are: And how, A most terrible viall poured out upon the well-favoured harlot; and how the Lord is bringing into contempt not only honourable persons (with a vengeance) but all honourable holy things also.*

Wholsome advice, with a terrible threat to the Formalists: And how BASE things have confounded base things: And how base things have been a fiery chariot to mount the Author up into divine glory and unspeakable Majestie: and how his wife is, & his life is in that beauty, which maketh visible beauty seem meere deformity.

CHAP. 6. *Great ones must bow to the poorest peasants, or else they shall rue for it; No material sword or humane power (whatsoever) but the pure spirit of universall love, who is the eternall God, can breake the necke of tyranny, oppression, and abhominable pride and cruell murther, &c. A catalogue of severall Judgments recited, as so many warning-pieces to appropriators, impropriators, and anti-free communicants.*

CHAP. 7. *A further discovery of the subtlety of the well favoured harlot, with a parley between her and the spirit. As also the horrid villany that lies hid under her smooth words, and sweet tongue (in pleading against the letter and history, and for the Spirit and mistery, and all for her own ends) detected. Also upon what account the spirit is put, and upon what account the letter, &c. And what the true communion, and what the true breaking of bread is.*

CHAP. 8. *The wel-favoured harlots cloaths stript off, her nakedness discovered, her nose slit. Her hunting after the young man void of understanding, from corner to corner, from religion to religion: And the spirit pursuing, overtaking, and destroying her, &c.*

What a terrible thunder-clap i'th close.

A word from the Lord to all the Great Ones of the Earth (whom this may concerne) being the last Warning Piece, &c.

1 *The word of the Lord came expresly to me, saying, Sonne of man write a Roule, and these words, from my mouth, to the Great ones, saying, thus saith the Lord:*
Slight not this Roule, neither laugh at it, least I slight you, and cause all men to slight and scorne you; least I destroy you, and laugh at your destruction, &c.
2 *This is, (and with a witnesse, some of you shall finde it, to be) an edg'd toole; and there's no jesting with it, or laughing at ∴.*
It's a sharp sword, sharpned, and also fourbished——
No sleepy Dormouse shall dare to creep up the edge of it.
Thus saith the Lord, You shall finde with a witnesse, that I am now comming

to $\begin{cases} 1 & \textit{Informe} \\ 2 & \textit{Advise and warne} \\ 3 & \textit{Charge} \\ 4 & \textit{Judge and sentence} \end{cases}$ *you, O ye great ones.*

CHAP. I.

Containing severall strange, yet true and seasonable Informations, to the great ones. As also an apologeticall hint, of the Authors Principle, standing in the front.——

1 Thus saith the Lord, *I inform you, that I overturn, overturn, overturn.*[2] And as the Bishops, Charles, and the Lords, have had their turn, overturn, so your turn shall be next (ye surviving great ones) by what Name or Title soever dignified or distinguished) who ever you are, that oppose me, the Eternall God, who am UNIVERSALL Love, and whose service is perfect freedom, and pure Libertinisme.

*An Apologeticall hint concerning the Authors Principle, the result—is negative; hee speaks little in the affirmative because not one in a hundred, yea even of his former acquaintance, now know him, neither must they yet.

2 *But afore I proceed any further, be it known to you, That although that excellent Majesty, which dwels in the Writer of this Roule, hath reconciled ALL THINGS to himselfe, yet this hand (which now writes) never drew sword, or shed one drop of any mans blood. (I am free from the blood of all men) though (I say) all things are reconciled to me, the eternall God (IN HIM) yet sword levelling, or digging-levelling, are neither of them his principle.

Both are as farre from his principle, as the East is from the West, or the Heavens from the Earth, (though, I say, reconciled to both, as to all things else) and though he hath more justice, righteousnesse, truth, and sincerity, shining in those low dung-hils, (as they are esteemed) then in the Sunne, Moone, and all the Stars.

3 I come not forth (in him) either with material sword, or Mattock, but now (in this my day—) I make him my Sword-bearer, to brandish the Sword of the Spirit, as he hath done severall dayes and nights together, thorow the streets of the great City.

4 And now thus saith the Lord:

Though you can as little endure the word LEVELLING, as could the late slaine or dead *Charles* (your forerunner, who is gone before you—) and had as live heare the Devill named, as heare of the Levellers (Men-Levellers) which is, and who (indeed) are but shadowes of most terrible, yet great and glorious good things to come.

5 Behold, behold, behold, I the eternall God, the Lord of Hosts, who am that mighty Leveller, am comming (yea even at the doores) to Levell in good earnest, to Levell to some purpose, to Levell with a witnesse, to Levell the Hills with the Valleyes, and to lay the Mountaines low.

6 High Mountaines! lofty Cedars! its high time for you to enter into the Rocks, and to hide you in the dust, for feare of the Lord, and for the glory of his Majesty. For the lofty looks of man shall be humbled, and the haughtinesse of men shall be bowed downe, and the Lord ALONE shall be exalted in that day; For the day of the Lord of Hoasts, shall be upon every one that is proud, and lofty, and upon every one that is lifted up, and he shall be brought low. And upon all the Cedars of *Lebanon*, that are high and lifted up, and upon all the Oaks of *Bashan*; and upon all the high Mountaines; and upon all the Hils that are lifted up, and upon every high Tower; and upon every fenced Wall; and upon all the Ships of *Tarshish*, and upon all pleasant Pictures.

And the LOFTINESSE of man shall be bowed down, and the haughtinesse of men shall be laid low. And the Lord ALONE shall be exalted in that day, and the Idols he shall utterly abolish.

And they shall go into the holes of the Rocks, and into the Caves of the Earth, for feare of the Lord, and for the glory of his Majesty, when he ariseth to shake terribly the earth.

In that day a man shall cast his Idols of Silver, and Idols of Gold—to the bats, and to the Moles. To go into the Clefts of the Rocks and into the tops of the ragged Rocks, for feare of the Lord, and for the glory of his Majesty. For the Lord is now RISEN to shake terriblly the Earth, *Isa.* 2.10. to the end of the Chapter.

7 Hills! Mountains! Cedars! Mighty men! Your breath is in your nostrils.

Those that have admired, adored, idolized, magnified, set you up, fought for you, ventured goods, and good name; limbe and life for you, shall cease from you.

You shall not (at all be accounted of (not one of you) ye sturdy Oake) who bowe not downe before eternall Majesty: Universal Love, whose service is perfect freedome, and who hath put down the mighty (remember, remember your fore-runner) and who is putting down the mighty from their seats; and exalting them of low degree.

8 Oh let not, (for your owne sakes) let not the mother of Harlots in you, who is very subtle of heart.

Nor the Beast (without you) what do you call 'em? The Ministers, fat parsons, Vicars, Lecturers, &c. who (for their owne base ends, to maintaine their pride, and pompe, and to fill their owne paunches, and purses) have been the chiefe instruments of all those horrid abominations, hellish, cruell, devillish persecutions, in this Nation which cry for vengeance. For your owne sakes (I say) let neither the one, nor the other bewitch you, or charme your eares, to heare them say, these things shall not befall you, these Scriptures shall not be fulfilled upon you, but upon the Pope, Turke, and Heathen Princes, &c.

9 Or if any of them should (through subtilty for their owne base ends) creep into the Mystery of that forementioned* Scripture.

Isay 2:   And tell you, Those words are to be taken in the Mystery only; and they onely point out a spirituall, inward levelling (once more, for your owne sakes, I say) believe them not.

10 'Tis true, the History, or Letter, (I speake comparatively) is but as it were haire-cloth; the Mystery is fine Flax. My flax, saith the Lord, and the Thief and the Robber will steale from me my flax, to cover his nakednesse, that his filthinesse may not appeare.

But behold, I am (now) recovering my flax out of his hand, and discovering his lewdness—*verbum sat*—[3]

11 'Tis true, the Mystery is my joy, my delight, my life.

And the Prime levelling, is laying low the Mountaines, and levelling the Hils in man.

But this is not all.

For lo I come (saith the Lord) with a vengeance, to levell also your Honour, Riches, &c. to staine the pride of all your glory, and to bring into contempt all the Honourable (both persons and things) upon the earth, Isa. 23.9.

12 For this Honour, Nobility, Gentility, Propriety, Superfluity, &c. hath (without contradiction) been the Father of hellish horrid pride, arrogance, haughtinesse, loftinesse, murder, malice, of all manner of wickednesse and impiety; yea the cause of all the blood that ever hath been shed, from the blood of righteous *Abell*, to the blood of the last Levellers that were shot to death. *And now (as I live saith the Lord) I am come to make inquisition for blood; for murder and pride, &c.* [Ps. 9.12]

13 I see the root of it all *The Axe is laid to the root of the Tree* (by the Eternall God, *My Self*, saith the Lord) *I will hew it down.* [Matt. 3.10; Lu. 3.9] And as I live, I will plague your Honour, Pompe,

Greatnesse, Superfluity, and confound it into parity, equality, community; that the neck of horrid pride, murder, malice, and tyranny, &c. may be chopt off at one blow. And that my selfe, the Eternall God, who am Universall Love, may fill the Earth with universall love, universall peace, and perfect freedome; which can never be by humane sword or strength accomplished.

14 Wherefore bow down, bow downe, you sturdy Oakes, and tall Cedars; bow, or by my self Ile break you.

Ile cause some of you (on whom I have compassion) to bow &c. and will terribly plague the rest.

My little finger shall be heavier on them, then my whole loynes were on *Pharoah* of old.

15 And maugre the the subtilty, and sedulity, the craft and cruelty of hell, and earth: this Levelling shall up.

Not by sword; we (holily) scorne to fight for any thing; we had as live be dead drunk every day of the weeke, and lye with whores i'th market place, and account these as good actions as taking the poore abused, enslaved ploughmans money from him (who is almost every where undone, and squeezed to death; and not so much as that plaguy, unsupportable, hellish burden, and oppression, of Tythes taken off his shoulders, notwithstanding all his honesty, fidelity, Taxes, Freequarter, petitioning &c. for the same,) we had rather starve, I say, then take away his money from him, for killing of men.

Nay, if we might have Captains pay, and a good fat Parsonage or two besides, we would scorne to be swordsmen, or fight with those (mostly) carnall weapons, for any thing, or against any one, or for our livings.

16 No, no, wee'l live in despite of our foes; and this levelling (to thy torment, O mighty man) shall up, not by sword, not by might, &c. but by my Spirit, saith the Lord.

For I am risen, for I am risen, for I am risen, to shake terribly the earth, and not the earth onely, but the heavens also, &c.

But here I shall cease informing you.

You may for your further information (if you please) reade my Roule to all the rich Inhabitants of the earth.

Reade it if you be wish, I shall now advice you.

CHAP. II

Containing severall new, strange, yet seasonable Admonitions, and good advice; as the last warning to the Great Ones of the Earth. from the Lord.

1 Thus saith the Lord: Be* wise now therefore, O ye Rulers, &c. Be   *Sero sapiunt

Phyrges, sed
nunquam Sera est
ad Bonos mores
via.
1 Admonition to
great ones.

instructed, &c. Kisse the Sunne, &c. Yea, kisse Beggers, Prisoners, warme them, feed them, cloathe them, money them, relieve them, take them into your houses, don't serve them as dogs, without doore. &c.

Owne them, they are flesh of your flesh, your owne brethren, your owne Sisters, every whit as good (and if I should stand in competition with you) in some degrees better then your selves.

2 Once more, I say, own them; they are yourself, make them one with you, or else go howling into hell; howle for the miseries that are coming upon you, howle.

The very shadow of levelling, sword-levelling, man-levelling, frighted you, (and who, like yourselves, can blame you, because it shook your Kingdome?) but now the substantiality of levelling is coming.

The Eternal God, the mighty Leveller is comming, yea come, even at the doore; and what will you do in that day.

Repent, repent, repent, Bow down, bow down, bow, or howle, resigne, or be damned; Bow downe, bow downe, you sturdy Oakes, and Cedars, bow downe.

Veile too, and kisse the meaner shrubs. Bow, or else (by my self saith the Lord) Ile breake you in pieces (some of you) others I will teare up by the roots; I will suddenly deale with you all, some in one way; some in another. Wherefore

Each Begger that you meet
Fall down before him, kisse him in the street.

Once more, he is thy brother, thy fellow, flesh of thy flesh.

Turne not away thine eyes from thine owne FLESH, least I pull out thine eyes and throw thee headlong into hell.

3 Mine eares are filled brim full with cryes of poore prisoners, Newgate, Ludgate cryes (of late) are seldome out of mine eares. Those dolefull cryes, Bread, bread, bread for the Lords sake, pierce mine eares, and heart, I can no longer forebeare.

Werefore high you apace to all prisons in the Kingdome,

4 Bow before those poore, nasty, lousie, ragged wretches, say to them, your humble servants, Sirs, (without a complement) we let you go free, and serve you, &c.

Do this (or as I live saith the Lord) thine eyes (at least) shall be boared out, and thou carried captive into a strange Land.

5 Give over, give over, thy odious, nasty, abominable fasting, for strife and debate, and to smite with the fist of wickednesse. And instead thereof, loose the bands of wickednesse, undo the heavy burdens, let the oppressed go free, and breake every yoake. Deale thy bread to the hungry, and bring the poore that are cast out (both of houses and Synagogues) to thy house. Cover the naked: Hide not thy self from thine owne flesh, from a creeple, a rogue, a begger, he's thine owne flesh. From a Whoremonger, a thief, &c. he's flesh of thy flesh,

and his theft, and whoredome is flesh of thy flesh also, thine owne flesh. Thou maist have ten, times more of each within thee, then he that acts outwardly in either, Remember, turn not away thine eyes from thine OWN FLESH.

6 Give over thy midnight mischief.

Let branding with the letter *B*. alone.

4 Admonition to great ones

Be no longer so horridly, hellishly, impudently, arrogantly, wicked, as to judge what is sinne, what not, what evill, and what not, what blasphemy, and what not.

For thou and all thy reverend Divines, so called (who Divine for Tythes, hire, and money, and serve the Lord Jesus Christ for their owne bellyes) are ignorant of this one thing.

7 That sinne and transgression is finisht, its a meere riddle, that they, with all their humane learning can never reade.

Neither can they understand what pure honour is wrapt up in the Kings Motto, *Honi Soit qui Mal.y.Pense*. Evill to him that evill thinks.

Some there are (who are accounted the off scouring of all things) who are Noble Knights of the Garter. Since which—they could see no evill, thinke no evill, doe no evill, know no evill.

ALL is Religion that they speak, and honour that they do.

But all you that eat of the Tree of Knowledge of Good and Evill, and have not your Evill eye Pickt out, you call Good Evill, and Evill Good; Light Darknesse, and Darknesse Light; Truth Blasphemy, and Blasphemy Truth.

And you are at this time of your Father the Devill, and of your brother the Pharisee, who still say of Christ (who is now alive) say we not well that he hath a Devill.

9 Take heed, take heed, take heed.

Filthy blinde Sodomites called Angels men, they seeing no further then the formes of men.

10 There are Angels (now) come down from Heaven, in the shapes and formes of men, who are full of the vengeance of the Lord; and are to poure out the plagues of God upon the Earth, and to torment the Inhabitants thereof.

Some of these Angels I have been acquainted withall.

And I have looked upon them as Devils, accounting them Devils incarnate, and have run from place to place, to hide my self from them, shunning their company; and have been utterly ashamed when I have been seen with them.

But for my labour; I have been plagued and tormented beyond expression. So that now I had rather behold one of these Angels * pouring out the plagues of God, cursing; and teaching others to curse bitterly.

*Rev. 15, Judges 5, Revel. 10, Neh. 13. 25,

And had rather heare a mighty Angell (in man) swearing a full-mouthed Oath; and see the spirit of *Nehemiah* (in any form of man, or woman) running upon an uncleane Jew (a pretended Saint) and tearing the haire of his head like a mad man, cursing, and making others fall a swearing, then heare a zealous Presbyterian, Independent, or * spirituall Notionist,[5] pray, preach, or exercise.

11 Well! To the pure all things are pure. God hath so cleared cursing, swearing, in some, that that which goes for swearing and cursing in them, is more glorious then praying and preaching in others.

And what God hath cleansed, call not thou uncleane.

And if *Peter* prove a great transgressor of the Law, by doing that which was as odious as killing a man; if he at length (though he be loath at first) eat that which was common and unclean &c. (I give but a hint) blame him not, much lesse lift up a finger against, or plant a hellish Ordinance——against him, least thou be plagued, and damned too, for thy zeale, blinde Religion, and fleshly holinesse, which now stinks above ground, though formerly it had a good favour.

12 But O thou holy, zealous, devout, righteous, religious one (whoever thou art) that seest evill, or any thing uncleane; do thou sweare, if thou darest, if it be but (I'faith) I'le throw thee to Hell for it (saith the Lord) and laugh at thy destruction.

While Angels (in the forme of men) shall sweare, Heart, Blood, Wounds, and by the Eternall God, &c. in profound purity, and in high Honour, and Majesty.

13 Well! one hint more; there's swearing ignorantly, i'th darke, vainely, and there's swearing i'th light, gloriously.

Well! man of the earth! Lord *Esau*! what hast thou to do with those who sweare upon the former account?

Vengeance is mine, Judgement, Hell, Wrath &c. all is mine (saith the Lord), dare not thou to set thy foot so impudently and arrogantly upon one step of my Throne: I am Judge myself—Be wise, give over, have done—

14 And as for the latter sort of swearing, thou knowest it not when thou hearest it. It's no new thing for thee to call Christ Beel-zebub, and Beel-zebub Christ; to call a holy Angell a Devill, and a Devill an Angell.

15 I charge thee (in the name of the Eternall God) meddle not with neither, let the Tares alone, least thou pull up the Wheat also, woe be to thee if thou dost. Let both alone (I say) least thou shouldest happen of a holy swearing Angell, and take a Lion by the paw to thine owne destruction.

Never was there such a time since the world stood, as now is.

Thou knowest not the strange appearances of the Lord, now a daies. Take heed, know thou hast been warned.

16 And whatever thou dost, dip not thy little finger in blood any more, thou art up to the elbowes already: Much sope, yea much nitre, cannot cleanse thee, &c.

*This will come in request with you next; you may remember that Independency, which is now so hug'd, was counted blasphemy, and banishment was too good for it.

5 Admonition to great ones

Much more have I to say to thee (saith the Lord) but I will do it secretly; and dart a quiver full of arrowes into thy heart; and I will now charge thee.

CHAP. III

Containing severall dismall, dolefull cryes, and outcries. which pierce the eares and heart of his Excellent Majesty, the King of Kings. And how the King of Heaven chargeth the Great Ones of the Earth.

1 Thus saith the Lord, Be silent, O all flesh, before the Lord; be silent; O lofty, haughty, great ones of the Earth.

There are so many Bils of Indictment preferred against thee, that both heaven and earth blush thereat.

How long shall I heare the sighs and groanes, and see the teares of poore widowes; and heare curses in every corner; and all sorts of people crying out oppression, oppression, tyranny, tyranny, the worst of tyranny, unheard of, unnaturall tyranny.

—O my back, my shoulders. O Tythes, Excize, Taxes, Pollings, &c. O Lord! O Lord God Almighty!

What, a little finger heavier then former loynes?

What have I engaged my goods, my life, &c. forsooke my dearest relations, and all for liberty and true freedome, for freedome from oppression, and more laid on my back, &c.

2 Mine eares are filled brim full with confused noise, cries, and outcries; O the innumerable complaints and groanes that pierce my heart (thorow and thorow) O astonishing complaints.

Was ever the like ingratitude heard of since the world stood? what! best friends, surest friends, slighted, scorned, and that which cometh from them (in the basest manner) contemned, and some rewarded with prisons, some with death?

O the abominable perfidiousnesse, falseheartednesse; self-seeking, self-inriching, and Kingdome-depopulating, and devastating, &c.

These, and divers of the same nature, are the cries of *England*.

And can I any longer forbeare?

I have heard, I have heard, the groaning of my people. And now I come to deliver them, saith the Lord.

Woe be to *Pharaoh* King of *Egypt*.

You Great Ones that are not tackt nor tainted, you may laugh and sing, whom this hitteth it hitteth. And it shall hit home.

And this which followeth, all whom it concerneth, by what name or title soever dignified or distinguished.

3 You mostly hate those (called Levellers) who (for ought you know) acted as they did, out of the sincerity, simplicity, and fidelity of

their hearts; fearing least they should come under the notion of Covenant-breakers,[6] if they did not so act.

Which if so, then were they most barbarously, unnaturally, hellishly murdered; and they died Martyrs for God and their Countrey.

And their blood cries vengeance, vengeance, in mine ears, saith the Lord.

*Once more know, that Sword-leveling is not my principle; I onely pronounce the righteous judgements of the Lord upon Earth, as I durst.

4 Well! let it be how it will; these* Levellers (so called) you mostly hated, though in outward declarations you owned their Tenents as your owne Principle.

So you mostly hate me (saith the Lord) though in outward declarations you professe me, and seeme to owne me, more then a thousand whom you despise, and account worse than your selves, who are nearer the Kingdome of Heaven then your selve.

You have killed Levellers (so called) you also (with wicked hands) have slain me the Lord of life, whom am now risen and risen, indeed, (and you shall know, and feele it with a witnesse) to Levell you in good earnest. And to lay low all high hils, and every mountaine that is high, and lifted up, &c.

5 Well! once more, read *Jam.* 5, 1. to 7——Ye have killed the just——Ye have killed, ye have killed, ye have killed the just.

The blood cryeth in mine eares, Vengeance, vengeance, vengeance, vengeance is mine, I will recompence.

Well! what will you do with *Bray,*[7] and the poore prisoners elsewhere? You know not what you do.

You little know what will become of you.

One of you had best remember your dream about your Fathers Moule——[8]

6 Neither do I forget the one hundred spent in superfluous dishes (at your late great *London* Feast, for I know what——) when hundreds of poore wretches dyed with hunger.

I have heard a sound in mine eares, that no lesse than a hundred died in one week, pined, and starved with hunger.

Howle you great ones, for all that feast daies dole, &c. heare your doome.

CHAP. IV

How the Judge of Heaven and Earth, who judgeth righteous judgement, passeth sentence against all those Great Ones, who (like Oakes and tall Cedars) will now bow. And how he intends to blow them up by the roots.

1 Thus saith the Lord: All you tall Cedars, and sturdy Oakes, who

bow not down, who bow not down—

This sentence is gone out of my mouth against you, MENE, MENE, TEKEL.⁹

Thou art weighed in the ballances, and art found wanting.

God hath numbred thy Kingdome, and finished it.

And thou, and all that joyne with thee, or are (in the least degree) accessary to thy former, or like intended pranks, shall most terribly and most strangely be plagued.

2 There is a little sparke lies under (that huge heap of ashes) all thine honour, pomp, pride, wealth, and riches, which shall utterly consume all that is uppermost, as it is written.

The Lord, the Lord of Hosts, shall send among his fat ones, leanenesse; and under his glory he shall kindle a burning, like the burning of a fire, and the light of *Israel* shall be for a fire, and his holy one for a flame, and it shall burne and devoure his thornes, and his briers in one day.

And shall consume the glory of his Forrest, and of his fruitfull field, both soule and body (*i.e.* this shall be done inwardly and outwardly, and shall be fulfilled both in the history and mystery) and the rest of the trees of his Forrest shall be few, that a childe may write them.

And the Lord, the Lord of Hoasts, shall lop the bough with terror, and the high ones of stature shall be hewen down, and haughty shall be humbled, And he shall cut down the thickets of the Forrest with iron, and *Lebanon* shall fall by a mighty one, *Isa.* 10.

3 Behold, behold, I have told you.

Take it to heart, else you'l repent every veine of your heart.

For your own sakes take heed.

Its my last warning.

For the cryes of the poore, for the oppression of the needy. For the horrid insolency of proud man, who will dare to sit in my throne, and judge unrighteous judgement.

Who will dare to touch mine Annoynted, and do my Prophets harme.

For these things sake (now) am I arrisen, saith the Lord,

In Auxilium Patris בך

CHAP. V.

1 O *London, London,* my bowels are rolled together (in me) for thee, and my compassions within me, are kindled towards thee.

And now I onely tell thee, that it was not in vaine that this forme hath been brought so farre to thee, to proclaime the day of the Lord throughout thy streets, day and night, for twelve or thirteen days together.

And that I have been made such a signe, and a wonder before many of thine Inhabitants faces.

2 Many of them (among other strange exploits) beholding me, fall down flat at the feet of creeples, beggars, lazars, kissing their feet, and resigning up my money to them; being severall times over-emptied of money, that I have not had one penny left, and yet have recruited againe—

3 And now my hearts! you have been forwardly in all the appearances of God.

There is a strange one (now on foot) judge it not, least you be judged with a vengeance.

4 Turne not away your eyes from it, least you (to your torment) heare this voyce—*I was a Stranger, and ye tooke me not in.* [Matt. 25, 43]

Well I bow down before Eternall Majesty, who is universall love, bow down to equality, or free community, that no more of your blood be spilt; that pride, arrogance, covetuousnesse, malice, hypocrisie, self-seeking, &c. may live no longer. Else I tremble at whats comming upon you.

Remember you have been warned with a witnesse.

Deare hearts Farewell.

CHAP. VI.

A terrible word, and fatall blow from the Lord, upon the gathered Churches (so called) especially upon those that are stiled Anabaptists.

1 He that hath an eare to heare, let him hear what the Spirit saith against the Churches.

Thus saith the Lord: Woe be to thee *Bethaven, who callest thy self by the name *Bethel, it shall be more tollerable (now in the day of judgement, for *Tyre* and *Sydon*[)], for those whom thou accountest, and callest Heathens, then for thee.

2 And thou proud *Lucifer*, who exaltest thy self above all the Stars of God in heaven, shalt be brought down into hell; it shall be more tollerable for *Sodom* and *Gomorrah*, for drunkards and whoremongers, then for thee. Publicans and Harlots shall, Publicans and Harlots do sooner enter into the Kingdome of heaven, then you.

I'le give thee this fatall blow, and leave thee.

3 Thou hast affronted, and defied the Almighty, more then the vilest of men (upon the face of the earth) and that so much the more,

*The house of vanity.
*The house of God

by how much the more thou takes upon thee the name of Saint, and ashamest it to thy self onely, damning all those that are not of thy Sect.

4 Wherefore be it knowne to all Tongues, Kin[d]reds, Nations, and languages upon earth, That my most Excellent Majesty, the King of glory, the Eternall God, who dwelleth in the forme of the Writer of this Roll (among many other strange and great exploits) hath i'th open streets, with his hand fiercely stretcht out, his hat cockt up, his eyes set as if they would sparkle out; and with a mighty loud voyce charged 100. of Coaches, 100. of men and women of the greater ranke, and many notorious, deboist, swearing, roystering roaring Cavalliers (so called) and other wilde sparks of the Gentry: And have proclaimed the notable day of the Lord to them, and that through the streets of the great Citie, and in Southwark; Many times great multitudes following him up and down, and this for the space of 12. or 13. dayes: And yet (all this while) not one of them lifting up one finger, not touching one haire of his head, or laying one hand on his raiment.

But many, yea many notorious vile ones, in the esteeme of men (yea of great quality among men) trembling and bowing to the God of heaven, &c.

But when I came to proclaim (also) the great day of the Lord (among you) O ye carnall Gospellers.

The Devill (in you) roared out, who was tormented to some purpose, though not before his time.

He there shewed both his phangs and pawes, and would have torn me to pieces, and have eaten me up. Thy pride, envy, malice, arrogance, &c. was powred out like a river of Brimstone, crying out, a Blasphemer, a Blasphemer, away with him: At length threatning me, and being at last raving mad, some tooke hold of my Cloak on one side, some on another, endeavouring to throw me from the place where I stood (to proclaime his Majesties message) making a great uproar in a great congregation of people: Till at length I wrapt up my self in silence (for a season) for the welfavour'd harlots confusion, &c.

And to thine eternall shame and damnation (O mother of witchcrafts, who dwellest in gathered Churches) let this be told abroad: And let her FLESH be burnt with FIRE.

Amen, Halelujah.

FINIS

A SECOND

Fiery Flying Roule:

TO

All the Inhabitants of the earth; specially to the rich ones.

OR,

A sharp sickle, thrust in, to gather the clusters of the vines of the earth, because her grapes are (*now*) fully ripe. And the great, notable, terrible, (yet glorious and joyfull) day of the LORD is come; even the Day of the Lords Recovery and Discovery. Wherein the secrets of all hearts are ripped up; and the secret villanies of the holy Whore, the well-favoured Harlot (who scornes carnall Ordinances, and is mounted up into the notion of Spiritualls) is discovered: And even her flesh burning with unquenchable fire. And the pride of all glory staining.

Together with a narration of various, strange, yet true stories: And severall secret mysteries, and mysterious secrets, which never were afore written or printed.

As also, That most strange Appearance of eternall Wisdome, and unlimited Almightinesse, in choosing base things: And why, and how he chooseth them. And how (most miraculously) they (even base things) have been, are, and shall be made fiery Chariots, to mount up some into divine glory, and unspotted beauty and majesty. And the glory that ariseth up from under them is confounding both Heaven and Earth. With a word (by way of preface) dropping in as an in-let to the new Hierusalem.

These being some things of what are experimented.

Per AUXILIUM PATRIS בך

Howle, rich men, for the miseries that are (just now) coming upon you, the rust of your silver is rising up in judgement against you, burning your flesh like fire, &c.

And now I am come to recover my corn, my wooll, and my flax, which thou hast (theevishly and hoggishly) detained from me, the Lord God Almighty, in the poore and needy.

Also howle thou holy Whore, thou well-favour'd Harlot: for God, and I, have chosen base things to confound thee, and things that are.

And the secrets of all hearts are now revealing by my Gospell, who am a stranger, and besides my selfe, to God, for your sakes. Wherefore receive me, or els expect that dismall doom, Depart from me ye cursed, I was a stranger, and ye took me not in.

Printed in the Yeer 1649

CHAP. I.

The Authors Commission to write, a terrible wo denounced against those that slight the Roule. The Lords claime to all things; together with a hint of a two-fold recovery, wherethrough the most hypocriticall heart shall be ript up.

1. The Word of the Lord came expressely to me, saying, write, write, write.

2. And ONE stood by me, and pronounced all these words to me with his mouth, and I wrote them with ink in this paper.

3. Wherefore in the Name and Power of the eternall God, I charge thee burn it not, tear it not, for if thou dost, I will tear thee to peices (saith the Lord) and none shall be able to deliver thee; for (as I live) it is the day of my vengeance.

4. Read it through, and laugh not at it; if thou dost I'l destroy thee, and laugh at thy destruction.

5. Thus saith the Lord, though I have been a great while in coming, yet I am now come to recover my corn, and my wool, and my flax, &c. and to discover thy lewdnesse, *Hos. 2.*

Thou art cursed with a curse, for thou hast robbed me (saith the Lord) of my corn, my wool, my flax, &c. Thou hast robbed me of my Tythes, for the Tythes are mine, *Mal. 3.* And the beasts on a thousand hills, yea all thy baggs of money, hayricks, horses, yea all that thou callest thine own are mine.

6. And now I am come to recover them all at thy hands, saith the Lord, for it is the day of my recovery, and the day of my discovery, &c. And there is a two-fold recovery of two sorts of things, inward, and outward, or civil, and religious, and through both, a grand discovery of the secrets of the most hypocriticall heart, and a ripping up of the bowels of the wel-favoured Harlot, the holy Whore, who scorns that which is called prophanesse, wickednesse, loosenesse, or libertinisme, and yet her self is the mother of witchcrafts, and of all the abominations of the earth.

But more of this hereafter.

7. For the present, I say, Thus saith the Lord, I am come to recover all my outward, or civill rights, or goods, which thou callest thine own.

CHAP. II.

How the Lord will recover his outward things (things of this life) as Money, Corn, &c. and for whom, and how they shall be plagued who detaine them as their owne. Wherein also are some mysticall hints concerning Michaelmasse day, and the Lords day following it this year, as also of the Dominicall letter D. this year.

1. And the way that I will walk in (in this great notable and terrible day of the Lord) shall be thus, I will either (strangely, & terribly, to thy torment) inwardly, or els (in a way that I will not acquaint thee with) outwardly, demand all mine, and will say on this wise.

2. Thou hast many baggs of money, and behold now I come as a thief in the night, with my sword drawn in my hand, and like a thief as I am,—I say deliver your purse, deliver sirrah! deliver or I'l cut thy throat!

*For some special reason this poor wretch is here instanced.

3. Deliver MY money to such as * poor despised *Maul* of Dedington in Oxonshire,[10] whom some devills incarnate (insolently and proudly, in way of disdaine) cry up for a fool, some for a knave, and mad-man, some for an idle fellow, and base rogue, and some (true lier then they are aware of) cry up for a Prophet, and some arrant fools (though exceeding wise) cry up for more knave then foole, &c. when as indeed, ther's pure royall blood runs through his veins, and he's no lesse then a Kings Son, though not one of you who are devills incarnate; & have your eyes blinded with the God of this world, know it.

4. I say (once more) deliver, deliver, my money which thou hast to him, and to poor creeples, lazars, yea to rogues, thieves, whores, and cut-purses, who are flesh of thy flesh, and every whit as good as thy self in mine eye, who are ready to starve in plaguy Goals, and nasty dungeons, or els by my selfe, saith the Lord, I will torment thee day and night, inwardly, or outwardly, or both waies, my little finger shall shortly be heavier on thee, especially on thee thou holy, righteous, religious *Appropriator*, then my loynes were on *Pharoah* and the Egyptians in time of old; you shall weep and howl for the miseries that are suddenly coming upon you; for your riches are corrupted, &c. and whilst impropriated, appropriated the plague of God is in them.

5. The plague of God is in your purses, barns, houses, horses, murrain will take your hogs, O (ye fat swine of the earth) who shall shortly go to the knife, and be hung up i'th roof, except—blasting, mill-dew, locusts, caterpillars, yea fire your houses and goods, take your corn and fruit, the moth your garments, and the rot your sheep, did you not see my hand, this last year, stretched out?

You did not see.

My hand is stretched out still.

Your gold and silver, though you can't see it, is cankered, the rust of them is a witnesse against you, and suddainly, suddainly, suddainly, because by the eternall God, my self, its the dreadful day of Judgement, saith the Lord, shall eat your flesh as it were fire, *Jam.* 5. 1. to 7.

The rust of your silver, I say, shall eat your flesh as it were fire.

6. As sure as it did mine the very next day after *Michael* the Arch-Angel's, that mighty Angel, who just now fights that terrible battell in heaven with the great Dragon.

And is come upon the earth also, to rip up the hearts of all bag-bearing Judases. On this day purses shall be cut, guts let out, men stabb'd to the heart, womens bellies ript up, especially gammer Demases,[11] who have forsaken us, and imbraced this wicked world, and married *Alexander* the Coppersmith, who hath done me much evill. The Lord reward him, I wish him hugely well, as he did me, on ‑ the next day after *Michael* the Arch-Angel.

Which was the Lords day I am sure on't, look in your Almanacks,[12] you shall find it was the Lords day, or els I would you could; when you must, when you see it, you will find the Dominicall letter to be G. and there are many words that begin with G. at this time (GIVE) begins with G. give, give, give, give up, give up your houses, horses, goods, gold, Lands, give up, account nothing your own, have ALL THINGS common, or els the plague of God will rot and consume all that you have.

By God, by my self, saith the Lord, its true.

Come! give all to the poore and follow me, and you shall have treasure in heaven. Follow me, who was numbred among transgressors, and whose visage was more marr'd then any mans, follow me.

CHAP. III.

A strange, yet most true story: under which is couched that Lion, whose roaring shall make all the beasts of the field tremble, and all the Kingdoms of the earth quake. Wherein also (in part) the subtilty of the wel-favoured Harlot is discovered, and her flesh burning with that fire, which shall burne down all Churches, except that of the first Born, &c.

1. Follow me, who, last Lords day Septem. 30. 1649. met him in open field, a most strange deformed man, clad with patcht clouts: who looking wishly on me, mine eye pittied him; and my heart, or the day of the Lord, which burned as an oven in me, set my tongue on flame to speak to him, as followeth.

2. How now friend, art thou poore?

He answered, yea Master very poore.

Whereupon my bowels trembled within me, and quivering fell upon the worm-eaten chest, (my corps I mean) that I could not hold a joynt still.

And my great love within me, (who is the great God within that chest, or corps) was burning hot toward him; and made the lock-hole of the chest, to wit, the mouth of the corps, again to open: Thus.

Art poor?

Yea, very poor, said he.

Whereupon the strange woman who, flattereth with her lips, and is subtill of heart, said within me.

It's a poor wretch, give him two-pence.

But my EXCELLENCY and MAIESTY (in me) scorn'd her words, confounded her language; and kickt her out of his presence.

3. But immediately the WEL-FAVOURED HARLOT (whom I carried not upon my horse behind me) but who rose up in me, said:

,Its a poor wretch give his 6.d. and that's enough for a Squire or Knight, to give to one poor body.

,Besides (saith the holy Scripturian Whore) hee's worse then an Infidell that provides not for his own Family.

,True love begins at home, &c.

,Thou, and thy Family are fed, as the young ravens strangely, though thou hast been a constant Preacher, yet thou hast abhorred both tythes and hire; and thou knowest not aforehand, who will give thee the worth of a penny.

,Have a care of the main chance.

4. And thus she flattereth with her lips, and her words being smoother then oile; and her lips dropping as the honey comb, I was fired to hasten my hand into my pocket; and pulling out a shilling, said to the poor wretch, give me six pence, heer's a shilling for thee.

He answered, I cannot, I have never a penny.

Whereupon I said, I would fain have given thee something if thou couldst have changed my money.

Then saith he, God blesse you.

Whereupon with much reluctancy, with much love, and with amazement (of the right stamp) I turned my horse head from him, riding away. But a while after I was turned back (being advised by my Demilance)[13] to wish him cal for six pence, which I would leave at the next Town at ones house, which I thought he might know (*Saphira* like) keeping back part.[14]

But (as God judged me) I, as she, was struck down dead.

And behold the plague of God fell into my pocket; and the rust of my silver rose up in judgement against me, and consumed my flesh as with fire: so that I, and my money perisht with me

I being cast into that lake of fire and brimstone.

And all the money I had about me to a penny (though I thought through the instigation of my *quondam Mistris* to have reserved some, having rode about 8 miles, not eating one mouth-full of bread that day, and had drunk but one small draught of drink; and had between 8. or 9. miles more to ride, ere I came to my journeys end: my horse being lame, the waies dirty, it raining all the way, and I not knowing what extra-ordinary occasion I might have for money.) Yet (I say) the rust of my silver did so rise up in judgement against me, and burnt my flesh like fire: and the 5. of *James* thundered such an alarm in mine ears, that I was fain to call all I had into the hands of him, whose visage was more marr'd then any mans that ever I saw.

This is a true story, most true in the history.

Its true also in the mystery.

And there are deep ones couch't under it, for its a shadow of various, glorious, (though strange) good things to come.

7. Wel! to return—after I had thrown my rusty canker'd money into the poor wretches hands, I rode away from him, being filled with trembling, joy, and amazement, feeling the sparkles of a great glory arising up from under these ashes.

After this, I was made (by that divine power which dwelleth in this Ark, or chest) to turn my horse head—whereupon I beheld this poor deformed wrtech, looking earnestly after me: and upon that, was made to put off my hat, and bow to him seven times, and was (at that strange posture) filled with trembling and amazement, some sparkles of glory arising up also from under this; as also from under these ashes, yet I rode back once more to the poor wretch, saying, because I am a King, I have done this, but you need not tell any one.

The day's our own.

This was done on the last LORDS DAY, Septem. 30. in the year 1649. which is the year of the Lords recompences for Zion, and the day of his vengeance, the dreadfull day of Judgement. But I have done (for the present) with this story, for it is the later end of the year 1649.

CHAP. IV.

How the Author hath been set as a signe and a wonder, as well as most of the Prophets formerly. As also what strange postures the divine Majesty that dwells in his forme, hath set the forme in, with the most strange and various effects thereof upon the Spectators. Also his Communion with the spirits of just men made perfect, and with God the Judge of all, hinted at.

1. It is written in your Bibles, Behold I and the children whom the Lord hath given me, are for signs and for wonders in Israel, from the Lord of Hoasts, which dwelleth in Mount Sion, *Isa.* 8.18.

And amongst those who were set thus, *Ezekiel* seems to be higher then the rest by the shoulders upwards, and was more seraphicall then his Predecessors, yet he was the son of *Buzi (Ezek.* 1.) which being interpreted is the son of contempt; it pleases me (right well) that I am his brother, a sonne of *Buzi.*

2. He saw (and I in him see) various strange visions; and he was, and I am set in severall strange postures.

Amongst many of his pranks—this was one, he shaves all the hair off his head: and off his beard, then weighs them in a pair of scales; burns one part of them in the fire, another part hee smites about with a knife, another part thereof he scatters in the wind, and a few he binds up in his skirts, &c. and this not in a corner, or in a chamber, but in the midst of the streets of the great City Hierusalem, and the man all this while neither mad nor drunke, &c. *Ezek.* 5. 1, 2, 3, 4. &c. as also in severall other Chapt. amongst the rest, Chap. 12. 3. &c. Chap. 4. 3. Chap.24. 3. to the end. This *Ezekiel* (to whose spirit I am come, and to an innumerable company of Angels, and to God the Judge of all.)

3. (I say) this great Courtier, in the high Court of the highest heavens, is the son of *Buzi,* a child of contempt on earth, and set as a sign and wonder (as was *Hosea,* who went in to a whore, &c.) *Hos.* 2. when he (I say) was playing some of his pranks, the people said to him, wilt thou not tell us what these things are to us, that thou dost so, *Ezek.* 24.19. with the 3. verse and so forwards, when he was strangely acted by that omnipotency dwelling in him; and by that eternall, immortall, INVISIBLE (indeed) Majesty, the onely wise God, who dwells in this visible forme, the writer of this Roule, (who to his joy) is numbred amongst transgressors.

4. The same most excellent Majesty (in this forme) hath set the Forme in many strange Postures lately, to the joy and refreshment of some, both acquaintances and strangers, to the wonderment and amazement of others, to the terrour and affrightment of others; and to the great torment of the chiefest of the Sects of Professours; who have gone about to shake off their plagues if they could, some by crying out he's mad, he's drunk, he's faln from grace, and some by scandalising, &c. and onely one, whom I told of, by threates of caning or cudgelling, who meeting me full with face, was ashamed and afraid to look on me, &c.

5. But to wave all this.

Because the Sun begins to peep out, and its a good while past day-break, I'l creep forth (a little) into the mystery of the former history, and into the in-side of that strange out-side businesse.

CHAP. V.

The Authors strange and lofty carriage towards great ones, and his most lowly carriage towards Beggars, Rogues, and Gypseys: together with a large declaration what glory shall rise up from under all this ashes. The most strange, secret, terrible, yet most glorious design of God, in choosing base things to confound things that are. And how. A most terrible vial powred out upon the well-favour'd Harlot, and how the Lord is bringing into contempt not only honorable persons, with a vengeance, but all honorable, holy things also. Wholsome advice, with a terrible threat to the Formalists. How base things have confounded base things; and how base things have been a fiery Chariot to mount the Author up into divine glory, &c. And how his wife is, and his life is in, that beauty which makes all visible beauty seem meer deformity.

1. And because I am found of those that sought me not. And because some say, wilt thou not tell us what these things are to us, that thou dost so?

Wherefore waving my charging so many Coaches, so many hundreds of men and women of the greater rank, in the open streets, with my hand stretched out, my hat cock't up, staring on them as if I would look thorough them, gnashing with my teeth at some of them, and day and night with a huge loud voice proclaiming the day of the Lord throughout London and Southwark, and leaving divers other exploits, &c. It is my good will and pleasure (only) to single out the former story with its Parallels.

2. (*Viz.*) in clipping, hugging, imbracing, kissing a poore deformed wretch in London, who had no more nose on his face, then I have on the back of my hand, (but only two little holes in the place where the nose uses to stand.)

And no more eyes to be seen then on the back of my hand, and afterwards running back to him in a strange manner, with my money giving it to him, to the joy of some, to the afrightment and wonderment of other Spectators.

3. As also in falling down flat upon the ground before rogues, beggars, cripples, halt, maimed; blind, &c. kissing the feet of many, rising up againe, and giving them money, &c. Besides that notorious businesse with the Gypseys and Goalbirds (mine own brethren and sisters, flesh of my flesh, and as good as the greatest Lord in England) at the prison in Southwark neer S. *Georges* Church

Now that which rises up from under all this heap of ashes, will fire both heaven and earth; the one's ashamed, and blushes already, the other reels to and fro, like a drunken man.

4. Wherefore thus saith the Lord, Hear O heavens, and harken O

earth, Ile overturne, overturne, overturne, I am now [sta]ining the
pride of all glory, and bringing into contempt all the honourable of the
earth, *Esa.* 23. 9. not only honourable persons, (who shall come down
with a vengeance, if they bow not to universall love the eternal God,
whose service is perfect freedome) but honorable things, as Elderships,
Pastorships, Fellowships, Churches, Ordinances, Prayers, &c.
Holinesses, Righteousnesses, Religions of all sorts, of the highest
strains; yea, Mysterians, and Spirituallists, who scorne carnall
Ordinances, &c.

I am about my act, my strange act, my worke, my strange work,
that whosoever hears of it, both his ears shall tingle.

5. I am confounding, plaguing, tormenting nice, demure, barren
Mical,[15] with *Davids* unseemly carriage, by skipping, leaping,
dancing, like one of the fools; vile, base fellowes, shamelessely, basely,
and uncovered too before handmaids,—

Which thing was *S. Pauls* Tutor, or else it prompted him to write,
God hath chosen BASE things, and things that are despised, to
confound—the things are.—

Well! family duties are no base things, they ar[e] things that ARE:
Churches, Ordinances, &c, are no BASE things, though indeed
Presbyterian Churches begun to live i'th womb, but died there, and
rot and stink there to the death of the mother and child. Amen. Not by
the Devill, but (by * God) it's true.

Grace before meat and after meat, are no BASE things; these are
things that ARE. But how long Lord, holy and true, &c.

Fasting for strife and debate, and to smite with the fist of
wickednesse,—(and not for taking off heavy burthens, breaking every
yoke, *Esa.* 58.) and Thanksgiving daies for killing of men for money,
are no BASE things, these are things that ARE.

☞ Starting up into the notion of spirituals, scorning History,
speaking nothing but Mystery, crying down carnall ordinances, &c. is
a fine thing among many, it's no base thing (now adaies) though it be a
cloak for covetousnesse, yea, though it be to maintain pride and pomp;
these are no base things.

6. These are things that ARE, and must be confounded by BASE
things, which *S.Paul* saith, not God hath connived at, winked at,
permitted, tolerated, But God hath CHOSEN *&c.* BASE things.

What base things? Why Mical took *David* for a base fellow, and
thought he had chosen BASE things, in dancing shamelessly uncovered
before handmaids.

And barren, demure *Mical* thinks (for I know her heart saith the
Lord) that I chose base things when I sate downe, and eat and drank
around on the ground with Gypseys, and clip't, hug'd and kiss'd
them, putting my hand in their bosomes, loving the she-Gipsies
dearly. O base! saith mincing *Mical*, the least spark of modesty would

* That's a base
thing.

be as red as crimson or scarlet, to hear this.

I warrant me, *Mical* could better have borne this if I had done it to Ladies: so I can for a need, if it be my will, and that in the height of honor and majesty, without sin. But at that time when I was hugging the Gipsies, I abhorred the thoughts of Ladies, their beauty could not bewitch mine eyes, or snare my lips, or intangle my hands in their bosomes; yet I can if it be my will, kisse and hug Ladies, and love my neighbours wife as my selfe, without sin.

7. But thou Precisian,[16] by what name or title soever dignified, or distinguished, do but blow a kisse to thy neighbours wife, or dare to think of darting one glance of one of thine eyes towards her, if thou darst.

It's meat and drink to an Angel (who knows none evill, no sin) so sweare a full mouth'd oath, *Rev.* 10. 6. It's joy to *Nehemiah* to come in like a mad-man, and pluck folkes hair off their heads, and curse like a devill—and make them swear by God,—*Nehem.* 13. Do thou O holy man (who knowes evill) lift up thy finger against a Jew, a Church-member, cal thy brother fool, and with a peace-cods on him; or swear I faith, if thou dar'st, if thou dost, thou shalt howl in hell for it, and I will laugh at thy calamity, &c.

8. But once more hear O heavens, hearken O earth, Thus saith the Lord, I have chosen such base things, to confound things that are, that the ears of those (who scorn to be below Independents, yea the ears of many who scorn to be so low as carnall Ordinances, &c.) that hear thereof shall tingle.

9. Hear one word more (whom it hitteth it hitteth) give over thy base nasty stinking, formall grace before meat, and after meat (I call it so, though thou hast rebaptized it—) give over thy stinking family duties, and thy Gospell Ordinances as thou callest them; for under them all there lies snapping, snarling, biting, besides covetousnesse, horrid hypocrisie, envy, malice, evill surmising.

10. Give over, give over, or if nothing els will do it, I'l at a time, when thou least of all thinkest of it, make thine own child the fruit of thy loines, in whom thy soul delighted, lie with a whore—before thine eyes: That that plaguy holinesse and righteousnesse of thine might be confounded by that base thing. And thou be plagued back again into thy mothers womb, the womb of eternity: That thou maist become a little child, and let the mother *Eternity, Almightinesse,* who is universall love, and whose service is perfect freedome, dresse thee, and undresse thee, swadle, unswadle, bind, loose, lay thee down, take thee up, &c.

—And to such a little child, undressing is as good as dressing, foul cloaths, as good as fair cloaths—he knows no evill, &c.—And shall see evill no more,—but he must first lose all his righteousnesse, every bit of his holinesse, and every crum of his Religion, and be plagued, and confounded (by base things) into nothing.

By base things which God and I have chosen.

11. And yet I shew you a more excellent way, when you have past this.—In a word, my plaguy, filthy, nasty holinesse hath been confounded by base things. And then (behold I shew you a mystery, and put forth a riddle to you) by base things, base things so called have been confounded also; and thereby have I been confounded into eternall Majesty, unspeakable glory, my life, my self.

12. Ther's my riddle, but because neither all the Lords of the Philistins, no nor my Delilah her self can read it,

I'l read it my self, I'l (only) hint it thus.

Kisses are numbered amongst transgressors—base things—well! by bare hellish swearing, and cursing, (as I have accounted it in the time of my fleshly holinesse) and by base impudent kisses (as I then accounted them) my plaguy holinesse hath been confounded, and thrown into the lake of fire and brimstone.

And then again, by wanton kisses, kissing hath been confounded; and externall kisses, have been made the fiery chariots, to mount me swiftly into the bosom of him whom my soul loves, (his excellent Majesty, the King of glory.)

Where I have been, where I have been, where I have been, hug'd, imbrac't, and kist with the kisses of his mouth, whose loves are better then wine, and have been utterly overcome therewith, beyond expression, beyond admiration.

13. Again, Lust is numbered amongst transgressors—a base thing.—

Now faire objects attract Spectators eyes.

And beauty is the father of lust or love.

Well! I have gone along the streets impregnant with that child (lust) which as particular beauty had begot: but coming to the place, where I expected to have been delivered, I have providentially met there a company of devills in appearance, though Angels with golden vialls, in reality, powring out full vialls, of such odious abominable words, that are not lawfull to be uttered.

Words enough to deafen the ears of plaguy holinesse. And such horrid abominable actions, the sight whereof were enough to put out holy mans eyes, and to strike him stark dead, &c.

These base things (I say) words and actions, have confounded and plagued to death, the child in the womb that I was so big of.

14. And by, and through these BASE things (as upon the wings of the wind) have I been carried up into the arms of my love, which is invisible glory, eternall Majesty, purity it self, unspotted beauty, even that beauty which maketh all other beauty but meer uglinesse, when set against it, &c.

Yea, could you imagine that the quintessence of all visible beauty, should be extracted and made up into one huge beauty, it would appear to be meer deformity to that beauty, which through BASE things I have been lifted up into.

Which transcendent, unspeakable, unspotted beauty, is my crown and joy, my life and love: and though I have chosen, and cannot be without BASE things, to confound some in mercy, some in judgment, Though also I have concubines without number, which I cannot be without, yet this is my spouse, my love, my dove, my fair one.

Now I proceed to that which followes.

CHAP. VI.

Great ones must bow to the poorest peasants, or els they must rue for it. No materiall sword, or humane power whatsoever, but the pure spirit of universall Love, which is the eternall God, can break the neck of tyranny, oppression, abominable pride, and cruell murder. A Catalogue of severall judgements recited—as so many warning-pieces to Appropriators, Impropriators, and anti-free-communicants, &c. The strongest, yea purest propriety that may plead most priviledge shall suddainly be confounded.

1. Again, thus saith the Lord, I in thee, who am eternall Majesty, bowed down thy form, to deformity.

And I in thee, who am durable riches, commanded thy perishable silver to the poore, &c.

Thus saith the Lord,

Kings, Princes, Lords, great ones, must bow to the poorest Peasants; rich men must stoop to poor rogues, or else they'l rue for it.

This must be done two waies.

You shall have one short dark hint.

Wil.Sedgewick[17] (in me) bowed to that poor deformed ragged wretch, that he might inrich him, in impoverishing himself.

He shall gaine him, and be no great loser himself, &c.

2. Well! we must all bow, and bow, &c. And MEUM must be converted.—It is but yet a very little while; and you shall not say that ought that you possesse is your own, &c. read *Act.* 2. towards the end, chap. 4. 31. to the end, with chap. 5. 1. 2. to the 12.

It's but yet a little while, and the strongest, yea, the seemingly purest propriety, which may mostly plead priviledge and Prerogative from Scripture, and carnall reason; shall be confounded and plagued into community and universality. And ther's a most glorious design in it: and equality, community, and universall love; shall be in request to the utter confounding of abominable pride, murther, hypocrisie, tyranny and oppression, &c. The necks whereof can never be chopt off, or these villaines ever hang'd up, or cut off by materiall sword, by humane might, power, or strength, but by the pure spirit of universall love, who is the God whom all the world (of Papists, Protestants, Presbyterians, Independents, Spirituall Notionists, &c.) ignorantly worship.

3. The time's coming, yea now is, that you shall not dare to say, your silver or gold is your owne.

It's the Lords.

You shall not say it is your own, least the rust thereof rise up in judgement against you, and burn your flesh as it were fire.

Neither shall you dare to say, your oxe, or your asse is your own.

It's the Lords.

And if the Lord have need of an asse he shall have him.

Or if two of his Disciples should come to unloose him, I wil not (for a 1000. worlds) call them thieves, least the asse should slat[18] my braines out, my bread is not mine own, it's the Lords.

A rogo, to ask.   And if a poor * Rogue should ask for it—the Lord hath need of it—he should have it, least it should stick in my throat and choak me one way or other.

4. Once more, Impropriators! Appropriators! go to, weep and howl, &c. *Jam.* 5. 1. to the 7. the rust of your silver shall rise (is rising up) against you, burning your flesh as it were fire, &c.

That is (in a word) a secret, yet sharp, terrible, unexpected, and unsupportable plague, is rising up from under all, that you call your own, when you go to count your money, you shall verily think the Devill stands behind you, to tear you in pieces: You shall not put bread in your mouthes, but the curse shall come along with it, and choke you one way or other. All your former sweets shall be mingled with gall and wormwood: I give you but a hint.

It's the last daies.

5. Well! do what you will one can, know you have been warned. It is not for nothing, that I the Lord with a strong wind cut off (as with a sickle) the fullest, fairest ears of corn this harvest, and drop't them on purpose for the poore, who had as much right to them, as those that (impudently and wickedly, theevishly and hoggishly) stile themselves the owners of the Land.

6. It's not for nothing that such various strange kinds of worms, grubs, and caterpillars (my strong host, saith the Lord of Hosts) have been sent into some graine: Neither is in vain, that I the Lord sent the rot among so many sheep this last yeer; if they had been resign'd to me, and you had kept a true communion, they had not been given up to that plague.

7. It's not in vain that so many towns and houses have been lately fired over the heads of the Inhabitants: Neither is it in vain, that I the Lord fired the barning and ricks of a Miser in Worcestershire (this

yeer) the very same day that he brought in his own, as he accounted it.

On the very same day (I say) his barning and ricks were fired down to the ground, though multitudes of very expert men in the imployment came to quench it.

Of this the writer of this Scroule was an eye-witnesse.

8. Impropriators! Appropriators! Misers! a fair warning: More of you shall be served with the same sawce.

Others of you I'le deal withall in another way more terrible then this, saith the Lord, till you resign.—

Misers! 'specially you holy Scripturian Misers, when you would say grace before and after meat, read *James* 5. 1. to 7. & *Hosea* 2. 8,9,10.

CHAP. VII.

A further discovery of the subtilty of the wel-favour'd Harlot, with a Parley between her and the Spirit: As also the horrid villany (that lies hid under her smooth words, in pleading against the Letter and History, and for the Spirit and Mystery, and all for her owne ends) detected. Also upon what account the spirit is put, and upon what account the Letter. Also what the true Communion, and what the true breaking of bread is.

1. But now me thinks (by this time) I see a brisk, spruce, neat, self-seeking, fine finiking fellow, (who scornes to be either Papist, Protestant, Presbyterian, Independent, or Anabaptist) I mean the Man of Sin, who worketh with all deceiveablenesse of unrighteousnesse, 2 *Thes.* 2.

Crying down * carnall ordinances, and crying up † the Spirit: cunningly seeking and setting up himself thereby.

* Downe they must, but no thanks to him.
† Up it must, but no thanks to him.

I say, I see him, and have ript up the very secrets of his heart (saith the Lord) as also of that mother of mischief, that wel-favour'd Harlot, who both agree in one, and say on this wise to me.

2. 'Ah! poor deluded man, thou hast spoken of the Wisdome of 'God in a mystery, and thou hast seen all the history of the Bible 'mysteriz'd.

'O fool! who hath bewitcht thee, art thou so foolish as to begin in 'the spirit, and wilt thou now be made perfect in the flesh? keep thee to 'the spirit, go not back to the letter, keep thee to the mystery, go not 'back to the history.

'What? they dost talk so much of *James* 5. and *Hosea* 2. those words 'are to be taken in the Mystery, not in the History:

'They are to be taken in the Spirit, not as they [are] in the Letter.

Thus you have a hint of the neat young mans, and of the well-favour'd Harlots language.

3. But now behold I am filled with the Holy Ghost, and am resolv'd (*Acts* 13. 8,9,&c.) to set mine eyes on her and him, (who are no more twaine, but one) and say:

'O full of all subtilty and mischief, thou child of the Devil, thou 'enemy of all righteousnesse, wilt thou not cease to pervert the right 'ways of the Lord?

'Be it known to thee, or thou deceitfull tongue, that I have begun in 'the spirit, and will end in the spirit: I am joyn'd to the Lord, and am 'one spirit. The spirit's my joy, my life, my strength; I will not let it go, 'it's my delight.

'The mystery is mine (mostly) that which I most delight in, that's 'the Jewel. The historie's mine also, that's the Cabinet. For the Jewels 'sake I wil not leave the Cabinet, though indeed it's nothing to me, but 'when thou for thine own ends, stand'st in competition with me for it.

'Strength is mine, so is weaknesse also.

4. I came by water and blood, not by blood only, but by blood and water also.

The inwardnesse is mostly mine, my prime delight is there; the outwardnesse is mine also, when thou for thine own ends, standest in competition with me about it, or when I would confound thee by it.

5. I know there's no Communion to the Communion of Saints, to the inward communion, to communion with the spirits of just men made perfect, and with God the Judge of all.

No other Communion of Saints do I know.

And this is Blood-life-spirit-communion.

6. But another Communion also do I know, which is water, and but water, which I will not be without: My spirit dwells with God, the Judge of all, dwells in him, sups with him, in him, feeds on him, with him, in him. My humanity shall dwell with, sup with, eat with humanity; and why not (for a need) with Publicans and Harlots? Why should I turne away mine eyes from mine own flesh? Why should I not break my bread to the hungry, whoever they be? It is written, the Lord takes care of Oxen.

And when I am at home, I take a great care of my horse, to feed him, dresse him, water him and provide for him.

And is not poor *Maul* of Dedington, and the worst rogue in Newgate, or the arrantest thief or cut-purse farre better, then a 100. Oxen, or a 1000. such horses as mine?

7. Do I take care of my horse, and doth the Lord take care of oxen?

And shall I hear poor rogues in Newgate, Ludgate, cry *bread, bread, bread, for the Lords sake*; and shall I not pitty them and relieve them?

Howl, howl, ye nobles, howl honourable, howl ye rich men for the miseries that are coming upon you.

For our parts, we that hear the Apostle preach, will also have all things common; neither will we call any thing that we have our own.

Do you (if you please) till the plague of God rot and consume what you have.

We will not, wee'l eat our bread together in singlenesse of heart, wee'l break bread from house to house.

CHAP. VIII.

The wel-favoured Harlots cloaths stript off, her nakednesse uncovered, her nose slit, her hunting after the young man, void of understanding, from corner to corner, from Religion to Religion, and the Spirit pursuing, overtaking, and destroying her, with a terrible thunder clap ith close, &c.

1. And we wil strip off thy cloaths, who hast bewitch't us & slit thy nose thou wel-favoured Harlot, who hast (as in many things, so in this) made the Nations of the earth drunk, with the cup of thy forn[n]ications: As thus.

Thou hast come to a poor irreligious wretch, and told him he must be of the same Religion as his neighbours, he must go to Church, hear the Minister, &c. and at least once a year put on his best cloaths, and receive the Comm[u]nion—he must eat a bit of bread, and drink a sip of wine—and then he hath received, &c. he hath been at the Communion.

2. But when he finds this Religion too course for him, and he would faine make for another,

Then immediately thou huntest after him following him from street to street, from corner to corner, from grosse Protestantisme to Puritanisme, &c. at length from crosse in baptisme, and Common-Prayer-Book to Presbyterianisme, where thou tellest him he may break bread, with all such believers, who believe their horses and their cowes are their own; and with such believers, who have received different light from, or greater light then themselves; branded with the letter B. banished, or imprisoned fourteen weeks together, without bail or main-prise.

3. And here I could tell a large story, that would reach as far as between Oxonshire and Coventrey.

But though it be in the original copy, yet is is my good will and pleasure, out of my great wisdome, to wave the printing of it, and I will send the contents thereof, as a charge and secret plague, secretly into their breasts, who must be plagued with a vengeance, for their villany against the Lord.

Well! to return from this more then needful disgression, to the discovery, and uncovering of the wel-favoured Harlot.

Thou hast hunted the young man void of understanding from corner to corner, from religion to religion.

We left him at the Presbyterian—where such a believer, who believes his horses and his cows are his own, may have his child christned, and may himself be admitted to the Sacrament—and come to the communion.

And whats that?

Why after a consecration in a new forme, eating a bit of bread, and drinking a sip of wine perhaps once a moneth, why mother of mischief is this Communion?

O thou flattering and deceitfull tongue, God shall root thee out of the Land of the living, is this Communion? no, no, mother of witchcrafts!

5. The true Communion amongst men, is to have all things common, and to call nothing one hath, ones own.

And the true externall breaking of bread, is to eat bread together in singlenesse of heart, and to break thy bread to the hungry, and tell them its their own bread &c. els your Religion is in vain.

6. And by this time indeed thou seest this Religion is in vain.

And wilt therefore hie thee to another, to wit, to Independency, and from thence perhaps to Anabaptisme so called.

And thither the wel-favour'd Harlot will follow thee, and say thou must be very holy, very righteous, very religious.

And other Religions are vain.

And all in the Parish, all in the Countrey, yea all in the Kingdome, and all in the world (who are not of thine opinion) are without, are of the world.

Thou, and thy comrades are Saints.

(O proud devill! O devill of devills! O *Belzebub*!)

Well! (saith she) thou being a Saint must be very holy, and walk in Gospell-Ordinances saith the wel favour'd Harlot say and in envy, malice, pride, covetousnesse, evill surmising, censoriousnesse, &c. also.

And on the first day of the week, when the Saints meet together, to break bread, do not thou omit it upon pain of damnation.

By no means omit it, because thou hast Gospell Ordinances in the purity of them.

—Papists—they give wafers.—

Protestants—give—to all ith' Parish tagg ragg, and his fellow if they come.

But we are called out of the world, none shall break bread with us, but our selves, (the Saints together, who are in Gospell Order.)

Besides the Priests of England cut their bread into little square bits, but we break our bread (according to the Apostolicall practise) and this is the right breaking of bread (saith the wel-favour'd Harlot.)

Who hath stept into this holy, righteous Gospell, religious way, (Gospel-Ordinances so called) on purpose to dash to pieces the right breaking of bread. and in the room thereof thrusting in this vain Religion.

7. A Religion wherein *Lucifer* reigns, more then in any.

And next to this in the Independents (so called) both which damn to the pit of hell, those that are a 100. times nearer the Kingdome of heaven then themselves: flattering themselves up in this their vain Religion.

But take this hint before I leave thee.

He that hath this worlds goods, and seeth his brother in want, and shutteth up the bowells of compassion from him, the love of God dwelleth not in him; this mans Religion is in vain.

His Religion is in vain, that seeth his brother in want, &c.

His brother—a beggar, a lazar, a cripple, yea a cut-purse, a thief ith' goal, &c.

He that seeth such a brother, flesh of his flesh (in want) and shutteth up the bowels of his compassion from him, the love of God dwelleth not in him, his Religion is in vain: and he never yet broke bread—that hath not forgot his (*meum*).

9. The true breaking of bread—is from house to house, &c. Neighbours (in singlenesse of heart) saying if I have any bread, &c. it's thine, I will not call it mine own, it's common.

These are true Communicants, and this is the true breaking of bread among men.

10. And what the Lords Supper is, none know, but those that are continually (not weekly) but daily at it.

And what the true Communion is, those and those only know, who are come to the spirits of just men made perfect, and to God the Judge of all; all other Religion is vain.

Ay, saith the wel-favour'd Harlot (in the young man void of understanding) I see Protestantism, Presbytery, Independency, Anabaptism, are all vain. These coverings are too short, too narrow, too course for me, the finest of these are but harden sheets, and very narrow ones also.

I'l get me some flax, and make me both fine and large sheets, &c. I'l scorn carnall Ordinances, and walk in the Spirit.

Ay, do (saith the wel-favour'd Harlot) speak nothing but mystery, drink nothing but wine, but bloud, thou need'st not eat flesh, &c.

12. And so my young man starts up into the notion of spiritualls, and wraps up a deal of hipocrisie, malice, envy, deceit, dissimulation, covetousnesse, self-seeking in this fine linnen.

Being a hundred fold worse Devills then before.

But now thy villanie, hipocrisie, and self-seeking is discovering, yea discovered to many with a witnesse.

And though the true and pure levelling, is the eternall Gods levelling the Mountains, &c. in man. Which is the

Bloud-Life-Spirit levelling.

Yet the water, or weak levelling, which is base and foolish, shall confound thee.

And hereby, (as also by severall other strange waies, which thou art least of all acquainted withall[)]. I'l discover thy lewdnesse, and shew the rottennesse of thy heart.

I'l call for all to a mite, to be cast into the outward treasury.

And wil bid thee lay down all at my feet, the Apostle, the Lord, And this is a way that I am now again setting up to try, judge, and damne the wel-favour'd Harlot by.

Cast all into the Treasury, &c. account nothing thine owne, have all things in common.

The young man goes away very sorrowfull,—&c.

The wel-favour'd Harlot shrugs at this.—

13. When this cometh to passe, a poore wretch whose very bones are gnawn with hunger, shall not go about 13. or 14. miles about thy businesse, and thou for a reward, when thou hast hundreds lying by thee.

I will give thee but one hint more, and so will leave thee.

The dreadful day of Judgement is stealing on thee, within these few hours. Thou hast secretly and cunningly lien in wait, thou hast craftily numbered me amongst transgressors, who to thy exceeding torment, am indeed a friend of Publicans and Harlots.[19]

Thou hast accounted me a devil, saith the Lord.

And I wil rot thy name, and make it stink above ground, and make thy folly manifest to all men.

And because thou has judged me, I wil judge thee (with a witnesse) expect it suddainly, saith the Lord.

*Per Au*XILIUM PATRIS כֵן

Letter from Coppe to Salmon and Wyke

My Quintessence, my heart, and soule, my sal, and sol, my Wyke, (which being interpreted) is my soul and strongehold [.] here can I bee solitarie while sol shines upon me, and what weede I feare while I am in safetie in any Wyke, my Rockes stronge hold, which can neither bee surprised or the walls thereof sealed. I live in yor peace & freedome because I dwell in my selfe att Coventrie, Newgate (where I am) [(]for suspition of Blasphemie and Treason agt the State) is noe prison to mee while I am inthroned in my Triple heart wch is but one and triangular, which is as firme as a stone, when I my selfe (‡ heere & there ✕ and everywhere) raise uppe my selfe, the mighty shall bee afraid by reason of Breakings, they purifie themselves the sworde of him that layeth att mee cannot hold the speare, the dart, nor the Habergeon,[1] I esteeme iron as straw, & brasse as rotten wood, and Cahalter[2] as a spiders webb I count death as stubble, and laugh at the shaking of the speare. My deare salute all the saints in the Goale, Haile from the Gen[er]all to the Peddee's,[3] with an Holy Kisse. Love mee & love my dogge, I am soe backwards forever,

Alpha & Omega ABC.

poore pure Ceney & I can shake hands together when shee is in her's, and I in my Chamber, & hath sent you a thousand kisses. I have received the earnest penny [,] I would have had some more, but in Newgate wee are poore,

Noe more

To his dearest Mr Salmon, Mr Wike & Mr Butler[4] in Goale Coventrie.

[Reprinted from the Clarke Papers, Vol. 18, Worcester College, Oxford.]

A
REMONSTRANCE
OF
The sincere and Zealous
PROTESTATION
OF
ABIEZER COPPE

Against the

Blasphemous and EXECRABLE OPINIONS
recited in the Act of Aug. 10, 1650
The breach whereof, the Author hath (through
Mistake) been mis-suspected of, when he hath
not been in the least guilty thereof, &c.

Or, *INNOCENCE* (clouded with the name of
Transgression) wrapped up in silence;
But now (a little) peeping forth from under
the thick and black clouds of Obloquie,

Arising out of the sea of Malice in some, and out of Weakness,
Ignorance, and Mistake in others; who are by the Author much pitied,
and dearly beloved. And for their sakes primarily, as also for the
satisfaction of many, and information of all.

This ensuing
REMONSTRANCE, VINDICATION, AND *ATTESTATION*
is published

Per me   Abiezer Coppe,   —   de Newgate

Which is as a Preamble to a farther future Declaration
of what hath been, and now is; who hath
been so cloathed with a cloud, that few have known him.

London, Printed by JAMES COTTREL. 1651.

*Some said He is a good man; Others said, Nay but he
is mad, and hath a devil.*
*He is a wine-bibber, a glutton and a drunkard; a
friend of publicans and Harlots.*

But wisdom is justified of her children. [Lu. 7.34–5.]

I have patiently, cheerfully, and silently sustained (*through the malice, ignorance, mistake, and blinde zeal of Informers) a tedious twelve-months imprisonment in the common Goals of *Warwick*, *Coventry*, and that most infamous goal of *Newgate*, [I] Have been within these few days informed but my dearest friend, that

The two †Acts of May 10. and Aug. 9. 1650 were put out because of me; thereby secretly intimating that I was guilty of the breach of them. Whereupon, (after my long, and by many admired patience and silence) I thought good not so much for mine own sake (for my pure innocence supports me, and lifts up my head above all these things) but for the sake of others,

To present,

This ensuing Remonstrance, Vindication and Attestation; Resolving, by the help of the Omnipotent Omnipresent JEHOVAH (whom I purely *worship in the spirit* having *no confidence in the flesh*) [Phil. 3.3] to enlarge my self (when I enjoy my liberty) upon these things; and to all unprejudiced spirits (and perhaps to the silencing of them also) to give an account of my self, in reference to those Various Dispensations past and present, that I have been and am led into and thorow; as also, the removing of all stumbling-blocks, the clearing up of those mistakes, and the wiping away of those aspersions, which (through malice, weakness, ignorance, and mistake) have been cast upon me; who have been so concerned with a cloud, that not one amongst a thousand know me.

But for the present, I shall addresse myself to the Acts; and begin with that of Aug. 9th.[1]

In the Preamble of this Act the Parliament express their desires (**by all GOOD MEANS to propogate the Gospel &c.[)]**]Which is the desire of my soul. And it is always my fervent prayer to Him whose it is, That He is *the Prince of Peace*, [Isa. 9.6.], (*whose burden iseasie, and whose yoke is light* [Matt. 11.30.]; who *ruleth in righteousness*; who *judgeth not according to outward appeerence, but judgeth righteous judgement*) that he would, by his own out-stretched Arm, set it up. And I resolve never to give mine eyes any rest till I see it flourish: for it is my life.

They farther express

*All fleshly interests, carnall Gospellers, and pretenders to Religion, with some secret enemies (though seeming friends) to the State, combining together to incense them against me, because I have faithfully and boldy declared against their hypocrisie, pride, covetousness, self-seeking, and villainy, covered under the cloak of fleshly holiness and religion.

†Which were put out half a year after mine imprisonment.

Their desire to suppress (**Prophaneness and Wickedness, Superstition and Formality, &c.**)

The two former, my soul abhors, and I hate them with a perfect hatred; and have, by Life and Conversation, by Doctrine and Example (for many years) decried them; yea, even since I have been by all men (except those that knew me) cried up (as my *fore-runner* before me was by all sorts even of the most religious and righteous men, except a handful that knew him) for the worst of sinners, the vilest of persons; for a *Blasphemer, Devil*, &c.

And as for *Idolatry, Superstition and Idolatrous Formality*; Have any been a *Boanerges*[2] upon this account? (I speak as a fool.) I have thundered more against them then they all. And for my zeal herein, and against finer and subtler pieces of Formality, the coals were first kindled against me. And now the fire is at the highest: whereat I laugh; having sweet union with the Father and the Son; living in that Kingdom wherein dwelleth righteousness and peace; triumphing in *joy unspeakable, and full of glory*: [1 Pet. 1.8.] sweet Peace and pure Content being my continual repast. Neither do I repent

That the Almighty (whose I am, and who will do with his own what he pleaseth) Hath set me (as formerly he hath most of his Holy Prophets and Servants) as *A SIGNE and a WONDER—And—as a stumbling stone, and ROCK of OFFENCE to both the Houses of Israel,* &c,

*Isa. 8.18, 14, 15. Zech. 8.3, 8. (Men wondered at.) Their words wondered at, their carriage wondered at, their actions wondered at, &c. *As was Hosea, Hos. 1. 2.*

But to proceed.

The Act is bent against these ensuing Execreble Opinions &c. As (first) (**The denial of the necessity of Civil and Moral righteousness amongst men.**)

If there are such a generation of men, they stand or fall to their own master. As for me, I say concerning them, *O my soul! come not thou into their secrets: unto their assemblies, mine honour, be thou not united*, Gen. 49.6.

This Opinion (in the presence of the All-seeing God, in whose presence I am, and whom I serve) I utterly protest against. And in the same presence I most joyfully (to his praise) affirm, That that Golden Law, which is the Basis of all Civil and Moral righteousness amongst men; (Viz. *What soever ye would that men should do unto you, even so do you unto them, &c.*) is by the finger of God (in indelible letters) written as a Law of Life in my heart.

And here I can boldly say (as in reference to the grace of God) though in all humility (as in reference to myself) challenge the whole world, and say, *Whose ox have I taken? or whose ass have I taken? or to whom have I done any wrong?* [Exod. 22.1,4.] Whom have I dealt unjustly with? where is ever a drop of blood that I have shed? whom have I defrauded of a shoo-latchet or a thred? &c.

Herein do I make my boast of God all the day long, and in him do I triumph and rejoyce, though I am (to my joy also) numbered amongst Transgressors, and the chiefest of them prefered before me; many of them being released, and * set at liberty; and I (patiently and silently) lie by the walls, as having a visage more marred then any man's, &c.

But I proceed

And avowedly protest, that I hate and detest, yea (in the presence of God) protest against all those blasphemous Opinions or Tenents recited in page 980,[1] from the thirteenth line thereof to the seventh and twentieth line of pag. 891.

And many, or most of them, I will particularly hint at:

As primely this.

I do not **Vainly, ignorantly, and blasp[h]emously affirm myself or any other creature, to be very God**: neither was this Tenet (or any of the rest that follow) ever mine.

But this I have and do affirm, and shall still upon the house tops affirm, and shall expire with the wholesome sound, and orthodoxical opinion, That God Christ is in the creature. (CHRIST IN YOU *except you are reprobates*, 1 Cor.) [2 Cor. 13.5–7] The contrary assertion is the Blasphemie of Blasphemies, &c.

Again, I disavow, disown, detest and protest against that Opinion which holdeth that (**God dwelleth in the creature and nowhere else,** &c.) I live in that sound and orthodox opinion of Omnipresence; of which I can speak feelingly knowingly powerfully: whereof I formerly (in the time of mine own righteousness, which was as menstrous rags; and in time of my fleshly wisdom, which was *enmity to God) spake of formally, ignorantly, notionally (onely) like a Parot in a Cage.

And as for the **Righteousness, holiness of God**, &c. I had rather be cut to pieces than speak against it: for it is my Life. And whatever I have spoken against Righteousness and Holiness, it hath been against that Righteousness of Man, which is *as menstrous rags &c.* and against that carnal mock holiness, *pseud*-holiness of man which is a cloak for all manner of Villany; upon which the vengeance of God is and hath been proved forth &c.

And as for **Uncleaness, prophane Swearing, Drunkeness, Filthiness, Brutishness** &c. I declaim against them, as unholy &c.

As also, for **Lying, Stealing, Cozening, and defrauding others**, my soul abhors.

Further, I hold, declare and maintain, that **Murther, Adultery, Incest, Fornication, Uncleaness, Sodomie** &c. are things sinful, shameful, wicked, impious, and abominable, in any person &c.

Or that **Heaven and Happiness consisteth in the acting of these or such things**; and the rest, as they follow in pag. 981, are things that I disown, disavow, and protest against.

I shall conclude with this Affirmation and Asseveration:

That there is Heaven, and Hell, Salvation and Damnation. Heaven

*At which I envie not, &c. but take notice of, as do some hundreds also besides me.

*Isai
*1 Cor.

*Isai

for all those that repent of their sins, that *cease to do evil, and learn to do well.* [Isa. 1.16–7.] Heaven, for all them that are washt, purg'd and cleansed, by the Spirit of our God. Heaven, For all them that have Christ, the King of Glory, Eternal Majestie, in them. And Hell and Damnation, to all *that touch the apple of his eye*, that oppose *the Lord's Annointed*, and that *do his Prophets any harm.* [1 Chr. 16.22; Ps. 105.15.)

It was in my thoughts to have said something concerning the Act of May 10; but, upon reading thereof, I see nothing in it but what is contained in that of August; and therefore my labour is saved.

And I shall only adde a word or two concerning Liberty and Community.

As for Liberty, I own none but *the Glorious liberty of the sons of God*, which I *and the whole creation groans* after [Rom. 8.23] And I do from my heart detest and protest against all Sinful liberty, or that is destructive to soul or body.

And as for Community, I own none but the Apostolical, Saintlike Community spoken of in the Scriptures. So far as I either do or should own Community, that if flesh of my flesh be ready to perish, I either will or should call nothing that I have mine own: if I have bread, it shall or should be his; else all my Religion is vain, I own for dealing bread to the hungry, for cloathing the naked, for the *breaking of every yoke*, for the *letting of the oppressed go free.* [Isa. 58.6] I am or should be as my heavenly Father, who is kinde to all, loving to all, even to the ungodly, &c. Matt. 6. I can (through grace) pity those that are objects of compassion, and out of my poverty and penury relieve those that are in want. *And if this be to be vile,—&c.*

Yet.

Know all men by these Presents, That I am utterly against That Community which is sinful, or destructive to soul or body.

Ita testor, ABIEZER COPPE.

POSTSCRIPT

I have only one more word, and for the present I have done.

There are several Pamphlets[3] extant against a People called RANTERS; two whereof bear this inscription in their brazen foreheads, (Published by Authority) else the malice and simplicity of the Pamphleteer should have been still laughed at onely, and yet (upon another account) pitied by men.

For the present, I will only give—to understand, that the Pamphlets are scandalous, and bespattered with Lyes and Forgeries, in setting me in the front of such actions which I never did, which my soul abhors; such things which mine eyes never beheld, such words which my tongue never spake, and mine ears never heard.

All like that false aspersion,—Viz. that I was accompanied to Coventry with two she-disciples, and that I lay with two women there at once. Which two she-disciples were Captain Beak, and Other Souldiers, who have hurried me from Goal to Goal; where I sing Hallelujahs to the righteous Judge, and lie in his bosome, who is everlasting loving kindness. Amen.

HALLELUJAH

FINIS

Copp's Return

to the wayes of TRUTH:
IN A
Zealous and sincere PROTESTATION
Against severall Errors;

And in a
Sincere and zealous TESTIMONY to several Truths:

OR,
Truth asserted against, and triumphing over *Error*;
And the Wings of the
Fiery flying Roll clipt, &c.

BY

ABIEZER COPPE

---

the (supposed) Author of the Fiery flying Roll.

Herein is also something hinted concerning the *Author*, in reference to
the sinfulness and strictness of his Life.

With a little t'uch of what he hath been, and now is; Sparkling here and
there throughout these Lines,
And in the Preface.

Also a Letter of Mr *Durie's*, with several Proposals of great
concernment, hereunto since annexed:

And by the aforesaid Author (*A.C.*) faithfully, & fully answered, &c.

*I have seen the wickednesse of folly, and the foolishness of madness.
And now I apply my heart to wisdome.* Ecclei.
JOSHUAH *the High Priest* (was) *cloathed with filthy garments. And
the Angel saith, take away the filthy garments from him, and set a
mitre on his head*—Zech. 3.

London, Printed by *Tho. Newcomb.* 1651.

THE CONTENTS.

1. The Preface or Epistle Dedicatory. Wherein is hinted what the Author has been, and now is.

II. The severall Errors protested against:

1. That there is no sin.
2. That there is no God.
3. That Man, or the meer creature, is very God.
4. That God is in man, or in the creature, and now where else.
5. That Cursing and Swearing is no sin.
6. That Adultery and Fornication is no sin.
7. That Community of wives is lawful.

All which you may find in the Pages where the contrary Truths are asserted.

III. The several Truths asserted.
1. That there is sin.
2. That there is a God:
3. That Man, or the meer creature, is not very God.
4. That God is not confined in man, or is in the creature only, and no where else: But is omni-present; or everywhere.

5. That Swearing, and Cursing, is a sin.
6. That Adultery and Fornication is a sin.
7. That Community of wives is unlawful.
    Wherein is also something concerning
    Community in general, and concerning
    Liberty hinted at.
IV.   The Conclusion.

Some principal things in the second part (or Answer to
M. Durie's Proposals), contained.

The prime and principal motives inducing me to desire
my enlargement:
1. What Sin is.
2. That sin is sin; whether men imagine it to be so, or
   no.
3, & 4. That men do not please God as well when
   they sin, as when they sin not.
5. Some things concerning the Law of God.
6. Concerning God, and the souls of men, &c.
How we are partakers of the Divine Nature: wherein
    is something hinted concerning our spiritual
    filiation. And concerning our spiritual and
    mystical fraternity and union with Christ.
7. Something concerning the Resurrection of the
   body, and the last Judgement.

TO THE

Supream Power,

THE

PARLIAMENT

of the Common-wealth of

ENGLAND

And to the Right Honourable the

COUNCEL OF STATE,

appointed by their Authority.

Right Honourable,

I Am *exceedingly sorry, that I am fallen under your honours displeasure.*

And the rather because I am perswaded that you take no delight to lay heavy burthens upon any, nor to afflict any above measure.

And although I have FORMERLY wondered at my sore, tedious, and long continued imprisonment, under which unsupportable burthen I extreamly groan.

And the rather in respect of my poor weak disconsolate wife: (whom I left in perfect health and strength) and my small innocent children.

Shee being brought (almost) to deaths dore, with continual and sore languishing for my tedious imprisonment.

And for the space of above half a year, and to this day is under the Physitians hand, to our great Grief and charge:

Besides that unspeakable and continual charge (which in several respects) I lie at, and for the space of a year and half have lien at in prison.

Which hath wasted and almost utterly undone mine and me, that I have scarce clothes to hang on my back.

And all that little that I have at home, ruined and spoiled, &c.

And all my poor innocent children scattered here and there in several places. to our great care, Grief, and charge.

Although I say I have formerly wondered at the tediousnesse, and long continuation of my imprisonment, yet in all humility, I stoop to, and humbly acknowledge your Justice. And do not (now) much admire at my imprisonment.

First, in that I have been so slow, slack, and negligent in making any addresses to you;

Which indeed I resolved not to do: neither could I at all do it stil whatsoever came from me, came (Ex intimis medullis) from my very soul and heart; as these—that I now humbly present you withall do.

And secondly, because I am given to understand, that your Honours have been extreamly laden, and your ears filled brim full of complaints against me* which have arose from a kinde of zeal in some, from inveterate malice in others.

From ignorance, weakness, mistake, misapprehensions, and misunderstandings in others.

Which hath been occasioned by some bypast, and indeed, strange actions and carriages. And by som difficult, dark, hard, strange, harsh and almost unheard of words, and expressions of mine.

Of which I shall make bold to give first your honours, and then the * world a brief account.

And if your please,

(Thus)

With this introduction,
And a touch of what, and where I have been afore this strange appearance. (Thus)

As the Lord of old took fleshly Israel by the hand, and led them from place to place: pitching and removing their Tents (from place to place) hundreds of times (for the space of 40. years together) in the wilderness, &c.

So hath he took me by the hand, &c.

And hath transacted and done over the same things (in a spiritual sence) pitching and removing my tents from place to place.

Setting, and seating me in various forms.

In all which I have lived and acted zealously and conscientiously. Never stirring a foot, till I clearly apprehended this voice (All along.)

*Arise, get thee hence, remove thy Tent, &c. to such a place, &c.

And so removing me from grosser, and impurer, to finer and purer forms, &c.

And at length he set me, and seated me in that—

Which is (now) most in request, though it hath formerly been muchly

*Herein I honor, & humbly submit to the Magistrate, an[d]only speak of those several sorts of informers against me, &c.

*This I have been advised to, and am also bound in conscience to do in several respects, and amongst the rest, that I might be a warning to others—and amongst other things—that he that thinks he stands, may take heed lest he fall, &c.

*In this I do not in the least degree intend any thing concerning the sinfulness of my life, the *opposed: and they of that way persecuted.*

And for which I myself have (some years since, to my joy and comfort) sustained a 14 weeks close imprisonment, even for that way, which did, and now doth, fling dirt in the face of all other waies—affirming all other—to be false waies, and worships. And that onely to be the Gospel way, back'd on with many presidents and precepts, and plain texts of Scripture.

When I dwelt there—I walked most zealously, and most conscientiously: and I then shined gloriously in the eyes of many hundreds, who lived with me in that Region.

But at length, I did for a season leave that way: and thought that I was shewn a more excellent way, living and triumphing in joy unspeakable, and full of glory, in the power, spirit, and life of that which I was groaping after in the figure, flesh, form and outside, &c. I was fed *with such dainties, that the tongue of men & angels cannot express.

Unfathomable, unspeakable mysteries and glories, being clearly revealed to me.

Past finding out by any human search, or its sharpest discernings, &c.

But at length the terrible, notable day of the Lord, stole upon me unawares, like a thiefe in the night.

Even that DAY burst in upon me, which burneth like an oven, and NO FLESH (no not the FLESH of FOWLES which sore aloft) can stand before it, Malach. cap. 3 *and* chap. 4.

So that I can very well take up Habbacuks *expresse,*

Hab. 3. *when I saw him—*

My bowels trembled, my lipps quivered, rottenness entered into my bones, &c.

Why?

Before him came the Pestilence, and burning coales at his feet, &c.

*And the cup of the Lords right hand, was put into mine hand, &c. *Hab. 2.

*And it was filled brim full of intoxicating wine, and I drank it off, even the dreggs thereof.

Whereupon being mad drunk, I so strangely spake, and acted I know not what.

To the amazement of some.

To the sore perplexity of others.

And to the great grief of others.

For I was (really, in very deed) besides my self.

And till that cup passed from me, I knew not what I spake or did.

And because I was as rich, and as great as Nebuchadnezzar *was; I was therefore to be served, as he was.*

Sure I am, (in a sense) I was.

In a spiritual sense: I was as rich, (I say) and as great as

author whereof was the divell. But concerning the various dispensations in way of that religion I have passed through, &c.

Viz. I was abundantly satisfied with the loving kindness of the Lord, &c. (which was clearly, purely, and freely manifested to me) and with the light of his countenance, &c. living in peace, joy, and glorious consolation. And the Lord by his spirit (in his word) revealing and opening to me many glorious things which I neither saw nor understood afore, &c.

*which was the righteous judgement of the Lord, &c. upon me.

O the height! and depth! and length! and breadth! —how unsearchable are his ways! and his judgements past finding out, *Rom.*

Nebuchadnezzar, *and full as proud as he.*

Wherefore I'le (a little) dive into the mystery of that History Dan. 4:

For me thinks it is shewn to me that, that hits me——

In a mystical sense, I built a great Babel.

And (in the pride of my heart) I walking in the Palace of the Kingdome of Babylon, *i.e. recreating, and priding my self, in the pleasures of (that which I now see to be* בבל *) Babel, i.e. confusion.*

I said, is not this great Babel, which I have built, &c. whereupon my KINGDOME was taken from me.

And I was driven from MEN, Dan. 4. 32.

—From MEN,

i.e. That pure spark of Reason, (was for a season) taken from me. And I driven from it; from men, from RATIONALITY; from PURE humanity, &c.

And thus was I driven from MEN.

And I have been with BEASTS of the field, Dan. 4. 32, 33.

I have fed with BEASTS, &c.

I have eaten GRASSE with OXEN.

Have been conversant with BEASTS.

And have been company for BEASTS, &c.

And sure I am, (a) my hairs were grown like EAGLES feathers; and my nails like Birds CLAWES. (a) Dan. 4. 33.

And (now I am come to my self) I know it, and divers will know, (as many have felt) what I mean.——

But these daies are ended, Dan. 4. 34.

And I have lifted up mine eyes to Heaven.

And mine UNDERSTANDING is returned unto me. And I blesse the most high, and praise, and honour him that liveth for ever; whose dominion, is an everlasting dominion. And his kingdome is from generation, to generation.

(b) And all the inhabitants of the EARTH, are (b) Dan. 4.35. *reputed as nothing: And he doth according to his will in the Army of Heaven, and among the inhabitants of earth.*

And none can stay his hand: or say to him, what dost thou?

(c) And now I praise, and extoll, and honour the King of Heaven. ALL whose works are truth, and his waies judgement: and those that walk in pride, he is able to abase, &c. (c) Dan. 4. 37.

And now since, mine UNDERSTANDING is returned to mee.

I will dwell with my WIFE, as a man of knowledge:

I will love my little CHILDREN.

I will love all my BRETHREN, though of different statures, ages, and complexions, &c.

My strong Brethren, and my weak also, I will not offend .

My sickly ones I will pity, and visit, and be serviceable to them.

And my babe brethren, I will dandle on my knee; and do the best I can to quiet them, when they cry, and are crabbed, &c.

And with my brethren that are at age, I will dine and sup; with them I will talk and conferre.

With them I will eat, drink, and be merry in the Lord.

But I will hasten to a Conclusion,

Knowing that prolixity is not sutable to such personages, as your Honours are.

I will give but one hint: and I have done——

I have been (a long while) cloathed with filthy garments, and have lien in the channel.

Every one that hath past by me, have cast dirt upon me.

And I have lien still.

But now (in THESE—) I shake off the dirt, rags and all.

And I appear to your Honours, and to the world, in such an habit, as my penury will afford me.

I have patiently, and silently heard my self accounted, the father of mischief: and the grand authour of errors.

In many things I have been injuriously dealt withal: and several reports have gone of me, which have not been (in the least degree) true.

However, I have given offence to many, and grieved others:

For which my heart akes, my soul is grieved, and my and my bowels are kindled with compassionate tendernesse, and tender compassion towards them.

There are many * spurious brats, lately born: and because their parents have looked upon me as a rich Merchant they have took on them the boldnesse to lay them at my door, &c. *Errors broached

Some of them (indeed) look somewhat like my childen.

But however, to put all out of doubt,

Whether they are mine, or no: I will not be so full of foolish pity, as to spare them.

I will turn them out of doors, and starve them to death.

And as for those which I know are not mine own: I will be so holily cruel, as to dispatch them.

*I'll take those children young,*Ps.37. 10 in meet.

And dash their bones, against hard stones,

That lie the streets among.

As for my self,

Although I have been strangely acted,

☞   And by the Devil deluded.

Yet if I might gain a Kingdom, I could neither act, nor speak as I have done.

But I am resolved (by the grace of God) to give no offence (either in life, or doctrine) to any.

But both by life and doctrine, will decrie, whatsoever hath

occasioned out-cries against me. And hath offended God, your Honours, and grieved others. And I pay, hope, and believe, (that through the grace of God) my future deportment, to all sorts, shall make amends for what is by past.

These, with my self, I lay prostrate at your Honours feet:
For I am,

Right Honourable,

From the House of Bondage,
   where I live in the favour of
   the Prince of Peace.
   —NEWGATE.

Your humble, and faithful servant, and
   very, very poor prisoner,

The day of
   my Nativity, } 1619

May 30. And the day
   of my new- } 1651
   birth,

And,
Loving and peacefull to all men.

ABIEZER COPPE.

Truth asserted against,
AND
TRIUMPHING
OVER
ERROR.

Now I will lay the Axe to the root of the Tree,
even to this grand Error, (viz.) This

I. ERROR
That there is no sinne.

Concerning this Error,
1. I dis-own, detest, and protest against ıt.
2. I assert and prove the contrary, (*viz*)

I. ASSERTION.

I Assert and prove,
   That there is sinne:
 For, there is not a just man upon Earth, that doth good, and sinneth
not, as it is written, *Ecclesiast. 7. 20.*

Every man on earth living here below, sinneth: is (ἁμαρπλθ)i.e. A sinner, a sinner all over: full, brim-full of sin.

And of sinners, I am the chief.

And this (with unspeakable grief, sorrow of soul, and anguish of Spirit) I began to see in my tender years, when my heart melted like wax before the Lord.

And because I have been set as a Beacon on a hill, it will not be amiss to speak something concerning myself, in reference to sin. (And the rather because by wofull experience, I know as much as any man in the world, that there is sin, and what is sin.

And how, and wherein I have sinned; and what it hath cost me.

All which will illustrate this assertion——which I will mostly dwell upon. The contrary *Error* being the ground and Foundation of all the *Errors* which many suppose I am (or rather have been) *poysoned withall.)

*If I have drunk any deadly poyson it can do me no harm. *Mat.* 16. 18. THE Physitian hath given me a pure purge, and a powerful antidote. &c.

But to leave this *Parenthesis*, and to return to what I was saying.

When I was about 13 years old, sin began to lie at the dore.

The sight whereof was the Resurrection of several passions in me: as hatred, fear, grief, &c. And I began to flie from it, as from the face of a Serpent: arming myself against it, as against the deadliest enemy: setting a strict guard, making the watch as sure as I could.

*Psal. 39

Watching my thoughts, my actions; and watching my words, that I might not *offend with my tongue.*

Whereupon I writ upon Scrouls of Parchment, this inscription, (*Yea yea, nay, nay.*)

And sewed them about my rists.

So far was I, even from (*Faith, and Troth Oaths.*) From petty Oaths, or the least appearance of evill and sinfull speaking: that if I heard any one say, (*O Lord, O Christ, O God,* &c.) upon any trivial occasion, my flesh trembled thereat, it was even as a dagger to my heart.

And God is my Record, that in 27 years since, no such word proceeded out of my mouth.

*Exod. 20.

I looking upon (*O Christ, O God,* &c.) as a great breach of that pure Commandment, which saith *Thou shalt not take the name of the Lord thy God in vain,* &c.

And from the age of 13. and so forward, I began to take and keep a dayly Register of my sins, and set them down in a Book.

And in my evening and midnight prayer, (prayer by heart so called) I did constantly in that part of prayer called *Confession,* (with grief of soul, sighs and groans, and frequently with tears) confess over my sins.

When none saw me, but his that searcheth the heart, and tryeth the reins: and when no ear heard me but his that made the ear.

I also tyed my self for several years together, to read 9.6. and at least 3 chapters in the Bible every day: and much of the Scripture did I learn by heart.

I was in private, and most secret Fasting often.

Tears were my drink: dust and ashes my meat.

And sack-cloth my clothing.

Zeal, Devotion, and exceeding strictness of life and conversation, my life.

Neither is there, or was there any (even the highest and strictest) way of Religion, but I have zealously walked in it, as many hundreds can bear me witness.

But all this while I could not, neither to this day, can I see any thing in my self but sin.

And all my prayers tears, sighs, groans, watchings, fastings, humiliations, &c. besmeared over with filth and uncleanness.

And in the presence of the heart-searcher, and rein-tryer, I speak it: I have wept over my tears, because I could weep not more: not better, &c.

And have been greatly humbled for my humiliation, because it was not greater, not better.

And asham'd of all, because sin hath clinged so close to them all.

Besides those innumerable sinfull thoughts, words and deeds, which have invironed me about on every side.

This that I have now hinted in reference to the strictness of my life, is not blowing a Trumpet in mine own praise——

I have felt it like pangs of death: I speak it with sorrow and shame: and all to this purpose.

That I might proclaim, *There is sin, sin with a witness.*

And now do *I* lift up * my voice like a Trumpet, herein do I cry aloud, and spare not my self.   **Isa. 58.1. to the 8. verse.*

Nor——to shew the house of *Jacob* their sins, &c.

And if the righteous scarcely be saved, where shall the sinner and ungodly appear?

If our prayers, tears, sighs, groans, humiliations, (take all i'th'lump—) righteousnesses can scarcely be saved,—*justified* in themselves, &c. where shall our stark staring wickednesses, &c. appear?

O Sin! Sin! Sin!

There is Sin.

Murther, Theft, Adultery, Drunkenness, Swearing, Cursing, Uncleanness, Uncleanness, Covetousness, Pride, Cruelty, Oppression, Hypocrisie, Hatred, Envy, Malice, Evil surmising is sin.

Nothing but villany, sin, and transgression in me, the chief of sinners.

In man——

In every man.

There is none righteous; no, not one.

None that doth good; no, not one.

All are Sinners.

Thieves, little thieves, and great thieves, drunkards, adulterers, and adulteresses. Murtherers, little murtherers, and great murtherers. All are Sinners. Sinners All.

(*Rom.* 3. from the 9. to the 21. *verse.*)

What then? Are we better then they?

No, in no wise.

——*All are under sin.*

As it is written, there is none righteous; no, not one;—there is none that doth good; no, not one.

Their throat is an open sepulchre; with their tongues, they have used deceit. The poison of asps is under their lips.

Their mouth is full of cursing, and bitterness.

Their feet are swift to shed bloud.

Destruction, and misery, are in their ways.

THE WAY OF PEACE, have they not known.

Now we know, that what things soever the Law saith, it saith to them that are under the Law; that every mouth may be stopped; and all the world may become guilty before God.

Therefore by the DEEDS of the Law, shall no flesh be justified in his sight, &c.

But NOW the righteousness of God WITHOUT the LAW, is manifest—But

(Verse, 23.)—ALL have sinned, &c.

Verse 21. All the world (*is*) become guilty before God.

Guilty, guilty, my Lord.

All are full of sin.

I,—and the Nation.—

Ah! sinfull I.

Isa. 1. 4. 5. 6. 7. 10. 11. 12. 13. 14. 15. 21. 23. 24. 26. 27.

*Ah! sinful nation. A people laden with iniquity. From the sole of the feet even to the HEAD: there is no soundness in it: but wounds, and bruises, and putrified sores.

To what purpose is the multitude of your sacrifices to me saith the Lord? &c.

When you come to appear before me, who hath required these things at your hands, &c.

The new Moons and Sabbaths, the Calling of ASSEMBLIES, I cannot away with: it is INIQUITY, even the solemn meeting: And when you spread forth your hands, I will hide mine eyes from you: yea, when you make many prayers, I will not hear.

Your hands are full of bloud.

How is the faithfull City become an harlot? It was full of judgement, righteousness lodged in it, but now murtherers.

The Princes are rebellious, and companions of Thieves:

EVERY ONE loveth gifts, and followeth after rewards—(But) I will restore thy judges at the first, &c.

(And) Zion shall be redeemed with JUDGEMENT, &c.

And, now † O my God, I am ashamed, and blush to lift up my face, to thee my God. For we have sinned.   †*Ezra 9. Dan: 9.*

We, our Kings, our Rulers. Our Priests, our Judges,

All have sinned, and gone astray.

Do sin, are sinners.

Wo be to us, we are sinners.

Wo be to the inhabitants of the Earth——

That EARTH is full of sin.

There is sin, sin with a witness.

Ita testor
ABIEZER COPPE.

Let this suffice for the first assertion.

That there is sin.

And let this, as also divers other things in the following *Assertions* serve as sharp shears to clip the wings of the *Fiery flying Role*: which insinuats several blasphemous opinions, and which insinuats that nothing is otherwise a sin, then as men imagine it to themselves to be so: Which I utterly disown, and protest against, (as may be more fully seen in my answer to Mr. *Duries* Proposal to me concerning sin, &c.)

Wherefore I say, let the wings of the *Fiery flying Role* be clipt (by this large Tract concerning sin, and by that which follows, with my answer to Mr. *Dury*) and let it be thrown headlong into its own place, the Lake of fire and brimston, and the great Abyss from whence it came.

And let me mourn that, I, and the whole world be in darkness, and are involved in   *Sin and wickedness.*

II. ERROR.

That there is no God.

Concerning this *Error,*

First, I utterly disown, detest, and protest against it, as a horrid blasphemous opinion.

And although I have been slanderously reported of in this particular (as in divers others) yet I challenge the whole world to prove or affirm to my face, that ever I affirmed any such thing.

Yea, I can with joy, and boldness (in the presence of the *All-seeing God*) affirm, that I never said it in my heart, much less with my mouth,

That there is no God.

II. ASSERTION.

(But on the contrary I affirm and know.)
That there is a God.

O God is a *Spirit*, having his being in himself; yea, he is that (*Ens entium*) that *being of beings*, as that Sacred and unfathomable word (יהוה) *Jehovah*, (from הוה) imports.   *Jo. 4.

He is the (*Summum bonum*,) the chiefest good.

The fountain of life and light.

He is the *Alpha, and *Omega*, the first and the last, the begining and the ending, &c.

He is said to be the God of love & peace, (*Phil. 4. Rom. 15.*)

And a man of War. (*Exod. 15.*)

The Lyon, and Lamb. (*Revel. 5.*)

The Branch, and Root. (*Isa. 11.* with *Rev. 22.*)

A jealous God. (*Exod. 20*)

And the God of mercies. 1 *Cor.*

And all these (seemingly) cross denominations, do finely, and secretly declare him to be ALL, in ALL, according to the Scriptures, 1 *Cor.* 15. 28. *Colos.* 3. 11.

The heavens and firmament; day and night, &c. all his works praise him. And all things declare his glory.

Yet the tongue of men and angels is altogether unable to speak him forth to the full.

And as for myself.

I must not, I cannot, I dare not say anymore, but silently adore him, With,

O the height, the depth, the length, the breadth, how unsearchable! &c.   *Rom. 11:

Of him, and from him, and to him, and through him are ALL THINGS. And he is ALL in ALL, God blessed for evermore. *Amen.*

Rom. 11. 26. chap. 9. vers. 5. 1 *Cor.* 8. 6 chap. 11: vers. 12. 2 *Cor.* 5. 18 *Colos.* 1. 16. 17. 20: *Ephes.* 1. 23. and chap. 4. vers. 5.

*Concerning this, see more at large in that piece of *Hieroglipical* Divinity, in the preface to *Rich. Coppins* book.

III. ERROR.

That man, or the meer Creature, is very God.

Concerning this Error.
  First I disown, detest, and protest against it.
  Secondly, I affirm the contrary, *viz.*

III. ASSERTION.

That not any man, or the meer creature is very God.

For, First, the creature is mortall, 1 *Cor.* 15.
But God is immortall, 1 *Tim*. 1. 17. 1 *Tim*: 6. 16.
Secondly, the Creature is visible.
But God is invisible, 1 *Tim*. 1. 17. *John* 1. No man hath seen God, at any time, &c.
Thirdly, the creature is limited, and is weakness.
But God is unlimited Almightiness.
He is where he pleaseth, doth what he pleaseth, *Eccles.* 8. 3.
He is unlimited.
He sets up a brazen Serpent, when he pleaseth, *Numb*. 21. 8. 9.
And grinds it to powder, when he pleaseth, 2 *Kings* 18. 4.
He institutes Circumcision when he pleaseth, and commands it, upon pain of Excommunication and death, &c.
  Gen. 17. 10, 11. to the 28 verse, chap. 21. 4. chap. 34. 15. 17. 22. 24. *Exod*. 12. 44. 48. *Lev*. 12. 3. *Josh*. 5.3. 5.7. *Acts* 7. 8.
  All these Scriptures, I quote on purpose to shew how strictly God enjoyned Circumcision.
  And what penalties were laid on them that were not obedient herein, &c.
  But unlimited Almightiness dasheth that to pieces, which he made. Nuls his own Acts, Statutes, Laws, and strict Ordinances.
  Nothings this great thing, Circumcision.
  As it is written.
  Verily Circumcision is nothing, &c. 1 *Cor*. 7. 19.
  And they which preached, That, up, which God (upon pain of death) once set up. Were accounted (by the holy Apostle, who was inspired with the holy Spirit) The worst of gain-sayers, unruly, vain talkers, and deceivers, *Tit*. 1. 9,10.
  Yea, the preaching and practising of that, for which there were so many, so great precepts, and presidents, so large examples, and strict commands, was (at length) a horrid indignity to God, Christ, and the Gospel, &c. *Gal*. 5. 2,3. chap. 6. 12,13.
  And sure there's something i'th' winde——
  Certainly the meer creature is not very God.

For the meer creature is limited, and weakness.

But God is unlimited Almightiness.

He doth what he pleaseth.

He saith, thou shall not kill, *Exod.* 20.

And yet he bids *Abraham* slay his son, &c.

He saith, Thou shalt not commit Adultery, *Exod.* 20.

And fly Fornication, *Acts* 15. 20,29. *chap*: 21. 25. 1 *Cor.* 6. 18. *Ephes.* 5. 3. *Col.* 3. 5. 1 *Thess.* 4. 3.

And yet he saith to Hosea, Take a whore—a wife of whoredomes, and get children of fornication, *Hos.* 1. 2. *chap.* 3. 1,2,3. Love a woman, beloved of her friend: yet an Adulteresse. &c.

Certainly the meer creature, is not very God: for the creature is limited weaknesse.

But God is unlimited Almightiness.

And doth whatsoever he pleaseth.

And who hath enjoyned him his way? Or who can say, thou hast wrought iniquity? Or who can say to him, what dost thou? *Job* 36. 23. *chap.* 9. 12.

Fourthly, the meer creature is finite.

But God is infinite. *Ergo,*

The meer creature is not very God.

I might in this argument run (*ad infinitum*)

But let this suffice: for God is my Record, this was never my tenent, though some slanderously, others maliciously, and some through ignorance, weaknesse, and mistake, have reported it of mee.

Neither do I know any one upon the face of the Earth, that affirmeth,

That the meer creature, is very God.

IV. ERROR.

That God is in man, or in the creature onely, and no where else.

Concerning this error,

1. I utterly disown, detest, and protest against it.

2. I affirm, that my holding forth the contrary, (even that sound, and Orthodoxal truth of Omni-presency) to the life: hath been one of the main stumbling blocks, whereat many have stumbled, have fallen, and have been broken.

And for which, many (who have talkt, and only talkt of Omni-presency,) have been offended at me. But—

3. I assert the very truth, which is contrary to this error, (*viz.*)

IV. ASSERTION.

That God is not confirmed in man, or in the creature only,
but is omni-present, or every where.

That eternal, invisible, only wise God. *Jehovah (ens entium)* the beeing of beeings, is not confirmed in man only, &c.

For I know that he is (*Hic, & ubique*) here, and there, and every where.

He is in the heights, in the depths, above, below.

He is the high and lofty, that inhabits eternity.

Yet dwelleth in the lowest heart, *Isa*. 57. 15.

Psa. 39. 7. to the 13. Whither shall I go from thy presence? If I ascend up into Heaven, thou art there: If I make my bed in Hell, behold thou art there, &c.

Yea, the darknesse hideth not from thee: but the NIGHT shineth as the DAY.

The DARKNESSE, and the LIGHT, are both alike to thee, &c.

He is in Heaven, Earth, Sea, Hell.

The God of the Hils, and of the Valleys also.

He is near, and afar off, &c.

He filleth all things, all places.

Can you have any more then all?

He filleth ALL in ALL, *Ephes*. 2. 23:

And I am filled full, with joyous amazement; and amazing joy: that I can write no more of this subject. But shout for joy, that I know that the omnipotent *Jehovah*, is omni-present.

(*Hallelujah, Amen.*)

For God is not confined in man, or in the creature only. For he is in himself.

And in ALL THINGS.

For (once more) He is ALL in ALL, *Coles*. 3. 11.

V. ERROR.

That Cursing and Swearing, is no sin.

Concerning this thing, I shall

First declare, that for the space of 27 years, I was as free from this sin (yea, I speak as a fool) more free from it, then any that I knew, as I have already hinted in the first Assertion; whether I refer you.

But (at length) God in his infinite wisdome, (amongst many other things, for this very end, to shew to me, that at my *very best estate, I was altogether vanity.   *Psal*. 39.

And to take me off from mine own base bottom.

And for the destruction of the pride of my flesh.

That I might no longer glory in my self, but glory in the Lord, &c. was pleased to turn me loose.

And being * born a wild ass colt; and the reins being laid in my neck: I proved so indeed.   *Job 11. 12.

For‖ I was almost in all Evil.   ‖Prov. 5. 14.

And was infected with this plague of Swearing, &c.

But after a while, the hand of God found me out:

And sent the pangs of death to take hold on me.

*The terrours of the Almighty were set in array against me: especially for this horrid sin of Swearing: which lay upon me as a burden too heavy for me to bear. The jawes of Hell continually gaping for me.   .   *Job

And I concluding myself to be (as often I cryed out, I was) in a far worse case then *Cain*, or *Judas*.

And for a long season, (*a*) I lay weltring in my bloud. (*a*) *Ezek*. 16. My (*b*) wounds stunk, and were corrupt. (*b*) *Ps*.

But at length, everlasting loving kindness cast his skirts of love over me, (even (*c*) when I was cast out to the loathing of my person) when none eyes pitied me, none had compassion on me. (*c*) *Ezek*. 16.

When prayers, tears, sighs, groans, fastings, all could not cure mee.

He by his own out-stretched arm, wrought wonderfully; embracing me in the arms of his tender compassion, and compassionate tenderness, saying to me, Live.

He poured both wine, and oile into my wounds, and made (d) the bones which he had broken, to rejoice. (d) *Psal*. 51.

And hath made me to sing.

Bless the Lord, O my soul, and all that is within me, bless his holy name.

Who forgiveth all thine iniquities, who healeth all thy diseases, &c.

I have (indeed) seen the wickedness of folly, and the foolishness of madness; and now I apply my heart to wisdome.

And therefore,

Secondly, I dis-own, detest, and protest against that error, which saith,

That Swearing and Cursing is no sin.

And in the third place, I come to the

V. ASSERTION
That Cursing and Swearing, is a sin.

First, Cursing is a sin;

Because it is against that pure percept of Christ:

Bless, I say, and Curse not, *Matt.* 5. 44. *Luke* 6. 28. *Rom.* 12. 14.

And that *Swearing is a Sin*;

First, I know it by woful, and most doleful experience.

I have found it so to be; with a witness.

Yea, with a vengeance, as I have afore hinted.

Furthermore, *Swearing is a sin.*

For it is a breach of that pure Commandment, which saith, *Thou shalt not take the name of the Lord thy God in vain.   **Exod.* 20.

Thirdly, it is a breach of that pure precept of Christ, which saith, Swear not at all, *Matth.* 5. 34. 36. *ch.* 23. 16. 18. 20, 21, 22.

Therefore above all things, Swear not——*Jam.* 5.

Fourthly, Swearing is a sin.

Because it pulleth down judgement upon a Land and Nation: as it is written, *Jer.* 23. 10:

Because of Swearing, the Land mourns:

Because of prophane swearing, vain swearing, false swearing, forswearing, and forc't swearing, the Land mourns:

And I mourn.

For that vengeance, and those clouds of bloud which hang over this Nation: unless the glorious beams of that bright Sunne, the Prince of peace, and God of love dispel them.

But I proceed to the sixth Error.

VI. ERROR.

That Adultery, Fornication, and Uncleannesse, is no sin.

Concerning this Error,

First, I disown, detest, and protest against it:

Secondly, I lay down this assertion.

VI. ASSERTION.

That adultery, fornication, and uncleannesse is a sin.

First, because it is a breach of that pure precept, which saith,

Thou shalt not commit adultery, *Exod.* 20.

Secondly, it is a sin against a mans own body, (as it is written) 1 *Cor.* 6. 18.

He that commiteth fornication, sinneth against his own body.

And I doe not remember, (that throughout the Scripture) there is the like said of any other sin besides.

Thirdly, it is against all these ensuing, wholesome, pure, precious Precepts, and Scriptures.

Acts 15:20. 29. *ch.* 21. 25. 1 *Cor.* 6. 18. *Col.* 3. 5. 1 *Thess.* 4. 3.

And as for all uncleanness, let it not be once be named among you. *Ephes.* 5. 3.

And so I proceed to the Seventh Error, which hath some affinity with this; (*viz.*)

VII. ERROR.
That Community of Wives is lawful.

Concerning this Error,
Firstly, I disown, detest, and protest against it:
Secondly, I lay down this assertion; (*viz.*)

VII. ASSERTION.

Wherein is also something hinted concerning community in the general, and concerning liberty.

That Community of Wives is unlawful.

First because it is a breach of that pure Precept.

1 *Cor.* 7. 2. Let every man have his own wife, and every woman her own husband.

Secondly, this tenent, is a corrupt opinion, that Christ hates; which is briefly hinted in that of *Revel.* 2. 6.

This thou hast, that thou hatest the deeds of the *Nicolaitans*, which I also hate.   I will add,

Thirdly, that it is destructive to the dearest, and nearest relations, and the occasion of multitudes of miseries and perplexities.

Fourthly, it is destructive to the (*bene esse*)—Well beeing of a Common wealth.

And here I think good to give a hint of community in the general, because I understand, I have been by some traduced, and by others mistaken, concerning it.

I shall only here say,

That there is something (by some) contended for, in the name of community: which may prove meerly pernicious, and exceedingly destructive in several respects.

But for mine own part,

I shall (*ex animo*[1]) in the presence of God, declare to the whole world, and here recite what I have formerly written, in my Remonstrance——   Thus,

As for community, I own none but that Apostolical, saint-like community, spoken of in the Scriptures.

So far I either do, or should own community, that if flesh of my flesh, be ready to perish; I either will, or should call nothing that I have, mine own.

If I have bread, it shall, or should be his, else all my religion is in vain. I am for dealing bread to the hungry, for cloathing the naked, for the breaking of every yoak, for the letting of the oppressed go free. I am, or should be as my heavenly Father, who is kind to all, loving to all, even to the ungodly, &c. *Mat.* 6.

I can (throug[h] grace) pity those that are objects of my compassion, and out of poverty and penury relieve those that are in want.   Yet,

Know all men by these presents, that I am utterly against that community which is sinful, or destructive to soul or body, or the well beeing of a Common-wealth.

And as for liberty,

I do from my heart detest and protest against all sinfull liberty, or that is destructive to soul or body; or the (*bene esse*) the well beeing of a Common-wealth.

I own none other, long for none other; but that * glorious liberty of the sons of God.   *Rom.* 8.

Which God will hasten in its time.

Conclusion.

Till then, though I have been (through my over-much zeal, and through the weakness and mistake of others, an offence to many:

Yet (through grace) I will * give no offence for the future, either to Jew or Gentile, or to the Church of God.   *Cor.* 10. 32,33.

And resolve (by the grace of God) to live at peace with all men.

And I give the world to understand, that those that are godly, sincere, and conscientious in their waies: (let them bee where they will) I own them, love them: they are the very joy of my soul. I will neither be offended * at my weak brother, which eateth hearbs. Nor judge my strong brother, which eateth meat.   *Rom.* 14.2.

Neither will I judge my brother that * observeth a DAY: if to the Lord he observeth it.   *Rom.* 14.

Nor judge him that observeth not a day: if to the Lord he observeth it not.

To the Lord of the Conscience,

And to the Lord of ALL,

Even to the Lord, I leave you all,
And in the Lord, I love you all.
And in him,

Farewell, Amen.

A Preamble to the ensuing Proposals, and Answers.

*Since the finishing of my former—this ensuing Letter, with
the several Proposals therein contained, were sent to me by
the Reverend M. Dury, which with my full and faithful
Answer thereunto, may be aptly added as a second part to
the former Tract.*

*And to winde up all, it is thought expedient that my last
Letter, (to my worthily respected and faithful friend)
concerning this business, &c.*

> *Be annexed as a Conclusion of All——*

M. Coppe,

Although we all who conferred with you yesterday, came with some
fore-stalment against you (as by our Discourses you might well
perceive) yet when we parted from you, I found, as in myself, so in all
the rest, that your Declarations to us had left an impression in us, that
you were ingenuously open in what you then said; and that we had the
cause to believe that you were really sensible of, and truly penitent for
that which you had formerly done: which being so, you ought
conscientiously to bethink your self, how to give satisfaction unto the
world of the truth of your conversion. Let me therefore give you an
opportunity, to testifie unto all, that which was declared unto us, and
did seem a true evidence of your repentance: if then you would as in
the fear of God by way of Letter to some of us, lay open your sense
concerning the things which I shall now lay before you, you would do
yourself much right, in our opinion who conferred with you, and it
will bee an advantage towards the accomplishment of your desires as
God may direct us to improve it.

First, then, although the tediousness, and other inconveniences of
your imprisonment, may be lawful and natural motives to you to
desire a releasement; yet it will bee expedient for your own comfort, to
make it appear before God to your own conscience, that you
dessemble not your repentance to flatter him with your lips, (for God
cannot be deceived) and before men whose eyes are upon you, that
you make not a fair profession being effectually converted only to gain

your liberty; that then as a Sow, you may return again to wallow in the mire: I say, it will be very expedient, that you clear up these things, both to yourself, and to other men; for as you ought to suspect your self, so others will be ready to suspect you of this.

Secondly, you will do well to speak fully and plainly your sense of the things whereof I discoursed with you, after that you had opened your self in the things taken notice of by us, in your Preface, *viz.*

Concerning Sin; What you understand it to be? Whether any thing be otherwise a sin, then as men imagine it to themselves to bee so? Whether men please God as well when they sinne, as when they sinne not? And whether to act most sinne, bee the nearest way to perfection? And what you think of these Tenets; and whether the Fiery Flying Roll, doth not insinuate them to be Truths, and dispose men to receive them as such?

Concerning the Law of God declare your sense of it; as whether it is not a rule to all men of their life in thoughts, words, and deeds? where the infallible testimony thereof is to be found, whereunto all men must appeal and submit; and whether there be else where any truth of God to be believed besides that which is witnessed by every mans spirit unto himself?

Concerning God and the souls of men, what you think of him? and whether he hath not a being before, and out of all creatures in himself from eternity? what difference there is between the nature of mens souls, and his being? and in what sense we are said to partake of the Divine nature, 2 *Pet.* 1. 4.

Concerning the resurrection of the body, and the last judgement, what you believe thereof? and whether you think these things to be past already, as to any men living on earth, yea or no[.]

The third thing which I have to offer unto you, is the consideration of the circumstances whereby your sins are highly aggravated, and for which you should use means to make your repentance the more remarkable.

First, in respect of your own person; for you have been a preacher, and a leading man; now a sin in such a person is more dishonourable to God, and to the holy profession, then in other men; therefore their repentance ought to be more remarkebly satisfactory then other mens repentance.

Secondly, in respect of the publick and noted manner of your failings, you ought proportionably to make your humiliation the more publick and notable.

Thirdly, in respect of the greivousness, and hainousness of the actions in themselves, they being of a very deep dye; you ought to wipe them away with the greater contrition before God; and to evidence your turning from them with the greater abhorrency thereof before men; and with the more care of giving a ful assurance to the

State that you shall never return thereunto again.

Fourthly, in respect of the hurt which your Doctrine and perswasion, or example hath done to the souls of other men; whereof som you have led into the waie of perdition, who perhaps will never be reclaimed; & others you have so scandaliz'd that the way of truth is evil spoken of by them: all which should lie heavily upon your spirits all your days; that from henceforth you should strive to make so much the more amends, by being more examplary in holiness, then ever you have been in disoluteness.

If you will express your thoughts concerning these things, and pray to God to direct you both in thinking and expressing you will do that which becometh your ingenuitie; and add to the satisfaction which was wanting in your former discourse, and is now expected to be improved for your good, by

your willing servant in
Christ, John Dury.

June 23. 1651.

For his much honoured Friend Mr Dury.

SIR,

I have joyfully and thankfully received yours, with your wholsom advise therein contained.

And I give you to understand,

That

My desires jump with your requirings, and in the laying open of my sense, concerning the things which you lay before me.

And first concerning the nature and grounds of my desires, in my reference to my releasement, *&c.*

And therein——first Negatively.

I do not desire or seek after my Liberty, to this end, That I might return again, and wallow in the mire.

For I had rather die a thousand deaths, then do so: or desire so to do.

Neither do I, or did I dissemble my repentance, or flatter God with my lips.

For all those fair professions, sparkling through my Book, and those which (so solemnly in the presence of God, and before you with seriousness, and sorrow of heart, and tears in mine eyes,) I made, came from the bottom of my soul; cordially, fervently, and compunctionately: as the searcher of the heart knows, my conscience also bearing me witness.

And although (as you say, and I know) the tediousness, and several other inconveniences of mine imprisonment may be, and are lawful and natural motives to me, to desire a releasment.

Yet I say, and give you to understand, (and that from the bottom of my heart) these are not the main motives——

But the prime, chief, and principal, is

That I might be in a better way, place, posture, and capacity to glorifie God, then I possibly can be in here.

For how can I sing the songs of my God in a strange land, &c.

I do in the presence of God (even from my soul) with grief, gasp, and cordially, and feelingly breath out those groans.

Wo is me, that I am constrained to sojourn in Mesech, and to inhabit in the tents of Kedar, &c.

Truly, Sir,

I have a long, long while eaten * Grass with Oxen.   *Vid.*
Preface to my last book. p. 7. [p. 130]

Verbum sat—

These, and the like—are the prime grounds of my groaning under the burden of my imprisonment: which next to my sins is one of the heaviest, &c.

And so I come to your other Proposals.

And first to the first, which runs thus:

Prop. I. *What do you understand sin to be?*
Answ. In general, I understand sin, (which is my most unsupportable burden) to be the transgression of THE Law.

Against which we (in innumerable wayes) transgress; in thoughts , words, deeds; in omissions, commissions, ignorance, weakness, and presumption, &c.

But to your second, *viz.*

Prop. II. *Whether any thing be otherwise a sin, then as men imagine it to themselves to be?*

Answ. I answer, That sin, is sin in itself, yea, (as the Apostle saith) †
exceeding sinful.   †*Rom.*

Even every breach, (yea, the least breach) of the THE Law, is sin. Whether men imagine it to be so or no.

For instance:

Adultery is a sin, whether men imagine it to be so, or no.

Even adultery——of all sorts; corporal, or spirituall; which the whole Land, and every mans heart (even the heart of the purest and strictest) is brim full of, if they could see it.

But ALL adulterers (I say) of all sorts, whether corporal, or spiritual: and S. *James* his † adulterers and adulteresses, are sinners, do sin, whether they imagine so, or no.   †*James.* 4. 1. *to the* 6. *vers.*

Yea, *heart-adultery, and eye adultery, lust in both, in either is sin, sin with a witness. *Mat.* 5. 28.

Whether men imagin[e] it to be so or no.

But I know it so to be: and (with a witness) have found it so to be:

And still I remember, and shall never forget that I heard a reverend Divine (when I was about sixteen years old) affirm, That

*Whereof those are greatly guilty that cry out of adultery & uncleaness in others, &c.

heart-adultery, &c. was worse then the act of adulterie, &c. It being the father and spirit of adulterie.

As also (many times) reaching such objects which were (at that time—) free from the like lust, &c.

I do not say that I am of his opinion.

But sure I am, this express hath (hundreds of times) wounded me to the very heart; and hath (for many years) stuck as a dagger in my soul; and hath cost me hot waters, even many, many showrs of tears; and innumerable sighs and groans, &c.

And let him that is without sin (in this particular) cast the first stone at adulterers, and adulteresses.

And (for my part, as I have been cut and wounded, wounded to the heart for this: so will I throw stones (as fast as I can drive) at ADULTERY, at all sorts of adultery: in my self, and others, which I know to be sin, and sin of a deep dye: Yea, a crimson crime, whether men imagine it to be so or no.

And so is swearing, and cursing, &c. a sin, as I have * to my great grief, and sore smart found it to be: and I once more proclaim it so to be.

Whether men imagine it to be so or no.

And so is drunkness of all sorts (and there are various sorts thereof) a sin.

Whether men imagine it to be so or no.

And theft of all sorts (and there are several sorts thereof) a sin.

Whether men imagine it to be so or no.

And murther of all sorts (and there are several sorts thereof, and several sorts of Murtherers) a sin.

Whether men imagine it to be so or no.

And there are thousands of Drunkards, thieves and murtherers (of several sorts) who stroak themselves on the head, and say, I thank God, I am not as this drunkard, th[ie]f, or as this murtherer, &c.

And yet go away no more justified then the worst of Publicans and sinners.

But for my part I will not justifie any of these in my self, or in others.

For once more, I say, and know, that drunkenness of all sorts: theft of all sorts, is a sin.

Whether men imagine it to be so or no.

And so is pride, covetousness, hypocrisie, oppression, Tyranny, cruelty, unmercifulnesse, *despising the poor and needy, who are in vile raiment, &c.   *Jam. 2.

A sin.

Whether men imagine it to be so or no.

And so is doing unto others, as we would not be done unto ourselves, &c.

A sin.

Whether men imagine it to be so or no.

And the laying of Nets, Traps, and Snares for the feet of our neighbours, is a sin.

Whether men imagine it to be so or no.

And so is the not undoing of heavy burthens, the not letting the oppressed go free: the not breaking every yoak, and the not dealing of bread to the hungry, *&c.* and the hiding ourselves from our own flesh, *&c.*

A sin.

Whether men imagine it to be so or no.

And let this suffice for answer to your second *Proposal,*

Wherein I affirm,

That sin is sin whether men imagine it to be so or no.

And as for the FIERY FLYING ROLL,

I disclaim, declaim, and protest against it which doth (to use your own apt expression) *insinuate the contrary.*

Also I once more, disclaim, declaim, and protest against all other Errors, and blasphemous opinions therein insinuated, *&c.*

As my large, free, cordial professions to you, and what I have now written on this point, and that which here followeth.

As also the assertion of so many truths, in my former writings, together with those many protestations against mine own errors, as also against others that I have not been tackt or tainted with, do clearly demonstrate to all ingenuous, and unprejudiced spirits.

Even to all, unless to those that will be satisfied with nothing: but rejoyce to add afflictions to my bonds, and to spit out their inveterate and secret malice against me, *&c.*

But to the Lord I leave them. And to him I refer my cause who Registers my groans, and hears the sighing of the prisoners.

And knows the sincerity of my heart which he hath given me;

And I proceed to the rest of your Proposals.

Which (I humbly conceive) might have been more aptly proferrd to the authors of such *Assertions,* from whence your proposals have their rise, *&c.* then to me who am not the father of them nor did ever own them, *&c.*

And for my part I am indisposed to meddle with other mens matters.

And am also filled with various perplexities, griefs, and languishments, & so compassed about with so many inconveniencies with weaknesse of my body, and various distempers both of body and minde; and altogether wanting all manner of accomodations: being also sorely put to it for place—and opportunity.

That I am very unfit for these things.

However (so well as I can) I proceed to your 3, and 4, Proposals, *viz.*

III. and } Propos. *Whether men please God as well when they sin,*
IV.   }   *as when they sin not?*
                        And,
Whether to act most sin, be the nearest way
    to perfection?

Answ. I answer, That I disown, detest, and protest against this opinion, as erronous and blasphemous.

And contrary to the whole tenure of Scripture:

As also contrary to mine own experience.

For I am perswaded,

That never any man hath lien more under the wrath and heavy displeasure of God for sin, then I have done.

And as for the Scriptures, they affirm,

That when God saw that the wickedness of man was great upon the earth: and that every imagination of the thoughts of his heart, was only *Evil* continually: it repented the Lord that he had made man on the earth, and it grieved him at his heart, and that he was sore displeased thereat—he said,—

I will destroy man whom I have created, both man and beast, *&c. Gen.* 6. 5,6,7. 11,12,13.

The time would fail to summ up all the Scriptures to this purpose. *&c.*

Neither can I at this time in this place, be in a capacity to do it.

But I go on.

When Israel, Gods peculiar (seperated people) had sinned, *Num* 14.

The Lord said, how long will this people provoke me? I will smite them with the pestilence, &c. vers. 11,12.

And again how long shal I bear with this evil congregation? as truly as I live your Carcasses shall fall in the wildernesse, *&c.* vers. 27,28,29.

Again, they ceased not from their own doings, but have transgressed, &c.

And the anger of the Lord was hot against Israel, *&c. Judg.* 2. 19. to the end of the chap.

And Chap. 3. 7,8,9,10,11,12. 1 *King.* 11. from vers. to the 12.

These, and 100 more—yea, the whole current of the Scripture holds forth what I affirm, and maintain.

That God is highly displeased with men for sin, *&c.*

And that to act sin is the highest way to perfection, is a thing I never heard started before; neither did I ever hear of any that held it.

It is a Tenet so simply and sinfully absurd, That I abhor it.

And therefore I utterly disown it, detest it, and protest against it as so.

And I know and affirm, That the more sinful any one is, the more imperfect—and divellish. For (*he that committeth sin, is of the Divel*, &c) according to the Scripture, and God who is perfect sinneth not: and is displeased with them that do sin.

And so I come to your fift *Proposal*, viz.

    V. Propos. *What is my sense of the Law of God.—&c.*

Answ. In answer hereunto,

First, I declare and affirm the Law to be *holy, and just, and good, &c.   **Rom.* 2.

Secondly, That is a rule to all men of their lives, in thoughts, words, and deeds, &c.

And that the infallible testimony thereof is to be found in the word of God, whereunto all men must appeal and submit: and which they must believe: neither are they to adhere to any thing that is without, or contrary to the word, &c.

*And that the holy Scriptures are able to make——wise unto salvation, through faith which is in C. Jesus, &c.   *2 *Tim.* 3. 15,16.

And all the Scripture is given by inspiration of God, and is profitable, &c.

And so I come to your 6. *Proposal*, viz.

    VI. Propos. *What I think of God, and the souls of men,* &c.

Answ. I answer,

Concerning God (of whom I have, and doe write, with fear and trembling, &c.) I have spoken at large, in several particulars, in several Chapters, or under several Heads, in my Manuscript, called, *Truth Asserted*, &c. *Assertion* 2,3,4, from P. 8. to the 11.[2]

To all which I shall add this affirmative to your (now) *Quare*, viz.

That God hath a being before, and out of all creatures, in him self, from eternity.

And as for the difference between the nature of mens souls, and his being.

I believe,

That he hath his being in himself.

And men have their souls from him, &c.

   And concerning our partaking of the Divine nature, &c.

This is my sense,

That we are partakers of the Divine nature, through our Mystical, and Spiritual Filiation[3], &c.

For as the son of man partakes of his fathers nature, so the sons of God (in a glorious spiritual, and unspeakable manner) partake of his nature.

As it is written, *Because we are sons, therefore hath he given us his spirit, &c.   **Rom. Galat.*

And the love of God is shed abroad in our hearts, &c.

We are partakers of the Divine nature.

Through the glorious, Mystical, unfathomable, Spiritual union which we have with Christ, and his in-dwelling in us, &c:

And concerning this union, and in-dwelling so much is throughout the Scripture:

First, Typified.

Secondly, Metaphoriz'd.

Thirdly, Alegoriz'd.

Fourthly, Prophesied.

Fifthly, Promised, (*That it should be made manifest.*)

Sixtly, In plain Scripture tearms expressed.

And

Seventhly, Joyful and gloriously experienced.

This glorious Mystery (I say) which hath been* hid from ages, and from generations, &c.   *Colos*. 1. 26. 27.

Is held forth (in the Scriptures of truth) in Types, Allegories, Metaphors, Prophecies, promises in plain tearms, and all this confirmed by joyful experience.

And now being * he that sanctifieth, and they that are sanctified are—one, and he is not ashamed to call them brethren.   *Joh*.6 *Heb*.2.

And being he is * in them,—dwels in them. &c, *Joh*:16. *Col*.1. 26,27. 2 *Cor*.6. 16.

And being in him dwels ALL the fulness of the God-head bodily——&c.

Of his fulness we all receive, *Joh*. 1 *Colos*.

Wherefore I say, of and from, and through him——through mystical, spiritual, filiation, fraternity, unity, and in-dwelling, *We are partakers of the Divine nature.*

And so I come to your seventh Proposal, *viz*

VII. Propos. *What I think of the resurrection of the body, &c.*
And the last judgement, &c

Answ. To this I answer,

First, That I am no *Saduce*, and am as unwilling to be a *Pharisee*.

Secondly, concerning these points: I have never discoursed, preached, or writ anything.

Thirdly, I believe the resurrection of the body, &c.

According to the Scriptures, and especially——that of 1 *Cor*. 15. 35. to the 54.

And concerning the great day of Judgement;

I believe,

That the dead, both small and great, shall stand before God the

Judge of all, and the Books shall be opened, and the dead shall be judged out of those things which are written in the Books, according to their works, *Rev.* 20. 12.

Neither do I think these things to be past already as to any man living on Earth. But the contrary.

And as for those things which you offer to me, concerning the circumstances whereby my sins are aggravated, &c.

I have took them into my sad and serious consideration.

And those—with divers others—have been set home upon my spirit by the hand of God, &c.

And as for my repentance, and turning from them; and for the satisfaction of all, &c. I doe not desire that what I have spoken, and to that purpose written, may be put under a bushel: or confined in a corner, but that it might fly abroad, to that end, &c.

And furthermore, in what way and places soever divine providence shall dispose of me, I shal not cease to publish it, and what God hath wrought in me.

And as for my giving assurance to the State——which you speak of I neither have assurance of my self; nor can I have it from man.

But my assurance is in God: in whom I have hope, and full affiance, That (through his grace) I shall never return thereto again.

As I have humbly, sincerely, and cordially (both in my humble Petition to them, and in several other places of my writing) exprest.

And that my future deportment in all things, shall make amends for what hath been by-past, &c.

And thus have I faithfully, sincerely, (and as I conceive) fully fulfilled mine own desires, and answered your requirings, in adding to what I have formerly written, and to all my large professions, and protestations, &c.

This Anwer to your several *Proposals*, &c.

All which, I hope, (according to your promises——) will be improved for my good:

For which I pray, and hope, &c: And which also I humbly expect from you.

Hoping (that according to your profession, and those good thoughts I have of you) you will look upon me, upon my expressions, and writings; and upon my condition (which in several respects, is very sad) as your own.

—*Considering also your self*——

That I may finde by experience, that the golden Law of all true Righteousness—and love, is written in your heart.

The tenure whereof runs thus:

Whatsoever you would that men should do unto (and for) you,
Even so do you unto (And FOR) them.

For this is the LAW, and the Prophets.

And I am

Honoured SIR,
*Your humble and faithful servant
in THE LORD,*

Newgate, June 28.
1651.

ABIEZER COPPE.

For his much Honoured friend, Mr. Marchamont Nedham.

M. *Nedham!*
*My humble service, sincere respects, and hearty commendations to you
presented, &c.*

Although I have been (by sickness, weakness, and various distempers
of body and mind) impeded, &c.

Yet I have at length finished these.

And now I present them to you.

As for my former Writings, which you and the other Gentlemen
lately received; I cannot question, but that I have (now) fully fulfilled
your desires, and requiring, therein.

By deleating what might prove offensive to any.

By altering, correcting, and amending other things. And

By explicating some other things that might appear dubious, or
difficult.

And herein I have not omitted the least clause—

Wherefore I cannot question but that it may now pass.

And as for M. *Duries*—

I have faithfully, sincerely, (as as I conceive) fully (and I hope,
satisfactorily) answered his Letter, and those various Proposals therein
contained, &c.

And concerning your last—*About the Fiery Flying Roll*, &c.

—Thus:

Although (in the former Copy of my Book, *Page 5, 6.*) I spoke
concerning the blasphemous opinions which it insinuated only by way
of question and supposition, &c. yet now doe I there, and more at
large elsewhere,

First, positively acknowledge, that it doth so——

As you may see there, and more at large, in my answer to M. *Dury*.

And, Secondly, there is not any one, from the greatest to the least
error, therein insinuated, which I do not (both cordially, and
zealously) declaim and protest against, &c.

And, Thirdly, I have faithfully (and I humbly conceive) fully,
asserted Truths: contrary to every one of the Errors therein insinuated,

and to divers other Errors which I have not been (in the least degree) takct or tainted withal, &c.

Which I hope may give full satisfaction. I having (according to your advise) proceeded therein roundly, freely, and fully.

And (now) my humble request to you is,

That you would please to prosecute your good enterprise—in my behalf, &c.

Truly, Sir,

Hope deferred, maketh the heart sick.

And my languishing expectations will be more grievous to me, then my tedious imprisonment: unless they are satisfied, &c.

These, and my sad condition (which is so indeed in several respects) I make bold to present to your Christian, charitable consideration.

Relying on your sweetness, and goodness, for a continuation of your former, and undeserved favours.

And I shall joyfully subscribe myself,

SIR,

NEWGATE,   *Your faithful servant, and a well-wisher*
June 28. 1651.   *to you, and your vertues.*

ABIEZER COPPE.

FINIS

Laurence Clarkson

A SINGLE EYE

All *Light*, no *Darkness;* or *Light* and *Darkness* One:

In which you have it purely Discussed

1. The Original of *Darkness.*
2. What *Darkness* is.
3. Why it is called *Darkness.*

As also

What God is *Within*, and what *Without*; how he is said
to be *One*, yet *Two*; When *Two* and not *One*, yet
then *One*, and not *Two.*

Likewise

A Word from the Lord touching the onely resurrection
of the Body, In, From, and To the Lord
With a certain parcel of *Quaeries* to be answered from
Heaven or Hell,

This revealed to L.C. one of the UNIVERSALITY.

Imprinted at LONDON, in the Yeer that the
POWERS OF Heaven and Earth *Was*, *Is*,
and *shall be* Shaken, yea Damned, till
they be no more for EVER.

Behold, the King of glory now is come
T'reduce God and Devil to their Doom;
For both of them are servants unto Me
That lives, and rules in perfect Majesty:
Though called God, yet that is not my Name,
True, I be both, yet am I not the same:
Therefore a wonder am I to you all,
So that to titul'd Gods ye pray and call,
Oh then my Creature, let me speak to thee;
Thy Worship, and thy God, shall dy truly.
Why dote ye Worldings? up and down being hurl'd
As he is, so are we even in this World;
And so are all things perfect, just and good;
Yea, all are sav'd by's Cross, his wounds and blood.
Where else is heaven, but in our present peace
From him? or hell, but when that this doth cease?
Fie then for shame, look not above the Skies
For God, or Heaven; for here your Treasure lies
Even in these Forms, Eternall Will will reigne,
Through him are all things, onely One, not Twain:
Sure he's the Fountain from which everything
Both good and ill (so term'd) appears to spring.
Unto this Single Eye, though Adams two
Cannot perceive, to Such, to All

                                        Adieu.

Having experience that his Majesty, the Being and Operation of all things, appeareth in and to the Creature under a two-fold Form or Visage, by which that becometh real with the Creature, which is but a shadow with this Infinite Being: So that from hence it ariseth, the Creature supposeth God to be that which is not, and that not to be, which is God.

Therefore hath his Majesty divulged his pleasure, that thereby he may take occasion to unfold himself in and to the Creature under such a prospect, that the Creature may know God, as he is known of God, that so from the clear appearance of God, the Creature may behold purely what God is, which as yet is manifest, the Creation in this Nation inhabiteth no other Region then the Women of Samaria: And therefore it is the cry of his Majesty is not fulfilled and obeyed, but by Churches, Saints, and Devils opposed and contemned: So that rare it is to find the Creature that is awaked out of his deep sleep, that hath shaked off the covering, so that he can from the clear Appearance of God say, the vail is taken away, and that he Believeth the Truth as it is in his Majesty.

In answer to this, I have travelled from one end of England to another, and as yet could find very few that could define unto me the Object of their Worship, or give me a character what that God is, so much professed by them; yet notwithstanding I could come into no City or Town, Nor Village, but there I heard the name God under one Form or another, worshipped that for God, which I had experience was no God: So that in the period of my Pilgrimage, I concluded there was gods many, and lords many, although to me but one God: Therefore at my return, I was carried out by God to hold forth to the Creature, the God yesterday, to day, and for ever.

To that end, in the perusal of his Majesties pleasure, you may notice what is intended, or rather, in the ensuing Treatise recorded, having for the present but only presented to you a Map, in which you may take a full view what that God is thou pretends to Worship, whether he be Infinite, or Finite; whether he be subject to passion and affection; whether he behold the actions of the creature as the Creature esteems them, and whether he can be changed by thy prayers, so as to expiate and judgement, or produce a deliverance, yea whether he be all, and in all, or but all in part, that is to say, whether one act be good, another evil, one light, another darkness; and if so, reason from Scripture declareth, God is passionate, God is affectionate, and if either, then changeable.

But by forms and spiritual God like forms he is professed, and so worshipped as a God that beholds evil and good; so passionate with the one, and affectionate with the other, so that in conclusion they imagine him as themselves, not infinite, but finite, therefore it is, one Act in God is conceived two in themselves, to wit, one Act Adultry, another Honesty; when if Reason were admitted, and thereby Scripture interpreted, then should they observe in that Act they call Honesty, to be Adultry, and that Act so called Adultry, to have as much honesty as the other, for with God they are but one, and that one Act holy, just, and good as God; This to me by Reason is confirmed, and by Scripture declared, *That to the pure all things are pure*: [Tit. 1.15] So that for my part I know nothing unclean to me, no more then it is of it self, and therefore what Act soever I do, is acted by that Majesty in me, as in the ensuing Treatise will appear what Acts they are, the nature of Acting them; and in the period: how I esteem them: So that I weigh not how I am judged, in that I judge not myself. So to conclude, the censures of Scripture, Churches, Saints and Devils, are no more to me than the cutting off of a Dog's neck.

Vale.

ISAIAH 42.16.
I will make Darkness Light before them.

The God of gods hath cast me on this Subject, to the end he may take occasion to unfold himself what he is in himself, and how he maketh out himself in his Appearance to the creature.

To that end, be pleased to peruse the precedent verses, and you will find what occasioned these terms in this Text; In brief you may behold the Original thereof arise from the present state of the Gentiles, they being then as it were Prisoners, and in the state of darkness; So that in reference to their bondage; Christ called the Son of God was promised, to redeem them from the Region of Darkness; that notwithstanding they had worshipped that for God which was no god, yet now is the time come, now is the day that God will plunder them of their Idols, that God will enlighten their dark understandings, as in my Text, *God will make darkness light before them.*

Notwithstanding, it may be supposed by some, that the connexion hereof doth only concern the Gentiles, yet let me tell thee, I find that God is not so limited in his pen, inke, and paper, but that he can and will make the darkness of the Jew light, as well as the Gentile; yea, the darkness of you as any other: for never was there more superstition, more darkness in the Churches than now, and therefore never more need to have the light of God expel those dark mists that at this time is spread over all opinions in the Kingdom: So that now doth the time draw neer that the sayings in his text shall appear in the unfoldings of the Spirit, *God will make darkness light before them.*

Being now ar[r]ived at the wished Haven, all the difficulty will be how to unload the Vessel fraughted with such hidden pearls, how to make merchandise of them, how to unfold this Subject to your capacity, how to give you the mind of God, in such terms as God appears in you.

And that the more I find these unfoldings of God in this, seem to appear contrary to most that is quoted in the History; *I will make Darkness Light,*

How is it possible, when there is no Communion, no correspondency but enmity? Yea, so great, that they cannot dwell in one house, lodge in one bed, but devour one another; for where darkness is, light is not, and where light appeareth, darkness is gone; yet notwithstanding you hear, *he will make darkness light.*

So that the first thing I mind from hence is, *The he will not take darkness away, and in the room thereof place light, but that which in Scripture is called darkness, and by the Creature believed darkness, shall be made light.*

Secondly, we shall enquire, *Whether that in Scripture, or by the Creature entitled darkness, be darkness with God or no?*

To this end you may read Light and Darkness as both alike to God. So then it appeareth but a darkness in the Creatures apprehension, so but an imagined darkness; for saith the Text, *God is light and in him no darkness.* So that you see, whatsoever or however it is called darkness in Scripture, yet it is none with God[.] Then

Thirdly, I shall search *Whether that in Scripture or by the creature called God, admit of any other title* but unus (*to wit*) One himself, and *if I find there is but one Being, one God, and that all that is be light with God, then shall I not cease till I find the Original of Darkness, what it is, and why it is called darkness, &c.*

First, I find in his Divine Being, in his Essence, there is but one God; the history declareth the same. *I am what I am: I am the Lord, and there is none else: There is no other God beside me*: [Isa. 45. 5] with varieties of Scripture to this purpose. So then it is cleer by the History, That the Being and Essence of God admits not of the plural but singular.

So that there is but one God, whose name is *Light*, so called God; for, that which God is, is God (*to wit*) God is light, then that light is God; for what God saith he is, that is himself, but God saith, He is light, therefore Light is God; so from the Scripture where God saith *Let there be Light*, it is no more then if he had said, Let there be God, and there was God, for God is light. For,

You have heard the Scripture holds forth but one God, which God is Light; yet the same Scripture holds forth not only light but lights; as [Gen. 1.] *verse 14 Let there be Lights, and that Lights in the Firmament of the Heaven*: So that God made two great Lights, that is to say, The light of the Sun, the light of the Moon, Stars, fire and candle. From hence take notice, that though but one God, yet divers Lights, and that all made by God; for he that said *Let there be light*, said *Let there be Lights*: therefore he is called *The Father of Lights*, &c.

But then how shall we do with that place, *for God is light*, not lights; either he must be as well lights as light, or else, that all other lights but one hath a Being and Original besides God.

And if it appear that all lights, or that which is called light, though the light of the candle, be made by God, then the light of the candle is the light of God; but if all that is called light, to wit, the light of the Sun, Moon,

Stars, Fire, and Candle, have not their being in God, then not made by God; So it will follow, that there is not onely one, but two gods.

But the Scripture saith, *That God made the Light*, and *God made the Lights*: So that both light and lights were made by God, then had they their being in God; for all that he made were in him, of him, and to him, as well the Sun as the Moon, the Stars, the Fire, and the Candle, as any of them; So that in making of these, he made nothing but himself; for God is light, as well the one as the other.

But then, If God be light, then lights; so that we may as well say Gods as God; a God of the Sun, another of the Moon; for in that God is light, he must as well be the light of the moon, as the light of the Sun, the light of the fire, the candle, as the stars.

Not denying but God is as well the light of the one, as the light of the other; yet notwithstanding that, God is but one light, and although called lights by God, yet they are but one light in God; to that end, he is called *The Father of Lights*, [Jam. 1.17] but one Father, though many lights. So that why they are but one light in God, God one light, and yet by God called lights, are in reference to their distinct appearance in those several bodies (to wit) the body of the Sun, the body of the moon; that as you see notwithstanding several beams from one Sun, yet in their rise from the Sun, they were but one in the Sun; nay indeed, they were nothing but the Sun, but after they issued out of the Sun, one this way, another that way from the Sun, then according to this divers appearance, it is no more called a Sun, but a Beam, not only Beam, but Beams, which when reduced to their Being, they are no longer called a Beam, but a Sun.

So why they are called lights, and yet but one light with or in God, it is but according to its divers appearances, which in the being is but one appearance, because he that is the being of the light, is the appearance of the light, in what kind of degree whatsoever.

So that now you may take notice, and in some measure behold what God is, and what is to be understood by those terms, *God is light, and light is God*; which if it be that light is God, to wit, the light of the Sun, Moon, Stars, Fire and Candle, which if the light appearing in these, and held forth by these, be the light of God, Why may not the whole Creation say with their brother *Jacob, Surely, God were in these, and we knew it not?* [Isa. 45.14.]

But may be you will say, the light that is there recorded, is not to be understood in the Light of the Sun, Moon, &c. but a light that is quoted in these several Scriptures, to wit, a divine and Scriptural light, by which a creature beholds and enjoy[s] God.

However, God that is light appeareth in you, discovering to you that the light in the creature is not the same light of the Sun, yet the appearance of light in me, sheweth me (and that from Scripture declareth to me) that one is as much divine as the other; no more precious (simply in it self) then the other: for as you have heard, though Lights, yet but one Light with God: so that all that is light, is nothing but God; for Light is Light, and God is light: this may well in some measure be beleeved. But now to the matter in hand, *I will make darkness light, and crooked things straight*, &c.

Whether it is intended the darkness of the night to become the light of the day, or it is the Dark, as in several portions of Scripture is recorded: yea it is intended that you call the darknesse in the Creature, which darknesse is sin, hell, and misery: this darknesse he will make Light, Heaven, and Felicity; for in God is no darknesse, sin nor misery; yet this will he make Light. So that now I come to the place where I told you I would shew you the rise of Darknesse, what it is, and why it is called Darknesse.

To this end you shall find in Scripture a two-fold Power, to wit, more Powers than one, yet notwithstanding there is no Power but of God, and the Powers that be, are ordained of God. From hence you may observe the connexion hereof run in the plural, not Power, but Powers; a Power of darknesse, a Power of light, a Power in the wicked, a Power in the Godly; yet you have held forth in the same Scripture but one God.

So then, as it hath been proved, and I beleeve by you all will be granted, that the power of Light, Life and Salvation, cometh from God; the Power that acteth in the Godly, hath its rise from God, but then, What shall we say to the Power of darknesse, that Power in the wicked? for in them is a great Power, as saith the Prophet, *I have seen the wicked in Great Power* [Ps. 37. 35.] (instance) the Power in *Esau*, in *Pharoah*, the Power in *Herod* and *Pilat*, by which they crucified Christ, from whom came this Power? the Scripture saith, from above, (to wit) from God: yet this was the Power of darknesse, of sin: was it not a sinfull act to crucifie Christ? that I know you will all conclude it was a wicked act; and yet this act was according to the will of God, as saith the History, *By the Power of God the Kings of the Earth stood up, and the Rulers were gathered together, against the Lord and, against his Christ* &c. [1 Cor. 2.5; 2 Cor. 6.7; 13.4.] What had they Power from God to destroy the Son of God? was this the will of God? so saith the Scripture, by the Power of God they had gathered together: what to do? Nothing but what thy heart and thy Councel determined before to be done.

Well friends, consider this Power in *Pilat*, was a dark sinful Power, yet it came from God; yea, it was the Power of God, as is recorded: *I form light, I create darkness, I form peace, I create evil*. [Isa. 45.7] So that let it be a Power, whatsoever, in whomsoever, whether in Flesh or Spirit, wicked or Godly, it is the Power of God, yea, came from God. So that in time, he will make this Power of darknesse a Power of Light; that whereas you have called and condemned one Power for a dark sinfull Power; you shall have it appear to you, as now it is to me, that it's a Power of Light; for you have heard this Power came from God, this Power of Darknesse: yet God is Light, and in him no darknesse.

So that consider, though two Powers, yet they have but one womb, one birth; to both Twins, both brethren, as *Esau* and *Iaakob*, then if Twins, if brethren, then one Flesh, one Nature yea, of the self same Nature of God, from whom they came, as well *Esau* as *Iaakob*, *Pharoah* as *Moses*, *Pilate* as *Christ*: I say, although these be distinct, in reference to their several operations, as two streams runneth contrary ways, yet they are but of one Nature, and that from one Fountain: Herein it appeareth but a seeming opposition; instance the Tide, what striving for Victory; yet but one Water, yea and that from one Ocean. So is the case with these Powers, one opposite to the other, contending it for Victory, till at last, one overcomes another, as the Tide the stream.

Thus you may take nature from whence darknesse hath its rise, only from God.

Secondly, What Darknesse is; nothing but light with God.

Thirdly, why it is called Darknesse, is but only in reference to the Creatures apprehension, to its appearance; so nothing but imagined Darknesse: therefore his meaning is, that which appeareth now under the form of Darknesse, shall ere long appear in a Visage of Light, as saith the Text *I will make Darknesse Light before them*.

Again, it may be granted by you, as it hath been by some, that the Power or Powers are of God; yea that Power by which *Pharoah* persecuted Israel; that Power by which *Pilate* crucified Christ, yet it will not be granted that God gave the Power to do so; neither was it the Power, but a corrupt thought, or sinful imagination arising from the Devil, and their own wicked inventions.

Answer. Being now surrounded with the black Regiment, whose Commander is the Devil, and the whole legion consisting of the imaginations of the whole Creation, I have no way to escape this Camp and bottomlesse guilt but by breaking through the Bulwark and strong hold fortified against me.

So that being armed with a weapon of Majesty, I doubt not but that God in me shall cast down those strong holds and imaginations, yea every thing that exalteth it self against the Power of the most high.

To that end attend the nature of your objection, the sun thereof is to this effect, that a sinful act, or an act that is sinful, hath not its being in the Power of God, nor produced by the Power of God; no not that act of crucufying the Son of God, but from the Devil, and their sinful imaginations.

If them by whom the Objection was raised, didst nakedly understand the truth therein contained, I should not in the least molest thee, but in that thou declarest Truth not knowing it, I am engaged to unfold the same, that thou maist know it, for whereas thou sayest a sinful act is not produced by the Power of God, its Truth: for that which is not in the Power, cannot be acted by the Power: but an act that is sinful is not in God, nor the Power of God, therefore hath not its being in God, nor acted by the Power of God, for God is light, and in him no darknesse: but sin is darknesse, therefore sin is not in God.

So that yet, notwithstanding that, I must tell you as before I have related, that as all Powers are of God, so all Acts, of what nature soever are produced by this Power, yea this Power of God: so that all those acts arising from the Power, are as Pure as the Power, and the Power as Pure as a God.

So that hence it comes, there is no act whatsoever, that is impure in God, sinful with or before God.

Yet say you, there is a sinful act, or acts that are sinful; so that if all that is an act be produced by the Power of God, then why not the act that is sinful arise from the same Power, so sinful in and with God.

As I have said, so I say again, that those acts, or what act soever, so far as by thee is esteemed or imagined to be sinful, is not in God, nor from God, yet still, as I said, all acts that be are from God, yea as pure as God.

And yet notwithstanding that act, or so much of the act that thou apprehendest sin is not in God, nor simply in thyself: for indeed sin hath its conception only in the imagination; therefore; so long as the act was in God, or nakedly produced by God, it was as holy as God: but after there is an appearance in thee, or apprehension to thee, that this act is good, and that act is evil, then hast thou with *Adam* eat of the Forbidden Tree, of the Tree of knowledge of good and evil, then hast thou tasted of that fruit, which is not in God; for saith the Text, *Out of the mouth of the most High proceedeth not evil, but good*: [Lam. 3.38.] good but not evil; for God is good, and good is God: therefore it was he made all things good: yea that which is by you imagined evil, he made good: so that thou apprehending that from God which is not in God, doth of all his Creatures most abuse God, in making God the author of that which is not God, (to wit) Sin. But to the matter in hand, Thou hast heard all acts that are, had their being and birth from God, yea acted by God, to be plain those acts by thee called Swearing, Drunkenesse, Adultery and Theft, &c.[1] These acts simply as acts were produced by the Power of God, yea, perfected by the wisdom of God.

What said I, a Swearer, a Drunkard, an Adulterer, a Theef, had these the power and wisdom of God, to Swear, Drink, Whore, and Steal? O dangerous Tenent! O blasphemy of the highest nature! what make God the authour of Sin? so a sinful God! Well Friends, although the appearance of God in me be as terrible to you, as it were to *Moses* in the mount, yet notwithstanding, that what I have seen and heard, I do not in the least tremble, but rejoyce, that I have this opportunity to declare it unto you; however it may be received by you.

To that end consider what I said those acts called Swearing, Drunkenesse, Adultery and Theft, those acts, simply as acts, not as they are called (and by these imagined) Drunkenesse, Adultery and Theft, that is in and from thy imagination; for there is no such act as Drunkenesse, Adultery and Theft in God; though by his Power and Wisdom thou executest this act and that act, yet that appearance by which thou apprehendest and esteemest them to be acts of sin, that esteemation was not in God, though from God.

For indeed, it is but imagination, which is not, yea nothing in this, infinite being; for as I said before, so I say again, the very tittle Sin, it is only a name without substance, hath no being in God, nor in the Creature, but only by imagination: and therefore it is said; *the imaginations of your hearts are only evil continually*. [Gen. 8.21] It is not the body, nor the life, but the imagination only, and that not at a time, or times, but continually. Herein sin admitting of no form in it self, is created a form in the estimation of the Creature; so that which is not in God, is found to be in a something creature; as you have it related, *One Man esteemeth one day above another, another esteemeth every day alike*; [Rom. 14.5.] what to one is pure, to another is impure; herein it appeareth but a bare estimation.

To this end (saith *Paul*) *I know and am persuaded, by the Lord Jesus, that there is nothing unclean of it self, but to him that esteemeth any thing to be unclean, to him it is unclean*. [Rom. 14.14]

So that the extent thereof is in reference to all things, as well as meats and drinks; let it be what act soever. Consider what act soever, yea though it be the act of Swearing, Drunkenesse, Adultery and Theft; yet these acts simply, yea nakedly by, as acts nothing distinct from the act of Prayer and Prayses. Why does thou wonder? why art thou angry? they are all one in themselves; no more holynesse, no more puritie in one then the other.

But once the Creature esteemeth one act Adultery, the other honesty, the one pure, the other impure; yet to that man that so esteemeth one act unclean to him it is unclean, (as saith the History) there is nothing unclean of it self, to him that esteemeth it unclean; yea again and again it is recorded that to the pure all things, yea all things are pure, but to the defiled, all things are defiled: Yea the Prayer and Prayses of the wicked are defiled, as saith the History, *The Prayers of the wicked are abomination to the Lord*. [Prov. 15.8]

Observe not the act nakedly, as the act, for we find the Prayer and Prayses of some to be pure, though to others impure: impure to those acting, in relation to the title his apprehension, his Conscience in the improvement of them is defiled and condemned for a Swearer, a Drunkard, an Adulterer, and a theef.

When as a man in purity in light, acts the same acts, in relation to the act, and not the title: this man (no this man) doth not swear, whore, nor steal: so that for want of this light, of this single pure eye, there appeareth Devil and God, Hell and Heaven, Sin and Holynesse, Damnation and Salvation; only, yea only from the esteemation and dark apprehension of the Creature.

I will make darknesse light, rough ways smooth; not half light and half darknesse, not part rough and part smooth; but as it is said *Thou art all fair my Love, there is no spot in thee*. [Cant. 1.15,16; 4.1,7.] Observe, all fair my Love; in thee only is beauty and purity, withou defilement: my love my dove is but one, thou one, not two, but only one, my love: Love is God, and God is Love; so all pure, all, light, no spot in thee.

So that consider what act soever is done by thee, in light and love, is light, and lovely; though it be that act called Adultery, in darkness, it is so; but in light, honesty, in that light loveth it selfe, so cannot defile it selfe: for love in light is so pure, that a whore it cannot endure, but estranges it selfe from darknesse from whence whoredom has its first original. Love is so pure, that it will not lodge with two; but treads the steps of the Apostle, saying, *Let every man have his own wife*: [1 Cor. 7.2] when as darknesse is not ashamed to ly with his neighbours wife: for in light I declare that whoredom is the fruits of darknesse; therefore no compassion for light, who scorns the society of a whore indeed. Light is like *Susanna*, that had rather dy, then be defiled with harlots. Light; Yea, innocent *Susanna*, uncorrupted Light, must be accused, arraigned and condemned for that her accusers are guilty of: Yet fear not *Susanna*, thou shalt be vindicated, and thy accusers condemned.

So that is my Majesties pleasure to declare, again and again, that what acts soever is done by thee, according as thou esteemest it, yea according as thou beleevest it, so be it, so be it done unto thee; that is to say, if thou hast committed those acts in Scripture recorded for swearing, drunkeness, adultery and theft; and so acting apprehendest them, let me deal plainly with thee; to thee it is Sin; and for so sinning, thy imagination will pursue thee, arraign thee, and condemne thee for a Swearer, an adulterer and a theef.

When as on the contrary, thou are persuaded that those titles in Scripture, and thy apprehension recorded, for swearing, adultery, and theft, be no such acts, with thee, but only titles without thee; neither dost thou apprehend them any other, but pure acts, without title: then I declare, according to thy esteemation so is the act to thee, and for so doing, thy imagination, will not, cannot condemn thee, but say with the Apostle, *We know that an Idol is nothing*: [1 Cor. 8.4] what thou esteemeth Idolatry to is none: So that whatsoever I act, though it be that act you call swearing, adultery, and theft, yet to me there is no such title, but a pure act, for there is nothing that I do that is unclean to me, no more than it is unclean to it self.

And yet notwithstanding this, my priviledge doth not in the least approbate thee, yea thee that apprehendest the title to swear, whore or steal, &c. because to thee it is unclean, therefore not lawfull for thee; neither canst thou upon the bare report hereof, say, Well, if it be but as man esteems it, then I will esteem it so too.

Alas, friend, let me tell thee, whatever thy tongue saith, yet thy imagination in thee declares sad things against thee, in that thou esteemest them as acts of sin, thy imagination will torment thee for this sin, in that thou condemnest thy self, thou art tormented in that condemnation; with endless misery; so that I say, Happy is the man that condemns not himself in those things he alloweth of.

No matter what Scripture, Saints, or Churches say, if that within thee do not condemn thee, thou shalt not be condemned; for saith the History, *Out of thine own Mouth*, not anothers, *will I judge thee* [Lu. 19.22]: therefore, remember that if thou judge not thy self, let thy life be what it will, yea act what thou canst, yet if thou judge not thyself, thou shalt not be judged; For, *I came not into the World to condemn, but to save the World.* [John 12.47] But if the reproach and slander of Saints and Churches do cause thee to question thy self, then art thou ready to say within what they report without, I am guilty of what they accuse me: So that true is the saying, *O Adam*, thy destruction is of thy self.

But before I conclude touching how darkness is made light, sin holiness, and so all deformity converted into its own pure nature, it was my pleasure to treat something concerning the nature of this loss, that whether darkness in Scripture reconciled, and by the creature believed, be cast out as distinct from light, and so said to be damned, in that which is not light, not pure, but defiled.

In answer to that, the Lord declares that those filthy abominable works of darkness (by thee so apprehended) shall be destroyed and damned; But how, or where they shall be damned? that is in the saying of the Text, *I will make darkness light*: Oh that this were purely minded, then thou wouldst see that sin must not be thrown out, but cast within, there being in the Vat, it is dyed of the same colour of the liquor; as Saffron converts milk into its own colour, so doth the fountain of light convert sin, hell and devil into its own nature and light as it self; *I will make rough waies smooth*. Now it is damned and ramm'd into its only Center, there to dwell eternal in the bosom of its only Father: This, only this, is the damnation so much terrifying the Creature in its dark apprehension, that it shall be robbed and carried it knows not whither cryeth out I am damned, I am damned, being carried out of its former knowledge, now knoweth not where it is, therefore lamenting, *Master, Save me, I perish*, [Matt. 14.30] perished in its own Apprehension, yet saved in the essential. This much concerning *I will lead the blind by a way that they know not, and in paths they have not known: I will make darkness light, crooked things streight* &c.

A Word from the Lord touching Resurrection, there being reports not a few that I should deny the Resurrection of the body consisting of Flesh, Bloud and Bone. I answer, If I should not, Reason would arraign me for a mad man, Scripture would declare me anti-Scripturist, in favouring such a palpable Tenent of Darkness, which if rightly understood, affirm no such thing as the Resurrection of this Body: both which affirm, that what the body is made of, that is the life, perfection and happiness of the body; but the body consisting of flesh and bone, is made of the dust of the earth, therefore when thy body is reduced to its center, then (and not till then) is thy body alive, perfected in its happiness; not for thee to raise this body, it would declare thee a Tyrant; for as it is destructive for the Fowl to live in the water, or the Fish in the Firmament, so to raise thy body to a local place called Heaven, would to thy body become a Hell, for as the earth would become a Hell to the Spirit, so that place called heaven, would become a hell to the Body, for after it is laid in the grave, it is buried in its heaven, glory and happiness, where it shall rot and consume into its own nature for ever and ever.

Yet not denying but that body quoted in the History shall rise, which body hath several denominations, as *earthly, corruptible, dishonourable, weak, vile, and natural body*: [Rom. 1.23–27] all which doth make one cleer prospect, in which you may take a full view of what that body is made of shall rise, whether a visible body consisting of flesh and bone, or invisible body, consisting of the Sensitive within this body; To this end the History speaketh on this wise, *That we ourselves groan within ourselves, waiting for the redemption*, to wit, *our body*. [Rom. 8.23]

So that in light I declare, that the corrupt senses must put on incorruption thy mortal apprehension must put on immortality, that whereas before thou wast alive to five, dead to one, and dead to one, now thou shalt be dead to five, and alive to one. that lovely pure one who beholds nothing but purity, wheresoever it goeth, and what soever it doth, all is sweet and lovely; let it be under what title soever, thou art risen from title to act, from act to power, from power to his name, and that only one name, pure and undefiled; so that now thou art of purer eys than to behold any iniquity, so that Devil is God, Hell is Heaven, Sin Holiness, Damnation Salvation, this and only this in the First Ressurrection.

Yet here is no lodging, no safe inhabiting, in that thou art yet on the borders of Aegypt, only with *Moses* on Mount Hermon, only verbally, not practically, so short of the second Resurrection which is the life and power what thou saw, for till thou be delivered of that thou wast risen to, thou canst not say, *Death, where is thy sting? Grave, where is thy victory?* [1 Cor. 15.55]

Wonder not at me, for without Act, without Birth, no powerful deliverance, not only the Talkers, but the Doers; not only your Spirit, but your Body must be a living and acceptable Sacrifice; therefore till acted that so called Sin, thou art not delivered from the power of sin, but ready upon all the Alarms to tremble and fear the reproach of thy body.

Therefore my beloved ones, that supposeth your service is perfect Freedom, by having only light into anothers life, know this, that if light without life, thy service will be perfect bondage; and therefore it is when a creature is drawn forth to act in anothers life, instead of triumphing over sin, he will be conquered in sin; so that I say, till flesh be made Spirit, and Spirit flesh, so not two, but one, thou art in perfect bondage; for without vail, I declare that whosoever doth attempt to act from flesh, in flesh, to flesh, hath, is and will commit Adultry; but to bring this to a period, for my part, till I acted that, so called sin, I could not predominate over sin; so that now whatsoever I act, is not in relationship to the Title, to the Flesh, but that Eternity in me; So that with me, all Creatures are but one creaature, and this is my form, the Representative of the whole Creation: So that see what I can, act what I will, all is but one most sweet and lovely. Therefore my deer ones consider, that without act, no life; without life, no perfection; and without perfection, no eternal peace and freedom indeed, in power, which is the everlasting Majesty, ruling, conquering, and dancing all into its self, without end for ever.

The ensuing Queries

What that God is often recorded in Scripture, and by the Creature believed.

First. Whether he admit of a Corporeal Substance (to wit) flesh, blood and bones; and if so (as by some of the Creation is beleeved) then the Question will be Where his habitation hath been, is and will be, to the end of the world? I say, if God admit of a corporeal substance; whether then any other but a local place can contain that substance, or that he can be omnipresent in all places, and with all creatures at one time, in that substance, &c.

Secondly, Whether God admit of any other but a Spirit, so invisible? and if so, (as by others of his Creation beleeved) the Query is then, where its region hath been, is, and will be? I say, if God admit of no Corporeal substance, form, nor image, but only a spirit, whether then any other but an invisible habitation, an infinite boundlesse region can contain an invisible infinite boundlesse spirit.

Thirdly, If God be a Spirit, then whether a Spirit can be confined from any thing? and if confined, then we must observe these two things,

1. What he is confined from, or confined in?
2. What it is that doth confine God?

Fourthly, If God be a Spirit, and c[a]nnot be confirmed, then whether God be not infinite and omni-present in all places, and in all things: as well Hell as Heaven, Devil as Angel, Sin as Holinesse, Darknesse and as Light?

Fifthly, If God be infinite in all things: then whether all things are not finite in God? That if God be subject to nothing, then whether all things be not subjected to God, so as to do nothing without God, nor against God; but in the performance of the will of God, as well *Esau* as *Jacob*, *Pharoah* as *Moses*, *Pilat* as *Christ*: yea Sin, Devil, or any other instrument whatsoever?

Sixtly, Whether a creature, living in God, so as to know God, as he is known of God, be not infinite with and in God; and so all things finite unto him, as unto God; subject unto him, as unto God whether Devil, Hell, Sin, Death, or any other thing whatsoever?

Seventhly, If God be in all things, then in all men, the wicked as the godly? wherein then is the state of the wicked worse then the godly? yea, if God be in both, but have they not both one title, but are wicked, another godly?

Eightly, If God be in all things, then in all creatures that hath life whatsoever, so that wherein is man better then these, or hath any preheminence above these? yet if he have, by whom is it given: and the reason of so being given?

Ninthly, If God be in all, the wicked as the godly; why is not the wicked saved with the godly? but if not saved, what is that in the wicked more then the godly, that is damned? with the place where, and the nature of that damnation.

Tenthly, If God be in all, why are not all things in God? and if they be all comprehended as one in God; how commeth it they are two distinct from God, yea so titled from the Scripture? now if Scripture were indicted by God, the Question wil be, why it speaks not of things, as they are in God, but relates two distinct titles, two opposites; the one for God, the other against God? and whether that Scripture so contradictory be not the original or instrumental cause by which the Creation becomes blinded, divided, yea destroyed; in worshipping that for God, which in the Original is no God? I say, the Query will be whether the contradiction in the Scripture, be not the contradictions in the Creation: and that so long as there is this Scripture, there will be Religions, not Religious Forms, not Spirit, War, not Peace; envy, not Love; the teachings of men, not the teaching of God: yea in conclusion there will be gods, and not God: no not that God that is all in all, *Alpha* and *Omega*; the God yesterday and to day, and for ever.

FINIS

The Lost Sheep
FOUND:

OR,

The Prodigal returned to his Fathers house, after
many a sad and weary Journey through many
Religious Countreys,

Where now, notwithstanding all his former
Transgressions, and breach of his Fathers
Commands, he is received in an eternal Favor, and
all the righteous and wicked Sons that he hath left
behinde, reserved for eternal misery;

As all along every Church or Dispensation may
read in his Travels, their Portion after
this Life.

Written by Laur. Claxton, *the onely true
converted*
*Messenger of Christ Jesus, Creator of
Heaven and Earth.*

LONDON:
Printed for the Author. 1660.

... Sixthly, I took my journey into the society of those people called *Seekers*, who worshipped God onely by prayer and preaching, therefore to *Ely* I went, to look for *Sedgwick* and *Erbery*[1] but found them not, onely their people were assembled: with whom I had discourse, but found little satisfaction; so after that for *London* I went to finde *Seekers* there, which when I came, there was divers fallen from the Baptists as I had done, so coming to *Horn* in *Fleet lane*, and *Fleten* in *Seacoal-lane*, they informed me that several had left the Church of *Patience*, in seeing the vanity of *Kiffin*[2] and others, how highly they took it upon them, and yet could not prove their Call successively; so glad was I there was a people to have society withal; then was I moved to put forth a book which was the first that ever I writ, bearing this Title, *The pilgrimage of Saints, by church cast out, in Christ found, seeking truth*,[3] this being a sutable peece of work in those days, that it wounded the Churches; which book *Randel*[4] owned, and sold many for me. Now as I was going over *London-bridge*, I met with *Thomas Gun*[5] a teacher of the Baptists, who was a man of a very humble, moderate spirit, who asked me if I own'd the *Pilgrimage of Saints*? I told him yea: then said he, you have writ against the church of Christ, and have discovered your self an enemy to Christ. Then I said, it is better be a hypocrite to man then to God, for I finde as much dissimulation, covetousness, back-biting and envy, yea as filthy wickednesse among some of them, as any people I know: and notwithstanding your heaven-like carriage, if all your faults were written in your forehead, for ought I know, you are a hypocrite as well as I; which afterwards it was found out he had lain with his Landlady many times; and that he might satisfie his Lust, upon slighty erands, he sent her husband into the country, that so he might lodge with his wife all night; which being found out, so smote his conscience, that he privately took a Pistol and shot himself to death in *George-fields*. As all along in this my travel I was subject to that sin, and yet as saint-like, as though sin were a burden to me, so that the fall of this *Gun* did so seize on my soul, that I concluded there was none could live without sin in this world; for notwithstanding I had great knowledge in the things of God, yet I found my heart was not right to what I pretended, but full of lust and vain-glory of this world, finding no truth in sincerity that I had gone through, but meerly the vain pride and conceit of Reasons imagination, finding my heart with the rest, seeking nothing but the praise of men in the heighth of my prayer and preaching, yet in my doctrine through all these opinions, pleading the contrary, yea abasing my self, and exalting a Christ that then I knew not. Now after this I return'd to my wife in *Suffolk*, and wholly bent my mind to travel up & down the country, preaching for monies, which then I intended for *London*, so coming to *Colchester* where I had *John Applewhit, Purkis*, and some other friends, I preached in publick; so going for *London*, a mile from *Colchester*, I set my Cane upright upon the ground, and which way it fell, that way would I go; so falling towards *Kent*, I was at a stand what I should do there, having no acquaintance, and but little money, yet whatever hardship I met withal, I was resolved for *Gravesend*, so with much a do I got that night to a town called *Bilrekey*, it being in the height of Summer, and in that town then having no friends, and I think but six pence, I lodged in the Church porch all night, so when day appeared, I took my journey for *Gravesend*, and in the way I spent a groat of my six pence, and the other two pence carried me over the water; so being in the town, I enquired for some strange opinionated people in the town, not in the least owning of them, but seemingly to ensnare them, which they directed me to one *Rugg* a Victualler, so coming in, though having no monies, yet I called for a pot of Ale, so after a few words uttered by me, the man was greatly taken with my sayings, in so much that he brought me some bread and cheese, with which I was refreshed, and bid me take no care, for I should want for nothing, you being the man that writ *The Pilgrimage of Saints*, I have had a great desire to see you, with some soldiers and others, so for the present he left me, and informed Cornet *Lokier*[6] and the rest, that I was in town, who forthwith came to me, and kindly received me, and made way for me to preach in the *Blockhouse*; so affecting my doctrine, they quatered me in the Officers lodging, and two days after they carried me to *Dartford*, where there I preached; so against the next Lords-day came for *Gravesend*, and there preached in the Market-place, which was such a wonder to the town and countrey, that some for love, and others for envy, came to hear, that the Priest of the town had almost none to hear him, that if the Magistrate durst, he would have apprehended me, for I boldly told them God dwelled not in the Temple made with hands, neither was any place more holy then another, proving by Scripture, that where two or three were gathered in his name, God was in the midst of them, and that every Believer was the Temple of God, as it is written, *God dwelleth with a humble and contrite spirit*[Isa. 57. 15.]; So after this we went to *Maidston* and *Town-maulin*, and there I preached up and down, so at last having given me about five pounds, I went to my wife and promised in two weekes to return again, which I did, but I found not *Lokier* nor the rest so affectionate as before, for he had a gift of preaching, & therein did seek honor so suspicious of my blasting his reputation, slighted and persecuted me, so that I left them, and towards *Maidston* travelled, so one *Bulfinch* of *Town-maulin* having friends towards *Canterbury*, perswaded me to go with him, and so against the next Lords-day, having no steeple free, we had a Gentlemans barn free, where a great company was assembled: then for *Sandwich* I went, and up and down found friends, so coming to *Canterbury* there was some six of this way, amongst whom was a maid of pretty knowledge, who with my Doctrine was affected, and I affected to lye with her, so that night pervailed, and satisfied my lust, afterwards the mayd was highly in love with me, and as gladly would I have been shut of her, lest some danger had ensued, so not knowing I had a wife she was in hopes to marry me, and so would have me lodge with her again, which fain I would, but durst not, then she was afraid I would deceive her, and would travel with me, but by subtilty of reason I perswaded her to have patience, while I went into *Suffolk*, and setled my occasions, then I would come and marry her, so for the present we parted, and full glad was I that I was from her delivered, so to *Maidston* I came, and having got some six pounds, returned to my wife, which a while after I went for *Kent* again, but found none of the people so zealous as formerly, so that my journey was but a small advantage to me, and then I heard the maid had been in those parts to seek me, but not hearing of me, returned home again, and not long after was married to one of that sect, and so there was an end of any further progress into *Kent*. Then not long after I went for *London*, and some while remained preaching at *Bowe* in Mr. *Sterry's*[7] place, and *London-stone*, but got nothing; so to *Suffolk* I went, and having but one childe, put it to nurse, intending to go to my Parents in *Lancashire*: So leaving my Wife at my cousin *Andertons*, I hearing of *Seekers* in *Hartfordshire*, went thither, and at last was hired by Mr. *Hickman* to preach at *Peters* in *St. Albans*, so being liked, I was hired for a moneth longer, so fetcht my Wife, and there continued till such time the Town of *Sanderidge* took me for their Minister, and setled me in the Vicaridge, where Sir *John Garret*, Colonel *Cox*, and Justice *Robotom* came constantly to hear me, and gave me several Gifts, so that in heaven I was again; for I had a high pitch of free Grace, and mightily flown in the sweet Discoveries of God, and yet not at all knowing what God was, onely an infinite Spirit, which when he pleased did glance into his people the sweet breathings of his Spirit; and therefore preached, it was not sufficient to be a professor, but a possessor of Christ, the possession of which would cause a profession of him, with many such high flown notions, which at that time I knew no better, nay, and in truth I speak it, there was few of the Clergy able to reach me in Doctrine or Prayer; yet notwithstanding, not being an University man, I was very often turned out of employment, that truly I speak it, I think there was not any poor soul so tossed in judgement, and for a poor livelihood, as then I was. Now in this my prosperity I continued not a year, but the Parson being a superstitious Cavelier got an Order from the Assembly of Divines to call me in question for my Doctrine, and so put in a drunken fellow in my room: and thus was I displaced from my heaven upon earth, for I was dearly beloved of *Smiths* and *Thrales*, the chief of the Parish. Well there was no other way but for *London* again, and after a while sent my Goods for *Suffolk* by water: now at this I concluded all was a cheat, yea preaching it self, and so with this apprehension went up and down *Hartfordshire*, *Bedford*, and *Buckinghamshire*, and by my subtilty of reason got monies more or less; as of one at *Barton*, I had twelve pounds for the printing of a book against the Commonalty of *England*, impeaching them for traytors, for suffering the Parliament their servants, to usurp over them, judging the Common-wealth was to cut out the form, and shape of their grievances, and send it up to their servants the Parliament to finish, shewing, as the Common-wealth gave the Parliament power, so they were greater then the Parliament, with matter to the effect. And then being presented to a small parish in *Lincolnshire*, thither

I went, but finding no society to hear, I grew weary thereof, and stayd with some friends at *Oford*, so with a little monies went home again, and not long after going into *Lincolnshire*, I preached in several places, that at last Captain *Cambridge* hearing of me, and was much affected with me, and made me teacher to their Company, and said I should have all necessaries provided me, and a man alowed me; then I was well recruited and horsed, so that I judged it was the mercy of God to me, my distress being great, and my care for my family. Now after a while our Regiment went for *London*, so though I had preached in *Lincoln*, *Horncastle*, *Spilsby*, and many other places, yet they would excuse me for two moneths, having no need of preaching at *London*, so with what monies I had I went to my wife, and staid there a while, and so came for *London*: Now our Regiment being *Twisltons*[8], Quartered in *Smith-field*, but I Quartered in a private-house, who was a former friend of mine, asked me if I heard not of a people called *My one flesh*? I said no, what was their opinion, and how should I speak with any of them? Then she directed me to *Giles Calvert*. So that now friends, I am travelling further into the *Wilderness*, having now done burning of Brick, I must still wander in the mountains and deserts; so coming to *Calvert*, and making enquiry after such a people, he was afraid I came to betray them, but exchanging a few words in the height of my language, he was much affected, and satisfied I was a friend of theirs, so he writ me a Note to Mr. *Brush*, and the effect thereof was, the bearer hereof is a man of the greatest light I ever yet heard speak, and for ought I know instead of receiving of him you may receive an Angel, so to Mr. *Brush* I went, and presented this Note, which he perused, so bid me come in, and told me if I had come a little sooner, I might have seen Mr. *Copp*, who then had lately appeared in a most dreadful manner; so their being *Mary Lake*, we had some discourse, but nothing to what was in me, however they told me, if next [S]unday I would come to Mr. *Melis* in *Trinity-lane*, there would that day some friends meet. Now observe at this time my judgement was this, that there was no man could be free'd from sin, till he had acted that so called sin, as no sin, this a certain time had been burning within me, yet durst not reveal it to any, in that I thought none was able to receive it, and a great desire I had to make trial, whether I should be troubled or satisfied therein: so that

Seventhly, I took my progress into the *Wilderness*, and according to the day appointed, I found Mr. *Brush*, Mr. *Rawlinson*, Mr. *Goldsmith*, with *Mary Lake*, and some four more: now *Mary Lake* was the chief speaker, which in her discourse was something agreeable, but not so high as was in me experienced, and what I then knew with boldness declared, in so much that *Mary Lake* being blind, asked who that was that spake? *Brush* said the man that *Giles Calvert* sent to us, so with many more words I affirmed that there was no sin, but as man esteemed it sin, and therefore none can be free from sin, till in purity it be acted as no sin, for I judged that pure to me, which to a dark understanding was impure, for to the pure all things, yea all acts were pure: thus making the Scripture a writing of wax, I pleaded the words of *Paul, That I know and am perswaded by the Lord Jesus, that there was nothing unclean, but as man esteemed it,*[9] unfolding that was intended all acts, as well as meats and drinks, and therefore till you can lie with all women as one woman, and not judge it sin, you can do nothing but sin: now in Scripture I found a perfection spoken of, so that I understood no man could attain perfection but this way, at which Mr. *Rawlinson* was much taken, and *Sarah Kullin* being then present, did invite me to make trial of what I had expressed, so as I take it, after we parted she invited me to Mr. *Wats* in *Rood-lane*, where was one or two more like herself, and as I take it, lay with me that night: now against next [S]unday it was noised abroad what a rare man of knowledge was to speak at Mr. *Brushes*; at which day there was a great company of men and women, both young and old; and so from day to day increased, that now I had choice of what before I aspired after, insomuch that it came to our Officers ears; but having got my pay I left them, and lodged in *Rood-lane*, where I had Clients many, that I was not able to answer all desires, yet none knew our actions but our selves; however I was careful with whom I had to do. This lustful principle encreased so much, that the Lord Mayor with his Officers came at midnight to take me, but knowing thereof, he was prevented. Now *Copp* was by himself with a company ranting and swearing, which I was seldom addicted to, onely proving by Scripture the truth of what I acted; and indeed *Solomons* Writings was the original of my filthy lust, supposing I might take the same liberty as he did, not then understanding his Writings was no Scripture, that I was moved to write to the world what my Principle was, so brought to publick view a Book called *The Single Eye*, so that men and women came from many parts to see my face, and hear my knowledge in these things, being restless till they were made free, as then we called it. Now I being as they said, *Captain of the Rant*, I had most of the principle women came to my lodging for knowledge, which then was called *The Head-quarters*. Now in the height of this ranting, I was made still careful for moneys for my Wife, onely my body was given to other women: so our Company encreasing, I wanted for nothing that heart could desire, but at last it became a trade so common, that all the froth and scum broke forth into the height of this wickedness, yea began to be a publick reproach, that I broke up my Quarters, and went into the countrey to my Wife, where I had by the way disciples plenty, which then Major *Rainsborough*, and Doctor *Barker* was minded for Mr. *Walis* of *Elford*,[10] so there I met them, where was no small pleasure and delight in praising of a God that was an infinite nothing, what great and glorious things the Lord had done, in bringing us out of bondage, to the perfect liberty of the sons of God, and yet then the very notion of my heart was to all maner of theft, cheat, wrong, or injury that privately could be acted, though in tongue I professed the contrary, not considering I brake the Law in all points (murther excepted:) and the ground of this my judgement was, God had made all things good, so nothing evil but as man judged it; for I apprehended there was no such thing as theft, cheat, or a lie, but as man made it so: for if the creature had brought this world into no propriety, as *Mine* and *Thine*, there had been no such title as theft, cheat, or a lie; for the preventions hereof *Everard* and *Gerrard Winstanley* did dig up the Commons, that so all might have to live of themselves, then there had been no need of defrauding, but unity one with another, not then knowing this was the devils kingdom, and Reason lord thereof, and that Reason was naturally enclined to love itself above any other, and to gather to it self what riches and honor it could, that so it might bear sway over its fellow creature; for I made it appear to *Gerrard Winstanley* there was a self-love and vain-glory nursed in his heart, that if possible, by digging to have gained people to him, by which his name might become great among the poor Commonalty of the Nation, as afterwards in him appeared a most shameful retreat from *Georges-hill*, with a spirit of pretended universality, to become a real Tithe-gatherer of propriety; so what by these things in others, and the experience of my own heart, I saw all that men spake or acted, was a lye and therefore my thought was, I had as good cheat for something among them, and that so I might live in prosperity with them, and not come under the lash of the Law; for here was the thought of my heart from that saying of *Solomon*, Eccles. 3.19. *For that which befalleth the sons of men, befalleth beasts, even one thing befalleth them, as the one dieth, so dieth the other, yea they have all one breath, so that a man hath no preheminence above a beast; for all is vanity, all go into one place, all are of the dust, and all turn to dust again.* So that the 18th and 19th verses of *Ecclesiastes* was the rule and direction of my spirit, to eat and to drink, and to delight my soul in the labor of my minde all the days of my life, which I thought God gave me as my portion, yea to rejoyce in it as the gift of God, as said that wise Head-piece *Solomon*; for this then, and ever after, till I came to hear of a Commission, was the thought of my heart, that in the grave there was no more remembrance of either joy or sorrow after. For this I conceived, as I knew not what I was before I came in being, so for ever after I should know nothing after this my being was dissolved; but even as a stream from the Ocean was distinct in it self while it was a stream, but when returned to the Ocean, was therein swallowed and become one with the Ocean; so the spirit of man while in the body, was distinct from God, but when death came it returned to God, and so became one with God, yea God it self; yet notwithstanding this, I had sometimes a relenting light in my soul, fearing this should not be so, as indeed it was contrary; but however, then a cup of Wine would wash away this doubt.

But now to return to my progress, I came for *London* again, to visit my old society; which then *Mary Midleton*[11] of *Chelsford*, and Mrs. *Star* was deeply in love with me, so having parted with Mrs. *Midleton*, Mrs. *Star* and I went up and down the countries as man and wife, spending our time in feasting and drinking, so that Tavernes I called the house of God; and the Drawers, Messengers; and Sack, Divinity; reading in *Solomons* writings it must be so, in that it made glad the heart of God; which before, and at that time, we had several meetings of great company, and that some, no mean ones neither, where then, and at that time, they improved their liberty, where Doctor *Pagets* maid stripped her self naked, and skipped among them, but being in a Cooks shop, there was no hunger, so that I kept my self to Mrs. *Star*, pleading the lawfulness of our doings as aforesaid, concluding with *Solomon* all was vanity. In the interim the Parliament had issued forth several Warrants into the hands of Church-members, which knew me not by person, but by name, so could not take me, though several times met with me, that at last the Parliament to him that could bring me before them, would give a hundred pounds, so that one *Jones* for lucre of money, knowing me, got a Warrant to apprehend me, who meeting me in the four swans within *Bishopsgate*, told me he had a warrant from the High Court of Parliament to take me: Let me see it, said I, you have no power to serve it without an Officer, and so would have escaped, but could not the people so thronged about me, and a great tumult there was, some fighting with him for an Informer, but being a City Trooper, and some more of his Company with him, they carried me, as I take it, to Alderman *Andrews*, where they searched my Pockets; but having dropped an Almanack that had the names of such as sold my books for me, they found it, and carried it to the Parliament, so informed the House I was taken, and likewise desired to know what they should do with me, who gave Order to bring me by water to *Whitehall*-stairs, and deliver me to *Barkstead's*[12] Soldiers, where after a while a messenger was sent to take me into custody, where I was lodged in *Whitehall* over against the *Dial*, and two souldiers guarded me night and day, for which I was to pay; but some being of my principle, they would guard me for nothing, and a Captain of theirs would give me moneys; so after two days I was sent for before the Committee of Parliament to be examined: so being called in, they asked me my Name, my Countrey, with many such frivolous things; so coming to the business in hand, Mr. *Weaver* being the Chair-man, asked me if I lodged in *Rood-lane*? To which I answered, Once I did. Wherefore did you lodge there? Because I had a friend there of whom I hired a chamber. What company of men and women were those that came to you? To instance their names I cannot, but some came as they had business with me. Who were those women in black Bags that came to you? As now I know not. But Mr. *Claxton*, we are informed, you have both wives and maids that lodged with you there? Those that informed you, let them appear face to face, for I never lay with any but my own wife. No: for you call every woman your wife? I say I lye with none but my wife, according to Law, though in the unity of the spirit, I lye with all the creation. That is your sophistication, but deal plainly before God and Man, did not you lye with none in *Rood lane*, and other places, besides your wife? I do deal plainly as you, but I being a free born subject ought not to accuse my self, in that you are to prove your charge. Mr. *Claxton* confess the truth it, will be better for you: for we assure you shall suffer no wrong. What I know is trueth, I have, and shall speak. What did you at Mrs. *Croes* in *Rederiff*? I had conference with the people. As you were preaching, you took a pipe of Tobacco, and women came and saluted [y]ou, and others above was committing Adultery. This is more then [you] remembe[r]? No, you will not remember any thing against you: but surely you cannot but remember this *Almanack* is yours, and these mens names your own hand writing. Yea I did write them, was not these men your disciples? They were not mine, but their own. Did not Major *Rainsborough*, and the rest lye with other women? Not as I know. But Mr. *Claxton* do you remember this book is yours? I never saw that before, but may be some of the like nature I have. Why did not you write this Book? That you are to prove not. Here is the two first Letters of your name. What is that to me? it may serve for other names as well as mine. Did not Major *Rainsborough* and these men give you monies to print this Book? How should they give me monies to print that which neither I nor they knew of. This Book must be yours, for it speaks your language, suitable to your practise. I being but a stranger to you, how should you know my language or practise? Though you will confess nothing, yet we have witness to prove it. Let them be examined in my presence: So calling *Jones* [t]hat betrayed me, did you never see Mr. *Claxton* lye with no woman? I have heard him talk of such things, but saw no act. Though you cannot, there is some will, therefore Mr. *Claxton* deal plainly, that though you lay with none, yet did not you alow it none others? I saw no evil in them to disalow; And Gentlemen let me speak freely to you, Suppose I were your servant, entrusted with your secrets, and knew that you were Traitors against this present Power, would you take it well for me to impeach you, and bear witness against you? At which, either the Earl of *Denby*, or the Earl of *Salisbury* said, No: Such a servant deserved to be hang'd; at which they laughed and said, this was a case of another nature. I say as it is in the one, so it is in the other. Well then, Mr. *Claxton*, you will not confess the trueth. You say you have witness to prove it. However the trueth I have confessed, and no more can be expected. Do not you know one *Copp*? Yea I know him, and that is all, for I have not seen him above two or three times. Then they said, this is a sad principle, which if not routed, all honest men will have their wives deluded. One of them said, he feared not his wife she was too old, so they dismissed me to the place from whence I came, and said we shall report it to the House, that so with speed you may have your trial, but I think it was about fourteen weeks before I received the Sentence of the House, which took up the House a day and a half work, as *John Lilborn* said, stood the Nation in a Thousand pounds:[13] And thus they sate spending the Common-wealths monies, about friviolus things. Now having past some votes, at last they carried the day for my banishment, which vote that day was printed, and pasted upon many posts about the City of *London. That* LAWRENCE CLAXTON *should remain in* New bridwel *a moneth and a day, and then the High [S]heriffe of* London *to conduct him to the High Sheriffe in* Kent, *and so to be banisht* England, Scotland *and* Ireland *and the Territories thereof during life, and Major* Rainsborough *to be no longer Justice during his life.* Now when my moneth was expired, their Vote was not executed, so after a while I came forth of prison, and then took my journey with my wife to my house in *Stainfield*, and from thence I took my progress into Cambrigdeshire, to the towns of *Foxen* and *Orwel* where still I continued my .Ranting principle, with a high hand.

Now in the interim I attempted the art of Astrology and Physick, which in a short time I gained and therewith travelled up and down Cambridgeshire and *Essex, as Linton* and *Saffron-walden*, and other countrey towns, improving my skill to the utmost, that I had clients many, yet could not be therewith contended, but aspired to the art of Magick, so finding some of Doctor *Wards* and *Woolerds* Manuscripts,[14] I improved my genius to fetch Goods back that were stoln, yea to raise spirits, and fetch treasure out of the earth, with many such diabolical actions, as a woman of *Sudbury* in *Suffolk* assisted me, pretending she could do by her witch-craft whatever she pleased; now something was done, but nothing to what I pretended, however monies I gained, and was up and down looked upon as a dangerous man, that the ignorant and religious people was afraid to come near mee, yet this I may say, and speak the truth, that I have cured many desperate Diseases, and one time brought from *Glenford* to a village town wide of *Lanham* to Doctor *Clark*, two women and one man that had bewitched his daughter, who came in a frostly cold night, tormented in what then *Clerk*[15] was a doing, and so after that his daughter was in perfect health, with many such like things, that it puffed up my spirit, and made many fools believe in me, for at that time I looked upon all was good, and God the author of all, and therefore have several times attempted to raise the devil, that so I might see what he was, but all in vain, so that I judged all was a lie, and that there was no devil at all, nor indeed no God but onely nature, for when I have perused the Scriptures I have found so much contradiction as then I conceived, that I had no faith in it at all, no more than a history, though I would talk of it, and speak from it for my own advantage, but if I had really then related my thoughts, I neither believed that *Adam* was the first Creature, but that there was a Creation before him, which world I thought was eternal, judging that land of *Nod* where *Cain* took his wife, was inhabited a long time before *Cain*, not considering that *Moses* was the first Writer of Scripture, and that we were to look no further than what there was written; but I really believed no *Moses*, Prophets, Christ, or Apostles, nor no resurrection at all: for I understood that which was life in man, went into that infinite Bulk and Bigness, so called *God*, as a drop into the Ocean, and the body rotted in the grave, and for ever so to remain.

In the interim came forth a people called *Quakers*, with whom I had some discourse, from whence I discerned that they were no further than burning brick in *Egypt*, though in a more purer way than their fathers before them; also their God, their devil, and their resurrection and mine, was all one, onely they had a righteousness of the Law which I had not; which righteousness I then judged was to be destroyed, as well as my unrighteousness, and so kept on my trade of Preaching, not minding any thing after death, but as aforesaid, as also that great cheat of Astrology and Physick I practised, which not longer after I was beneficed in *Mersland*, at *Terington* and St. *Johns*, and from thence went to *Snetsham* in *Norfolk*, where I was by all the Town received, and had most of their hands for the Presentation, then for *London* I went, and going to visit *Chetwood* my former acquaintance, she, with the wife of *Middleton*, related to me the two Witnesses; so having some conference with *Reeve* the prophet, and reading his Writings, I was in a trembling condition; the nature thereof you may read in the *Introduction* of that Book (*Look about you, for the devil that you fear is in you*) considering how sadly I had these many years spent my time, and that in none of these seven Churches could I finde the true God, or right devil; for indeed that is not the least desired, onely to prate of him, and pray to him we knew not, though it is written, *It is life eternal to know the true God*, yet that none of them mindes, but from education believeth him to be an eternal, infinite Spirit, here, there, and every where; which after I was fully perswaded, that there was to be three Commissions upon this earth, to bear record to the three Titles above, and that this was the last of those three: upon the belief of this I came to the knowledge of the two Seeds, by which I knew the nature and form of the true God, and the right devil, which in all my travels through the seven Churches I could never finde, in that now I see, it was onely from the revelation of this Commission to make it known.

Now being at my Journeys end, as in point of notional worship, I came to see the vast difference of Faith from Reason, which before I conclude, you shall hear, and how that from Faiths royal Prerogative all its seed in *Adam* was saved, and all Reason in the fallen Angel was damned, from whence I came to know my election and pardon of all my former transgressions;[16] after which my revelation growing, moved me to publish to the world, what my Father was, where he liveth, and the glory of his house, as is confirmed by my writings now in publick; so that now I can say, of all my formal righteousness, and professed wickedness, I am stripped naked, and in room thereof clothed with innocency of life, perfect assurance, and seed of discerning with the spirit of revelation. I shall proceed to answer some Objections that may be raised, as unto what I have already asserted ...

Joseph Salmon

A Rout, A Rout,

Or some part of the
ARMIES QUARTERS
BEATEN UP,

By the DAY of the

LORD

Stealing upon Them.

Wherein is briefly discovered
the present cloudy and dark Appearance
of God amongst them.

By JOSEPH SALMON, a present Member of the
ARMY.

*He that hath an ear to hear, let him hear what the
Spirit saith.*
*Arise ye, and depart, for this is not your rest; it is
polluted, &c.*
*The weapons of our warfare are not carnal, but
mighty through God, to beat down strong holds,
&c.*

London, Printed for *G. C.* 1649.

A
W O R D
To the
Commanding Power
in the
A R M Y.

By your leave, Gentlemen,

I Hope, in these days of Liberty, I may be free to speak a word to my fellow Souldiers: I shall not trouble *You* with much at the present, for I know you have more trouble already upon your spirits, then you can well tell how to be rid of. My speech is intended especially (as I said before) to my fellow-Souldiers, those of the inferior rank and quality; I have very little from the Lord to declare to You as yet: All that I have to say, is this; That you go on as fast as you can with the Work you have begun, for the time draws nigh that is allotted you: Make haste (I say;) yet not more haste then good speed: Make a short work; but cut it short in Righteousness; for the Day is at hand, wherein he that helpeth and they that are holpen shall fall together. Gentlemen, you are the Rod of God, yea, the Rod of the Lords anger in his own Hand, the Almighty Arm acts you; and so it appears, for no manly glory can encounter with you: in this Day of the LORDS Wrath you strike thorow King, Gentry, and Nobility, they all fall before you: You have a Commission from the LORD to scourge *ENGLAND'S* Oppressors; do it in the Name of God, do it (I say) fully, hotly, sharply; and the same measure you mete, shall be met to you again; for the Lord will ere long cast his Rod into the fire of burning and destruction: It will be a sweet destruction, wait for it.

> *Gentlemen,*
> *Under an abrupt*
> *form I subscribe*
> *my self*
> *Yours in life*
> *and death,*

JOSEPH SALMON.

TO
The Fellowship (of SAINTS
scattered) in the ARMY.

Dear Hearts,

I *Know it will be a wonder to some of you, to behold this Frontispiece
faced with my Character; and truly it is as much my wonder as yours: I
little thought that ever God would have called me hither.*

Friends, I am yet amongst you, I own you, I can say Amen *to your
proceedings, although I cannot close with you in the managing of them. I
have a fellowship with you in the Lord: but I am distant from your dark and
fleshly enterprises.*

*You are a scattered seed amongst tares, and it is your name that upholds
the fame of the whole: You are that little leaven hid in the meal, whose
reputation seasons the whole lump; if it were not for you, this power of the
sword, would vanish and be annihilated. Behold, I shew you a Mystery, it is
yet hidden from many, yea most of you;* Thus saith the Lord of Hostes, The
Day is coming, and now is, when I will gather up my jewels in the Army
(from under this dark and carnal form of the Sword) into my self; where I
will be unto them Life, Liberty, Priviledg and Satisfaction, the fulness of
Arrears, and plenty of Accommodation; when they shall no more contend
with the world for outward Interest, but beholding all in Divine Fulness,
shall in the enjoyment of it sit down contented. *And this I partly see fulfilled
in my self and others.*

*But now it may be you will wonder why I yet remain amongst you, seeing
I am brought hither; I am sure many of your verdicts will pass upon me, I
shall not want the censure of most. But it is no matter; Cas[t] all your cruelty
and malice upon me; the Lord in me is mighty to bear it: I will own it all,
being willing to become sin from you, though the Lord in me knows no sin;
that you, together with me, may be presented in the Lord an eternal
righteousness.*

I have but this at present to say: I am now with you, as Mary *at the
Sepulchre, waiting to see the Lord: but he is risen. Your carnal affairs are the
Sepulchre where the Lord is buried to me; he is not here, he is certainly risen,
but where to see him in his next appearance, I wait: I must stand at the
Sepulchre till the voyce be uttered behinde me, which I beleeve will be
shortly, both to me and many others.* Till the day break, and the shadows flee
away, *Farewel my Beloved*, be thou as a Roe, or a young Hart upon the
mountains of *Bether.*

Sirs, I am yours,
JOS: SAL.

Farewell.

A ROUT, A ROUT,

OR,

Some part of the Army's Quarters beaten up, by the DAY of the LORD stealing upon them.

That Power (or Mystery) which acts all things, and by which whole man (in his councels, actions and engagements) is led out and disposed according to divine will and pleasure; I say, this Power (which is God) cometh forth and offers it self in a diversity of appearance, and still (by a divine progress in the affairs of the earth) moves from one power to another, from one dispensation to another, from one party to another; hereby accomplishing his eternal decreed design in and upon the Creature. This is manifest in all dispensations, civil and spiritual.

Time was, when God had faced the Jewish Ceremonies (those carnal manifestations) with a great beauty and splendor of divine Majesty: the Lord was there seen under that form to vail and hide his beauty and glory. In a time appointed he departed from them, went out of them, he would dwell there no longer; but he casts off that form or garment, and clothes himself with another, swallowed up that glory in another, the lesser in the greater; and then all the brightness and lustre of divine appearance resided in, and dwelt upon the flesh of the Son, as being a more true pattern, and exact resemblance of God the divine Power. But the Lord was not here in his appearance where he would be neither; and therefore having no resolution eternally here to tabernacle or abide, in the fulness of time he lays this form aside also. Though he was the Son, the dear Son, the only begotten Son, a Son so like the Father, yet he must not be spared, he must be crucified, the Lord will move hence also: whence note, That this divine Power (or Mystery) admits of no eternal habitation in any thing below it self.

Now as this Power (God) hath a dayly motion out of one dispensation spiritual into another, so also it is in civil or outward dispensations.

This I have found in my own experience, (by tracing this divine Power, in its going forth amongst the sons of Men) that it sometimes owns this, sometimes that form; sometimes this, sometimes that party, dayly moving from one to another as it pleaseth: now the Lord lives in all these, though in some darkly, in others more purely; and all these motions are as so many footsteps of God, whereby he gradually ascends out of the creature, into a more compleat image or likeness of himself.

Time was, when God dwelt amongst us in the darkness of absolute and arbitrary Monarchy: the face and beauty of divine mystery lived in it, deny it who can, that sees God in all things.

In this form of Monarchy God hath vailed his beautiful presence with a thick cloud of darkness: He hath made darkness his secret place, and his pavilions round about him have been thick clouds of the Sky. Though the image and brightness of God have dwelt in it, yet under such black darkness that man could never discern it. Tyranny, persecution, opposition, wil, nature and creature, hath been (as it were) that vail betwixt God and man in this dispensation; all this, and whatever you will call evil in Monarchy, the Lord was pleased to hide himself under, while resident in this carnal form. I know its difficult to see God in this darkness, the bright Sun under this black cloud: the naked and pure Spirit, under this foul habit and filthy attire; but he that cannot here discern God is blind, and sees not afar off.

God (having hitherto walked under this form) is now (and hath in these last days) come forth to rend this vail in pieces, to shake this form, to lay it waste, and clothe himself with another.

How God hath and does destroy Monarchy, and what it figures out to us.

The power and life of the King, and in him the very soul of Monarchy sunk into the Parliament, and here it lost its name barely, but not its nature; its form, but not its power; they making themselves as absolute and tyrannical as ever the King in his reign, dignity and supremacy; yet the Lord ascended a little nearer himself, by taking off this form (the Parliament) and hereby made way for his after-design.

We see in a short time, he lays aside that glorious shew and Idol (the Parliament) and clothes himself with the Army: And thus, both King, Monarchy and Parliament fell into the hands, and upon the swords of the Army: and thus the Army are to be the Executioners of that beast (Monarchy) which they had formerly wounded, and whose wound the Parliament had healed and salved over by a corrupt and rotten Treaty: all which doth figure out to me the stain of the glory of all flesh; as Monarchy (or arbitrary regal power) falls by the sword, so also shall that Kingly and Imperial power of all flesh be cut in sunder by the stroke of Divine Justice; for by his fire and by his sword will the Lord plead with all flesh, and the slain of the Lord shall be many: The Lord will kindle a burning under that glory wherein he hath formerly appear'd; God himself shall be the burning, the holy One shall be the flame, and all fleshly regality in us shall be the fuel which shall be burnt up and consumed. But we shall hence proceed to our former Discourse, and shall next in order consider

How God lives in the ARMY.

Thus far we see God hath moved from party to party, and its down at present in the Army; and here also God makes darkness his secret place, living under a poor, low, carnal form, and few can behold his beautiful presence under the power of the Sword. The Lord here besmears himself with blood and vengeance, deforms his own beauty, hides his aimable presence under a hideous and wrathful form.

And now in as much as God hath called me forth (from an impartial spirit) to declare my Light; I shall (from some clear experience of the Armies present condition) discover that dark and cloudy appearance of the supream Power (*God*) amongst them, whereby may be discerned how far below the pure appearance of the spirit, their present station renders them. And I am very confident, that which I shall say, the Lord will testifie and bear record the truth of the same upon the hearts of many amongst them. Friends! Look about you, for the Lord is now coming forth to rip up your bowels, to search your hearts, and try your reins; yea; to let loose the imprisoned Light of himself in you; and if the Lord by this doth not shake many of you, then say, That I have prophesied Lyes in the name of the Lord. Then let him that hath an ear to hear, hear what the Lord, the Spirit saith.

Thus saith the Lord, yea the Lord saith it:

That the present condition of the Army, or the present appearance of the supream Power amongst them, renders them in darkness, and far below the pure Light and Life of God.

That it is so, I offer my appeal thus.

First, let them and all others (who are spiritually wise) consider, by and from what principles God acts these men; I mean you Heroes of valour in the Army, you Grandees of the present power in the Kingdome: In patience possesse ye your soules till I shall race your foundation, and discover your principles, which God hath hitherto and still does act you in: they are either publick or private, common or (more properly) peculiar; your common and publick principles, are the outward liberty and freedom of the Nation, the establishment of outward Lawes, Liberties, and Priviledges; and some outward form of Gover[n]ment; which may correspond with your sence of Justice: what no farther yet? This is poor earthly Tabernacle, which God at present hath taken up in you; I wish I might not have cause to say, It is a speckled pretence under which your private interests resides: For I know this is the main spur that drives you on, (self-preservation:) This is your D[e]lilah, you[r] proper, private and peculiar principle: Resolved you are to save your Lives, and preserve your self-interest, though in this expedition you destroy all other powers and interests whatsoever: Herein, (though you walk, as men, very carnally) yet, Dear hearts I blame you not. I know God acts you in this cloud, he goes out with you in this darkness, and lets out his presence through this vail of self-preservation amongst you, he hath crowned you with fame, success and victory, while you have lived and acted in this earthly body of outward Liberty. But how far inferiour and below this is, to a Life in the purity of Divine light, (now God hath disclosed himself) I am in some measure able to discern.

You know not yet what it is to be dead to you own Interests, though you have professed a great deal of self-denyall, yet *I* profess many of you never knew what true self-denyall was; and what it is truly to be dissolved and dye out of your own carnal Interests: I know your honour and dignity is great in your hearts, your renowned enterprises call for merit: Your lives and safeties are also dear to you; it is so, so it must be, God will have it so: he lives in these low concernments, and yet your hearts cannot be imbittered or dis-ingaged from them: you hug them, you prize them, they are an object of your embraces. But I tell you (Sirs) God is going about to unbody himself in you, whilst you are embracing this body of self-safety and outward Liberty, he is dying and departing from it, though you see it not. And This know, That God will ere long leave you exceeding dark and dead in your enterprizes: I was alive once as well as you, and in my life I laboured amongst you (in my sphere) as much as another; but I am now dead with the Lord; I am at rest from my labour; Ah happy death! oh blessed loss! how far better is it O Lord to be dissolved and gathered up into thy rest, then to live the life of a worldly and carnall labour? and I know also that the hour of Gods judgement is come upon many of you: some of you have received your mortall wound already; I see you gasp and strugle in your confused and dark enterprizes. Let this silver probe but sink to the bottom of your wounded hearts, and something, without question, will speedily be discovered.

Ah Friends,—

If you saw your Interests in the Lord, your Lives and Liberties in the Lord, if you saw all yours in the Lord, you would think it a beggarly thing to contend for any thing, or to plead Gods quarrel with any that shall demand them of you. Doubtlesse, it is a poor, low, base, earthly Spirit, that raises contests, and seeks after the ruine and blood of creatures, for the enjoyment of that which at best is but a bitter-sweet, a well-being subject to all manner of casualties. Lo, This is the principle that God at present acts you by: It is the Lord in you, inhabiting his secret place; and because I see it is the Lord, I can embrace it, I can tender you in my bosom-affections, while you are carried forth in this carnal dispensation. Nevertheless, I will in part discover to you how far some are dead to their own Interest, and whither shortly you must be brought.

Those that live in the more pure knowledge and Life of God, see themselves (their Lives, Liberties, and all outward enjoyments) not their own, but the Lords, and theirs in the Lord, not a jot below him, or at the least distance from him,

If we have the Lord, we have enough, because he is all to us, and we the same fulnesse in him: Lo, this is life, libertie, and satisfaction. Now no outward losse or misery can make us unhappy: we may be persecuted; yet not forsaken, cast down, yet not destroyed; dying, and behold we live, in bondage, yet free; because the Lord is all this, and more to us. *To live, to us is Christ, and to die is gain.* If we have a portion of outward safety amongst others, we see it is the Lord; if not, it is the Lord; and where the Lord is, there is Liberty: God is to us light in darkness, glory in shame, beauty in deformity, liberty in bondage, we possess nothing, yet enjoy all things; suffering is our crown, death our life; yea, we live upon death dayly, we cannot live without it.

Again, We are also contented with the dispose of providence in any thing that may be called ours: If any party or power command us, our lives, liberties, or interest, it is the pleasure of the Father in us to give up all to them: we see a divine call in it, and can with alacrity yeeld obedience. Oh, it is a sweet smelling sacrifice, acceptable with the Father, when we (the son) are thus drawn forth to offer up our dearest Interests for the world. It may be you cannot in this apprehend me: it is no matter, the Father willeth it should be a mystery.

Yet farther:

Our Interest of Life and Liberty is at your service; if you call for it, take it; we are contented to be prodigal of it, to satisfie the blood-thirsty spirit of any man in the Kingdom.

While we are in the enjoyment of these outward things, we use them as if we used them not, being free to throw them off at the first demand: we are as free to suffer, to be trampled upon, to hang and burn, as to enjoy that outward liberty which you (so seriously and resolutely) press after. I tell you, Sirs, Suffering is our Conquest; While we are ground to pieces under any power whatsoever, all this while we trample upon them: debasing is our exalting; in that which you call misery and calamity, we are more then conquerors: We dare meet you (even you, whose courage hath excelled, whose fierce countenance makes the earth to tremble, you who are the present terror of the Nation) and appear in a naked posture before you; yea, throw your selves, lives, liberties, and all upon the edg of your cruelty; and we are sure, if you dare encounter with us here, we shall overcome you. Ah Sirs! When you see this way of conquest, you will throw your swords behind you in an holy despite and scorn; you shall lay all your honour in the dust, and by that sweet spirit of meekness shall destroy and subdue your enemies.

But secondly:

I wish you might be carried forth into a serious view of the manner of your present Actings. As your Principles are poor and beggarly, so also the manner of your Engagements[1] is dark and fleshly. This cloudy and vailed appearance of God amongst you, puts you upon preposterous designs, upon low and carnal Enterprizes: You have taken away *Charls* his life, because otherwise he would (it's likely) have taken yours. True, it is the good will of the Lord it should be so, I have nothing to say against it; the Lord in this cloud leads you forth to it, and in this you have plaid the parts of men acting under a fleshly discovery of things. You are led forth in a way of vengeance upon your adversaries; you sentence and shoot to death at your pleasure; it little moves you to trample upon the blood of your enemies; this is your Victory, Glory and Triumph. All this is well; you must tarry here till God moves higher amongst you.

I have only this to say to you:

Is it not a poor carnal thing for Saints, so high in profesion as you have been, to stand brangling with the world for a few carnal enjoyments? What, the sons of everlasting peace, and ingaged in a carnal combat? Well, it is the Lord; I am satisfied. But oh, that sweet and meek Spirit of Christ! Who, when he was reviled, reviled not again; was persecuted, but with patience under-went it, and committed himself to him that judged righteously. You cannot, you dare not commit your selves, your cause, your lives and liberties to the Lord, and nakedly, without any carnal opposition, surrender your Interest to a divine dispose: Nay rather, Shall not your swords soon be sheathed in the bowels of those who obstruct, or impede, your furious march in the road of self-preservation? Poor dear Hearts! It is the lowness, weakness and darkness of God by which you are led forth and acted. The Lord, ere long, will come forth in another appearance amongst you; he is coming out of darkness, his secret place, into a light and open view, he will let out a more pure glory upon you, when, in an holy shame, you will reflect upon your present Employments.

I tell you, dearly esteemed, it is a scorn to us, either to pick, or plead a Quarrel with any party, for an outward or carnal Interest; The Lord hath shewed us (and will shortly manifest to you) a more easie and sweet way of Victory; we can overcome by being conquered, we can lose all, and yet be savers in the conclusion.

Again, for I draw homewards.

The manner of your present Actings is in much fear, dread, darkness and confusion; it is your dayly thoughts and care how to complot your designs, and lay out your work so, as that you may save your selves, your honor and reputation, but all is too little, you must shortly part with all; your name, fame, success and victory must all be forgotten, yea, you your selves shall rejoyce at your own Overtures.

You are very fearful and jealous of your defamation; you are afraid to think of it: your spirits are involved in confusion and distraction, for fear lest your design should betray you. These are your imprisoned thoughts, I am very certain, but spiritual wisdom can discover them. The Lord knows that you lie under a sad weight of fear, terror and distraction: Fear, the pit, and a snare have taken hold on you, disorder and confusion abounds amongst you: You grope for the wall like the blind; you aim at Liberty and Priviledg, but you grope blindly after it, as knowing not which way to accomplish it; and thus many times you sit down weeping by the Rivers of

Babylon; you are oft so over-whelmed in these troubled waters of Liberty and Priviledg, that you are constrained to sink under the waves of sorrow and darkness: I know the Lord judges many of you, and throws you down by the sad and serious consideration of your actings; He turns your hearts, ways and enterprises upside down before you, and I know you are under dayly convictions of spirit. Thus the dark presence of God shuts you up in fear, and keeps you under bondage: The thick cloud of horror and confusion vails that sweet presence, and bright splendor of Peace and Liberty from you; but in an appointed time the mystery of light will break out in you, and upon you, when in the shinings of Divine Majesty, you will clearly and purely behold things in a naked appearance, when you shall see no cause of fear or trouble in any thing.

Those that live in love to all, see no cause to fear any; for there is no fear in love, perfect Love casts out fear: If you were in Charity with all men, you would fear no man; for Charity thinks no evil, it knows none, it fears none: All things are not yet reconciled to you, earth and heaven are not yet agreed; but you labour under a body and bulk of cursed enmity, and hence is the spring of all your fear and jealousie: If you could see all men, all interests, all power in the Lord, you would be offended at none, you would not fear any, but would, with a sweet, patient, contented, and quiet spirit, lie down under any thing coming from a Divine dispose. We see and behold our selves, (as in the Lord) without fear or jealousie, because we are really reconciled to all men, all designs, all interests; and all they that know us are carryed forth in a spirit of Love towards us. The reason why we are hated, despised, and trampled upon, is, because the world knoweth us not, they know not the Father in us.

In this state of ignorance we are the objects of scorn and contempt, and it is our Freedom and Liberty to be so: The Lord in us, and we in the Lord, and with him, travel together under the worlds infirmities, and because we see it the Fathers will, it is our meat and drink to do it; we love to sweat drops of blood under all mens offences: Throw all the wrath, malice, envy and scorn of man upon us, we fear it not, but in the Lord we are able to bear all, and suffer under it. Lo, thus we fill up behinde the measure of the sufferings of Christ in our flesh, the dyings of the Lord are manifested in us dayly: Here, O here's a way to bring forth peace and unity: the Lord is coming, (he is coming) to discover it: For by this death we ascend to a life, in all mens hearts and affections; after this cross of hatred, we are crowned (as most choyce and precious) in all mens love and esteem, when the spirit shall descend from on high, and be poured out upon them; they shall look upon us (whom in the Lord they have pierced) and mourn over us with a spirit of love and tenderness: Then shall we see of the travel of our souls, and be therewith satisfied.

Ah my dear Friends! my Soul travels again in birth with you, till the Lord be thus formed and brought forth in you: I know many of you are almost spent under you burthen; you are so lost in a wilderness of Confusion, That you desire and seek after a retired rest; you begin to loath your husks, and to have some desire after your Fathers table: I say no more, he that does come, will come, and will not tarry; behold, he comes with a recompence: you are afraid to lay down your Swords, lest you should lose your Liberties; but the Lord will recompence this seven-fold into your bosom, he is coming forth to make you free to suffer a blessed Freedom, a glorious Liberty, a sufficient recompence for the loss of all outward glories: Is it the loss of your Honor, Fame and Dignity that you are afraid of? The Lord is coming to make you glad to part with it, and with a holy rejoycing to throw it all behinde you: Ah friends! The Lord will honor you with meekness; you shall be the fame of the world, for true valor and spiritual courage; yea (now and not before) shall the desire of the Nations be towards you, their lamb-like spirits of meekness and innocency will be an enforcing invitation to the lion-hearted devourers of the world to feed together with you in your green pastures, and to drink of your quiet and still waters: when you are become children of this new birth, you shall be able to play upon the hole of the Asp, and to dwell with the Cockatrice in his den, oppression and tyranny shall be destroyed before you; the sons of your afflictors shall come bending to you: that God shall bring forth in you, shall attract the hearts of the world towards you, they shall throw down their crowns at your feet; and shall take hold of that skirt of Righteousness which is upon you, and say, We perceive of a truth, that the Lord is in you and amongst you. But in the mean time, you, together with the world, are shut up in darkness, and not truly discerning one another: you fear the world, and they are afraid of you; you are at a distance, involved in a bloody contest, an earthly, lustful, and carnal Warfarr.

{ *Where Live and Lie, and die together;* }
{ *Yet but a while, it's not for ever.* } *Farewell.*

Post-script.

Friends,

But one word more, and I have done. I told you before, and now I say it again, That your reputation is the fame and glory of this present Army; you (I know) are the main supporting Pillars of it. I will tell you *what I see in this*, more plainly then I have hitherto declared. I see the Lord, *our spiritual Sampson*, hath laid his hands of almighty power upon (*You*) these Pillars of this woodden Fabrick, he will dis-joynt you, and shake you all to pieces, and in you the whole edifice of this swordlie Power shall be annihilated: the Lord will die with it,[2] in it (or rather out of it, and from it) and in this death he will destroy more then you have done all your lives time. The Lord will *here* take you napping, as you are eating and drinking, marrying, and giving in marriage to strange flesh, and the lake of divine burning shall consume you. Oh, it will be a glorious day; wait for it.

I have here offered a few things to a publique view, I know the wise ones amongst you will light it, and dis-regard it; the form, method and language invites not the curious and nice spirit of anie man; it hath no beautie upon it, though a great deal in it, which the Princes of this world cannot discern. It is indeed the foolish language of the Spirit; if you do not like it, retort it again, and I will carrie it where I had it; you are like yet to have no better from me. I was once wise as well as you, but I am now a fool, I care not who knows it: I once also enjoyed my self, but I am now carried out of my wits, a fool, a mad man, besides my self; if you think me any other, you are mistaken, and it is for your sakes that I am so.

And now Friends, *In him that was, is, and is to come*, I take my farewel of you: Remember what I say, (*is, was, and is to come.*) The Lord *was*, when you were lowest; he *is*, now you are highest; and he *is to come*, when you shall be nothing. *Even so, Come Lord Jesus, Come quickly.*

FINIS

Letter from Salmon to Thomas Webbe

My own heart bloud, from whom I daily receive life and being, in whom my eternall freedom is perfected, to whom is ascribed now and forever, Amen.

Thou art the Webb of my own spinning, I have laboured to bring thee forth in this glorious form that thou now livest; let me cloath myself with the Webb of my own travel. My dear thou art to me as a garment of Needlework,[1] I wear thee as my choicest robes of Royalty; because thou art as a vesture upon me, winde nor weather affright me not; the Northern gales and Borean blasts of cruelty, I know cannot pierce through thee, my garment of salvation. Well, to be brief, I know, my heart, thou art not altogether ascertained of my present state as appears by yours lately received. My love, thy patheticall lines, I did with much tendernesse accept, and I shall never forget thy live therein manifested. Cop, my, thy, own hart is gone to London; No other note from the Vulgar but hanging at least for him. The last week save one, a Souldier was burnt through the tongue for a businesse of the same nature. The glory of these things passeth multitudes both in City and Country, notwithstanding all their cruelty. For my own part I finde my Genius much elevated and heghtened, to look the worst of these casualties in the face, that can succeed these things; My condition outwardly is very poor, when lying here at great expences, yet am I made not to care for the future, although sometimes I scarce know over night how I shall be provided for on the morrow. Well, what my Titular Angel, the Gardian Genius will do with this handfull of earth, I know not, neither am at all troubled, but that if I live, my love to thee; if I die, I die to thee. So that whether living or dying I am thy

[J]o. Salmon.

Ten thousand salutes, alias holy kisses to thy dear wife, with whom is my heart; my tender respects to thy Uncle, my Father, his Spouse, my beloved my dear Mary, your maid: Eternal plagues consume you all, rot, sink and damn your bodies and souls into devouring fire, where none but those that walk uprightly can enter. Sirs, I wish you damnable well, because I dearly love you; the Lord grant we may know the worth of hell, that we may forever scorn heaven: For my own part I am ascended far above all heavens, yet I fill all things, and laugh in my sleeve to think what's coming: well I say no more, but farewel. From my Pallace of Royall Majesty, in the last year of this reign of the beast, and in the day wherein the neast of all hearts are ripening as fast as possible may be.

Coventry, April, 3rd. 1650.

[Printed from E. Stokes, *The Wiltshire Rant* (1652), p. 13.]

Heights in *Depths*

AND

Depths in *Heights*

OR

TRUTH

no less *Secretly* then *Sweetly*
sparkling out its GLORY
from under a *Cloud* of
OBLOQUIE.

Wherein is discovered the various *Motions* of an
Experienced Soul, in and through the manifold
dispensations of GOD.

And how the Author hath been acted in, and
redeemed from the unknown paths of darkness;
wherein, as in a wilderness, he hath wandered
without the clear vision of a *Divine Presence.*

Together with a sincere abdication of certain
Tenents, either, formerly vented by him, or now
charged upon him.

Per me JO. SALMON

Are they Hebrew? So am I. Are they Israelites? So am I.
Are they the Seed of Abraham? So am I.
The God and Father of our Lord Jesus Christ knowes
that I lie not.

London, Printed by *Tho. Newcomb* 1651.

AN
Apologeticall Hint
to the ensuing
Discourse.

READER,

This little Piece comes to thy view as a poore Pilgrim, void of that large accommodation which happily it may finde at its own home. I have here dressed it in a homely Language, and formed it as like my self as possible I could; if thou canst see so much wo[r]th in it, as to give it entertainment, I am bold to say (ere it part from thee) it will return thee satisfaction. It steales like a Thiefe upon the benighted world: However, bee not shy of it; for it shal take nothing from thee but what thou shalt bee made willing to part withall.

Lastly, *I* send it into the World, to discharge some debts which in my late Travels through Egypt land *I* left unsatisfied.

As more plainly thus:

It is not long since wherein that eminent appearance of light, which drawed out its glory upon my Spirit, and from thence gave a sweet and powerfull reflexe upon the World, did shrowd it selfe under a most sable and enigmaticall cloud of darknesse, and withdrew for a season, behinde the dark Canopies of Earth and Flesh; in which state the Hemispheare of my spirit was so bespread with obscurity, that *I* knew not whither *I* walked, or what *I* did.

Like Nebuchad-nezzar.

Thus was *I* led into paths that *I* had not known, and turned from a King to become a* Beast, and fed upon huskes for a season. After a while posting most furiously in a burning zeal towards an unattainable end: my manner of walking being adjudged by those in power contrary to the peace and civill order of the* Commonwealth) *I* was justly apprended as an offender: who never before had demerited any thing from them, except love and respect for my faithfull service, which upon all occasions I was ever free to offer as a due homage to the justness of their Cause.

Which indeed were no lesse, according to the present state of things.

I suffered above halfe a yeares imprisonment under the notion of a blaspheamer; which through want of air, and many other conveniences, became very irksome and tedious to my outward man.

Being now retired from the noyse of the world, and cloystered up from the usuall society of my friends, having my grates on the one side for a defence, and my doore fast bolted on the other, I had time enough afforded me to ponder my state and condition.

Upon which I summoned my heart to an appearance before the throne of divine Justice, where after a scrutinous and serious debate, I fownd that *I* had in many things, been led out and acted in the most undoing and destroying paths of darknesse.

Upon which *I* was for a reason deeply, yea intolerably sensible of these things; and multitudes of armed thoughts all at once beleaguered my soule, as if they had agreed with one consent to devour me.

In the middest of this trouble and distraction, *I* was led to consider that certanly Providence had some end in leading (or suffering me to bee led) into these appearances.

This stayed me, and got by degrees more ground upon my Spirit; in which to this day I can rejoyce and lift up my head above the most insulting and daring Fury: insomuch as I know the Lord had a speciall end to accomplish through all these declinings.

The rage of man shall turn to the praise of God, & for ever blessed be that *Grace* & *Love* which hath taught me to say from an inward experience of light, I thank God that I was made a servant of* sin. But to return: Having this clear conviction upon my spirits, I forthwith addressed my selfe to those who had been the causers of my then present confinement: and truly I will speak it to their everlasting praise, (especially some of them) they were as willing to embrace me & my desires (upon such faire termes propounded) as I could be to offer my selfe to them.

Major *Beak* (a man much honored in my thoughts, though once a professed enemy to me) upon the discovery of my mind to him, seemed to be much affected with my condition, & withall informed me of divers blasphemous expressions, which were vented in certain letters of mine which had lately been intercepted; which (after my humble request) hee offered to my view one or more of them: I drew out from them those expressions which most deserved my severest censure, arraigned them and condemned them as guilty.

I offered what *I* had done to Major *Beak*, together with a Petition to the Councel of State for my liberty. Who according to my desires, being in himselfe perswaded of my hearty and penitentiall remorse, did with all care and speed present the same in my behalfe, and so next under God became the onely means of my Release.

Not long after the Right Honorable Colonel *Purefoy* came down to *Coventry* with my discharge from the Councell, who after strict examination (and finding himselfe with the rest satisfied) presented my Discharge to the Mayor and Aldermen then present, which accordingly was received, and *I* set at liberty, ingaging to his Honour and the rest, that *I* would with all convenient speed declare my selfe in Print against those things which I was then charged withall, and still

All things shal work together for the best to them that love God.

am by many.

This then is one and not the least end of my exposing these lines to a publick view, that I may appeare to bee no worse then my word to them whose indulgencie in a time of need was sufficiently manifested towards me.

And truly had not this with some other weighty reasons prevailed with me, I should not have troubled the world with things of this nature. Onely. Therefore Reader take notice that my main ends in this business are,

1. To give a faithful account of the dealings of the most High towards me, as he hath led me along through manifold dispensations of himselfe.

2. To declare to all men what I now am, onely in what *I* am not: if thou (Reader) art so wise as to discover my spirit by what *I* shall here declaim, thou wilt spare me the labour of making an after profession of my Faith, which *I* confesse *I* shall hardly be drawn to declare to* any man.

Hast thou Faith, have it to thy selfe.

3. *I* now am made to speak, because *I* am almost weary of speaking, and to informe the world that silence have taken hold of my spirit. The thunderstrokes of the Almighty have to purpose uttered their voices in me, heaven and earth have trembled at their dreadfull sounds: the Alarm being over ther's silence now in heaven; for how long *I* know not.

I lie quietly secure in the Lord while *I* see the whole world consuming in the fire of envie one against another. I heare much noyse about me, but it serves onely to deafen me into the still slumbers of Divine rest. The formall world is much affrighted, & every form is up in Arms to proclaim open wars against it selfe: The Almighty power is dashing one thing against another, and confounding that which hee hath formerly faced with the glory of his own presence: Hee setteth up and casteth down, and who shal say, *What doest thou?* Come then, O my Soule, enter thou into thy Chamber, shut thy doores about thee, hide thy selfe in silence for a season till the indignation bee blown over.

Reader, I heartily bid the[e] farewel, commending thee into that bosome of love, where *I* rest,

Thine in silence.

Heights in Depths

AND

Depths in Heights

OR

TRUTH
no less *secretly* then *sweetly*
sparkling out its GLORY
from under a *Cloud* of

OBLOQUIE.

Vanitie of Vanities, All is Vanitie saith the Preacher.

The highest piece of wisdom, is to see wisdom it self but Vanity.

The whole world is a Circle, including nothing but emptiness.

*Wisdom it self is but a womb of Wind, whose wringing Pangs,   *Worldly.
pretend the birth of pure Substance, but in times revealing Order it am
its nothing, except travel for sorrow, whose high aspires, do cursorily
expire into an airy notion, even while it appears to be something, it
proves nothing.

Man walketh in a vain shew, he shews to be a man, and thats all.

Here is nothing that truly is, because it abides not; things onely   *Below.
appear to be, and so vanish.   *What God doth
    he doth for ever.

I am satisfied in nothing so much, as in knowing that *nothing can   *In the world
satisfie me.

We seem to live in the State of variety, wherein we are not truly
living, but onely in appearance: in Unity is our life: in one we are,
from one divided, we are no longer.

While we perambulate variety, we walk but as so many Ghosts or
Shadows in it, that it self being but the Umbrage of the Unity.

To descend from the oneness or Eternity, into the multiplicity, is to
lose our selves in an endlesse Labyrinth.

To ascend from variety into uniformity, is to contract our scattered   *In Eternity by
spirits into their original center and to find ourselves where we* were,   Gods decree.
before we* were.   *As to outward
    appearance

Certainly, when a man looks upon the face of things and with a serious inspection eyes the shaken Frame of them, he must conclude that there is something above and beyond all appearances, which can onely and alone satisfie.

If we look upon the Temporary, or more outward state of things; good Lord how subject is it to revolutions and vicissitudes? what is it that we can call certain, but onely uncertainty.

Behold the Lord maketh the earth empty and voyd; he layeth it waste: it reels to and fro like a drunkard: all its Foundations are out of course: one charge succeeds another, while the earth is become subject to a constant inconstancie.

The world travels perpetually, and every one is swoln full big with particularity of interest; thus travelling together in pain, and groaning under enmity: labouring to bring forth some one thing, some another, and all bring forth nothing but wind and confusion: this is certainly a great evil that God hath given men to be exercised withall under the sun.

If further we cast our eye upon these things which promise greater Stabillitie, (*viz*: formes of righteousness and Religion) alas how doth experience daily informe us, of the violent turnings and overturnings which are incident to these also?

*So farr as they are bare form.

Doth not the Almighty power blast these things daily, which hath been most in request amongst us? is he not dashing one forme against another as potters Vessels? what lively Characters of sudden mortalitie may we runn and read upon all* outward formes? what meanes this great noyse, and stir, that alarmes the world continually? the bitter contention, that intermixes it selfe with mens wayes and worships? the perpetuall clashings of one forme against another? The heaven of forme is passing away, which goes not without much clamour, strife and contention. Thus is it the Lords will that people shal labour in the fire, and weary themselves for very vanitie.

*As Adam, who desired to be as *God*, to know good and evill.
*I speak by deep experience.

The farther a man *reaches beyond himselfe to contemplate an incomprehensible glory, though his labour may be delightfull, yet his loss will prove very* extensive.

While with a swift winged ambition, we are transported into the sublimity of notion; the Scorching influences of the heavenly Splendor, meets us (as it were) with an untimely check; Singes the golden *plumes* of our soring fancies; & down we fal into unconceivable depths of darknes.

Ob. How then shall a man attaine to a onenes, and communion with this inaccessible glory?

Sol. Seeing there is no way probable for us (by our most lofty aspires) to interesse our selves in that

*Out of al our dross & tinn: for he is as a refiners fire

We must patiently expect its seasonable descenscion upon us; whose nature it is to* consume us into it selfe, and to melt us into the same nature and likenes:

And truly till this come, and thus manifest it selfe, all that man can doe to acquire satisfaction, does not multiply his sorrow upon his head, and augment cares upon his spirit. Vanitie, vanitie, all is vanitie.

It is but vanitie for me to write, vanitie for you to read. Words are but wind; you read you know not what, and perhaps I write I know not what: and so let it be till God will have it otherwise.

There is a set time for ever[y] purpose under heaven; vanity hath its time also; nay time it selfe is but a lengthened threed of vanitie; there's no reallity but in eternitie:

When time shall be no longer then will appear in their proper and perfect substance.

Well; to every thing there is a season; a time to* cast away stones, and a time to gather stones together, I know not very well which of these times I am now under, while I am thus busied: *A vane thing.

It may be I am not casting stones against the wind, (that is but vanity) However, (if so) methinks the wise reader might find some better employment, then to stand as a spectator of such folly and madnes.

Truly I would very willingly say nothing, & yet at present I am forced into a freedom to speak my mind:

If I speak any thing more then my reason dictates to me as truth; I am become a foole;

And yet I have not so much reason in me, as to make what I say appear reasonable to others: this is also vanity, and a sore travell. But to draw near to what I intend:

I have lived to see an end of all perfections; that which I now long for, is to see perfection it selfe perfected.

I have bin led out to seek the Lord in manifold appearances, I must now (by himselfe) be found in himselfe, who is the good it selfe, and nothing but this can satisfie: Take only this br[ie]f hint, for information.

*How the Author hath beene acted
in, and carried through various
and manifold appearances.*

No sooner had I attained to any maturity in a natural understanding, of common principles of morality, but I found in my selfe a secret longing to soar in a more celestiall orbe; (being partly convicted of a higher life than that of nature.)

This desire being kindled, and supplied with the timely breath of the Almighty, it soone begann to warme and afterwards to set my whole heart of a flame, which to this day could never be extinct; but hath ever since (like the ambitious sparke) made its constant ascensions, and earnest aspires, towards this heavenly center.

Receiving (after my noctural slumbers in nature's grave) some quicknings of a divine principle within me; I presently arose and (as it were) shooke of my night dresses, and appeared to my selfe, like the sunn, dawning out its refulgent splendor, from behind the darke canopies of the earth: I was not adorned in another hue, and devoutly resolved to tread the paths of a more princely dignity.

I presently set forth for heaven, the whole powers and faculties of my soule being infinitely ingaged thereunto, by some taste of the fruits of that good land, which received as pledges of divine love, and as the earnest of that more glorious inheritance, which I now waited for.

I now forsooke my owne kindred and my fathers house, withdrew my selfe from my former vanities, and willingly exposed my selfe to all the contempt and reproach of the world, that I might owne Christ, his cause, and people.

By this time (the honest presbyterian party) were looked most upon, as owners of, and sufferers for, the cause of God;

These, being newly crept out of the shell of Episcopacy, were hatched into a more pure and refined forme; and (after a small time) did seeme to hover gently, and sore sweetly, in a more sublimer region than the former.

With these I now joyned, and became a Zealous hearer and very great affecter of them; and truly did enjoy much of God in this station while the Lord appeared to me in it.

After a while, the notion of Independency offred it selfe upon the stage, to which I was willing to lend my audience (at least) and make proofe of its plausible proposalls. I understood they were a people, much decryed by the vulgaritie which made me imagine that there was something of God amongst them;

I saw they were a people farr excelling others in the strictnes of their forme; and (which most affected me) were gathered out of the world, and knit one to another in a more close, and comfortable bond of love, than any;

The more excelling lustre of this forme, (to me) darkned the beauty, and dim'd the glory of the other: my affections (upon the illumination of the understanding) were soone commanded and forth they runn with a great deale, of delight, to wel-com this newly received glory; in this forme I was concluded and shutt up for a season: wherein I also enjoyed much satisfaction:

Soone after, the doctrine of beleivers baptisme was much pressed by many: and this (though it were a much despised forme) I was yet free to make triall of it, and owne it so farr as I could see it hold a correspondencie with truth.

I (after some serious debate) was convinced that it was my duty to obey God in my subjection to that ordinance of water baptisme: I hereupon tendered my willing and chearful submission, and consulted not the flesh and blood in this business. In the hottest time of Persecution: I was made one eminent both in holding forth this way to the world, and also in an open suffering for the same.

By this time I began to think it was high time to settle, and not to expose my minde to such changes and alterations of things of this nature: Whereupon I here built me a Tabernacle, and was fixed in a peremptory resolve, That this and no other could lawfully be adjudged the way of God.

Then came that voice from the throne of the heavenly Almightiness: Arise and depart for this is not your rest.

I was make as truly sensible of this inwardly, as the eye is sensible of the light, or the ear of the outward sound.

I was certainly struck dead to all my wonted enjoyments.

Stript I was of my glory, and my Crown taken from my head, & I could see nothing but Vanity (and that legibly written) upon all my former travels.

I then had a clear discovery in my spirit, how far all my former enjoyments came short of that true rest which my soul had all along aimed at.

Here I stood for a season weeping with *Mary* at the Sepulcher: fain I would have found Christ where I left him, but alas he was risen: I found nothing in form but a few* signals of Mortality; as for Jesus, he was risen and departed.

> *A few grave clothes, or such like stuff

Thus have I followed Christ from his babe-ship, or infancy, to his Grave of mortality, running through life of Form in a bare knowledge of Christ after the Flesh, till I expired with him* into his death, and was sealed up in the Grave of most darke, and somnolent retires for a season.

> *As many of you as have been baptised into Christ, hath been baptised into his death.

Loath, full loath I was thus to shake hands with form, & to leave the terrestrial image of Iesus Christ; yet so it was designed that hee must goe to his father, and (although* I were ignorant of it) prepare a higher mansion in himself for me.

> *Like the disciples, who were ignorant of the promise of the Spirit.

When my 3. dayes (or set time) was expired, I begann to feele some quickning comfort within me; the grave stone was rolled away, and I set at libertie, from these deep and darke retires; out I came with a most serene and chearfull countenance, and (as one inspired with a supernaturall life) sprang up farr above my earthly center, into a most heavenly and divine enjoyment: Wrapt up in the embraces of such pure love and peace, as that I knew not oft times, where I were in or out of this fading forme.

Here I saw heaven opened upon me and the new Ierusalem (in its divine brightnes and corruscant beauty) greeting my Soule by its humble and gentle descensions:

Now I certainly enjoyed that substance, which all this while I had groped after in the shadow.

My water was turned into wine-form, into power; and all my former enjoyments being nothing in appearnce to that glory which now rested on my spirit.

Time would faile to tell, what joy unspeakable, peace unconceiveable; what soul ravishing delights, and most divinely infatuating pleasures my soul was here possest with.

I could cast my eye no where, but that presence of love presented it selfe to me, whose beatificall vision, oftimes dazeled me into a sweet astonishment:

In a word, I can give you no perfect account of that glory which then covered me; the lisps and slipps of my tongue will but render that imperfect, whose pure perfection surmounts the reach of the most strenuous and high flown expression.

I appeared to my selfe as one confounded into the abyst of eternitie, nonentitized into the being of beings; my soule split, and empited into the fountaine and ocean of divine fulness: expired into the aspires of pure life:

*Viz: the carnal self.

In breife the Lord so much appeared that* I was little or nothing seene; but walked at an orderly distance from my self, treading and tripping over the pleasant mountaines of the Heavenly land, where I walked with the Lord and was not:

I shall be esteemed a foole, by the wise world, thorough an over much boasting: otherwise I could tell you how I have been exalted into the bosome of the eternall Allmightines, where I have seene and heard,

*As to the weakness of many.

things unlawful, (I say* unlawful) to be uttered amongst men; but I shall at present spare my self the labour, and prevent the worlds inconsiderate censure.

The proud and imperious Nature of flesh, would willingly claim a share in this glorious work, for which cause happened a suddain, certain, terrible, dreadfull revolution, a most strange vicissitude.

God sent a Thorn immediately; hid himself from me by a sudden departure, and gives a speedy Commission to a Messenger of Satan to assault me.

*Note wel what I say, that was reserved pure in the life of Christ, while the flesh acted its part.

The Lord being thus withdrawn, & having carried away (in the bundle of his Treasures) the heart and life of that *new seed in me, there now remained nought behind but the man of sinne, who (for his pride) being wounded with the thorn of Divine vengeance, began by degrees to act its part.

This Thorn, I say was in the flesh (or fleshly principle) the spirit (or new man) that was preserved still in the heart of eternal love, and became a life occult, hid with Christ in God.

Angry flesh being struck at heart with the piercing dart of vengeance, begins to swell, and contracting all the evil humors of the body of death into one lump, to grapple with this throne of wrath, at last violently breaks out, and lets forth the very heart and coar of its pride and enmity.

The rankor and venom of this subtil serpent, now discovers it self, and being sore sick with a cup of pure wrath, disgorges its foul stomack upon the very face, and appearance of Truth.

I was now sent into a strange land, and made to eat unclean things in *Assyria*; walked in unknown paths and became a mad man, a fool amongst men.

Thus tumbling in my own Vomit, I became a derision to all, and even loathed by those by whom I had been beloved: being made drunk with a Cup of vengeance, every one begins to cast a squint eye towards me.

O the deep drunken bewitching, besotting draughts of the wine of astonishment that hath been forced upon me.

Well, my folly being discovered and the bowels of corrupt flesh being let out, I la[y] as a spectacle of scorn and contempt to every eye; yea my mothers children were angry with me, and even those were apt to censure me for a firebrand of hell, and hypocrite, a cast away, into whose hands when the Cup of the Lord shall come, they may appear as bad, if not worse then my self.

But most true it is, he that slippeth with his feet, is as a Lamp despised in the heart of him that is at ease.

Certainly if the Lord would but let loose the reins of mens hearts, they should soon discover as bad, or worse in themselves, as they hate and despise in others.

The time of many is now at hand; yea, it is come upon them, wherein the baseness and rottenness of their hearts are discovered; they walk with their insides outwards, and shew their nakedness and shame.

They are turned and tossed as a ball in a large countrey: reel, stagger, stumble and fall with the desperate intoxicating draufhts of wrath and madness: tumble up and down in their own filthiness and beastiality; and are become signs and wonders amongst men: yea, those that have been Rivals to the chiefest and most eminent in knowledge and enjoyment, have been puld down from the Throne, and set as mirrors of amazement in the world: Judged with a witnes both by God and man: judged in themselves, the damnation of whose flesh sleepeth not: Judged, censured, stripped, persecuted, imprisoned by others.

The hand of the Lord meets them continually, and the world knows not, considers not, their most heavy and sad pressures.

O God, that men could a little consider the several disposings of the eternal wisdom!

I would gladly offer one silent whisper in the ears of the world, and leave it to the wise, and ponderous judgement of every Christian,

Hark then—

Think you that those eighteen upon whom the Tower of *Siloam* fell were greater sinners then others? I tel you, nay—

Are their impieties on their foreheads? and are not yours in your hearts? is there not the same spring of enmity, root of bitterness, den of Darkness, and spawn of folly and madness in you as in them.

What if the Lord should tear off your large Phylacteries of religion and righteousness, and instead thereof stamp the foul image of that hidden enormity, which harbors secretly in your breast.

What if God should uncloke you, and strip you of your lovely garbes of pretended holiness, and should let that appear which is hidden under this pleasing vesture?

Consider, is there not in the best of you a body of death?

Is not the root of rebellion planted in your natures?

Is there not also a time for this wicked one to be revealed?

Do you think that God will not one time or other, one way or another discover and judge that flesh, which now seems to sleep securely under the specious pretences of righteousness.

You little think, and less know, how soon the cup of fury may be put into your hands: my self, with many others have been made stark drunk with that wine of wrath, the dregs whereof (for ought I know) may fall to your share suddenly.

I speak not this either to extenuate my own evil, or to cast approbries in the face of those who have (to the utmost) censured me; but rather to mittigate the severity of peoples spirits, and to give a by-hint of that doom and judgement, that is at hand upon the world.

For my own part, I do most ingeniously and candidly confess, that the worst of men cannot out-vie my iniquity. Hell it self cannot hatch that mischiefe, which my heart hath not been a receptable to imbrace; and if ever a proud Pharisee in the world dare stept up and plead his own innocency, let him cast the first stone at me: If every man be found guilty and there is none that doth good, why should we so unseemingly envy, and not rather pitty (and lament over) each others miseries.

But to return: being thus clouded from the presence of the Lord, I was violently posted through most dark paths, where I ever and anon stumbled and fell into the snare of open error and profaneness, led and hurried, (by what power let the wise judg) in a princple of mad Zeal, to tear and rend the very appearances of God, which I had formerly cherished in my brest.

Delighting my self in nothing but in that which rendred me most vile and ugly in the sight of all men, and glorying in nought, but my own shame.

I could not have imagined that such deadly poyson had lodged within me, had not the dreadful piercing lance of vengance, let it out before my face, and made it palpably manifest to all men.

I was indeed full sick of wrath, a vial of wrath was given me to drink; the heavenly pleasure would not excuse me a drop of it; which no sooner had flesh received, but it burst in sunder, polluted and defiled my wayes and actions, with its filthy poysonous nature;

Well——drink I must, but mark the riddle.

'Twas given me, that I might drink, I drank, that I might stumble, I stumbled, that I might fall: I fell, and through my fall was made happy.

It is strange to think, how the hidden and secret presence of God in me, did silently rejoyce while flesh was thus manifested;

I had a sweet rest and refuge in the Lord, even while my flesh was frying and scorching in the flames of ireful fury. *Spiritual I, or the new man*

I was ark'd up in the eternal bosome, while the flesh was tumbling in the foaming surges of its own vanity:

And although the beast ascended out of the bottomless pit, and cast out a flood of envy against me, yet I was preserved in the Lord from its insulting fury: and this I know is a riddle to many, which none but the true Nazarite can expound; and til he is pleased to unfold it, it pleases *Jesus Christ.* me it should lie dark.

But to conclude——

Thus have I been forc't into the strange paths of obscurity, driven up and down in a tempestuous storm of wrath, and split upon the rocks of dreadful astonishment; All the waves and billows of the Almighty have gone over me.

I am now at rest in the silent deeps of eternity, sunk into the abysse of silence, and (having shot this perilous gulf) am safely arrived into the bosome of love, the land of rest.

I sometimes hear from the world, which I have now forsaken; I see its Diurnals are fraught with the tydings of the same clamor, strife, and contention, which abounded in it when I left it; I give it the hearing, and that's all.

I meddle with none of them; though they are daily censuring me at their pleasure.

My lovely silence contributes to large a parcel of Peace to me, as that I would gladly be at Peace with all men: but yet such is the restless fury of the disturbed world, that it will not upon any terms enter into a league of concord with me.

I cannot inveigh against any form, party, or religious interest: it becomes not my sweet silence, to bawl and brawl with the unquiet spirits of men, who are therfore swoln with madness; and frenzy against me, because they cannot by their bitter emulation, either disturb the peace and rest of my spirit, or provoke me to a contest with them, upon such poor base and beggerly terms.

I see there is nought that can satisfie under the Sun.

And certainly were men possessed of that true enjoyment which they pretend to, they would be better satisfied, and more at peace in their spirits.

My great desire (and that wherein I most delight) is to see and say nothing.

My mind is wholly bent to contemplate that.

I have run round the world of variety, and am now centered in eternity; that is the womb out of which I was taken, and to which my desires are now reduced.

There is nothing in the world of so great amplitude, as to comprehend or contain my spirit within its measurable orb; something that is more durable, then any thing that is extant in the world, is that which my souls press after.

And in the interim I find my self mostly comprehended, and best satisfied in my still and silent reserves.

I am, or would bee, very little, or nothing in shew, yet I am, indeed, both what I would be, or may desire to be.

I am drawne, from off the stage out outward appearances, on which (of late) I have acted a most sad and Tragicall part: I am bound in the close Galleries with my beloved, where (under the sweet verge of his Love and the shadow of his wing) I am wooed to refresh my selfe with most mellifluous delights.

I am as the Lords Lillie amongst Thornes; I stand in a very fertile soyl: though it be a valley, yet its both fat, rich, and pleasant.

I cannot envy the Thornes that are about me, neither can they hurt mee: I grow quietly by them, stand peaceably amongst them, and they are made (against their wills) a defensive hedge about me.

In summ,

While I view with a serious inspection the state of things about me; I clearly perceive how every thing prides it self in a momentary state; when (alasse!) after it hath shewed it self, it suddenly is swallowed up by that being whence it first came.

Everything beares a constant and greedy motion towards the center; and when once we are wearied in the prolixity of variety, wee revolve into silence, where we are as if we had never been.

Every one stands up, *Vi & armis*, to plead the prerogative of his own interest; the World is so filled with Verbosity, that I am gladly constrained into silence, till I have time and opportunity to offer my minde amongst them.

I see partly what the end will be, but I must not declare, neither will the world hear it.

I have stept out of my silent Mansions, to offer these few words to the Vulgar view: how hardly I was perswaded to it, my own heart can evidence, and many in my behalf can testifie: some engagements urged me to it, more then any desire of mine to become publick.

I am quite a weary of popular applause, and I little value a vulgar censure; the benefit of the one, cannot at all affect me, nor the prejudice of the other much molest me:

I enjoy greater treasures in my happy silence, then all their creulty can make me capable of the want of.

Tis true I have lost a good name, and honorable esteem in the world.

I have also another name, which is a new one, which none can read, but he that hath it; non can blast with the least blot of infamy.

I can cheerfully bear the indignation of the Lord, for I have sinned:

It is not for me to reply against the dealings of the Eternal Wisdome: it is rather good for mee to bear the yoke in my youth, with a Christian silence and gravity.

I am made willing to give my *cheek to the smiter, to sit alone, (keeping silence) and put my mouth in the dust: any thing with the Lord, it is to mee very acceptable; nothing (without God) dares approach my quiet and still Mansions.

*In any Christian contest.

In a word: I am both to doe and to suffer all things thorow an Eternall Almightinesse: And resolved I am to gaine a conquest over the World, by prostrating my self a subject to their weakness.

I must submit to them, that I may raign over them; and even then I trample them underneath my feet, when I am most subdued to their will and pleasure.

Well——to draw neer to my chamber, (for it's bad standing without doors, while a storm is impending) I am to this day set upon the account of a blasphemer, a seducer: what not.

I will not say but I have given some former ground of suspition, both by my unwary walking, and heedless expressions.

Somewhat I have formerly vented in certain papers, which the weak stomacks of many can hardly digest: and truely I could heartily wish, that some expressions had been better pondered; and not so untimely exposed to a publick view: though I also beleeve, that if they were well chewed (and not so suddenly swallowed without relishing the nature of them) they would be better digested then they are.

Especially the book intituled divinity anatomized.

'Tis a vanity and sore travail, for a man to unbosom his life in the face of a confused multitide; and to offer it up to the rude censure of the (no less mercylesse then) ignorant world.

I clearly see that the understandings of men (for the most part) are too gross and corpulent, to turn and winde in the nice, and narrow criticismes of truth; their spirits too dull and plumbous[1] to mount above their wonted notorious and thread bare principles.

Whatsoever stands out of their Sphear, or bears, no proximity to their commonly received maximes; must presently be deemed as blasphemy, and sentenced to the infernal lake, as most odious and abominable.

That which men call truth today, they proclaim error to morrow and that which now is adjudged and condemned as error, anon is embraced and extolled as truth. That man certainly is not otherwise, that will regard the uncertain censures of men.

Truely for my part, as I sit still and behold how the over-busie world is acted; so I can quietly let them alone, to roul in their confused labyrinth: but because in many things I have offended; and the froward spirits of men are not easily courted to a pardon: I have here thought meet, to cite a small parcel of the most crying errors of the times; and (before I withdraw into my sweet and safe retires) spend a little time in sweeping them from my door: that so the evil of error, may not lie in the porch, to disquiet my blessed rest, and disturb the sweet slumbers of my silent mansions. Which done, I shall then as well resolvedly, as quietly bid adeue to the wretched world: and wrap my self up in my mantle of silence, where I shall refresh my defessed² spirit with the pure naps of divine pleasure, while the beloved is pleased to awaken me into a more active state.

Briefly then in one word.

I shall linck the most capital errors now extant, in one chain; and expulse them by a free vote, from having any future commerce with me, or claiming the least propinquity to my reformed jugement.

A sincere Abdication of cer-
tain Tenents, either for-
merly vented by, or now charged upon the
Author.

I am daily assured as one that holds these horrid opinions. *Viz.* That there is no Good; no Devil; no Heaven; no Hell; as one that denies the Scripture, and the blessed Trinity of the God-head; that saith there is no Sin; or otherwise that God is the author of Sin; these (among others of less consequence) are chiefly alledged against me: to all which I reply, as followeth——.

And first, of God.

Ps. 14, 1.

The fool hath said in his heart, there is no God. 'Tis the greatest folly and madness in the world to assert or give credit to it.

The wise man, whose eyes are in his head, cannot harbor such a motion in his heart.

Act. 17, 25, 26, 27, 28

I wholly banish such conceits from my minde; and on the contrary assert,

That God is that pure and perfect being in whom we all are, move and live; that secret blood, breath, & life, that silently courseth through the hidden veins and close arteries of the whole creation.

Everything both visible and invisible is fraught with his presence, & brim'd up with the plentiful distils of a divine life: he is both all and in all, he truly is, and there is nothing besides him that derives not power from him.

Col. 1, 16, 17.
Isa, 45.8.
Ps. 65.8, 9.10.,
&c.
Col. 3, 11
Isa. 54, 16

He hath but a weak eye, that sees not the sparkling beams of eternity, darting out their refulgent beauty in and through variety.

What madman or fool will then deny a divine and eternal being?

Where can we go, what can we do without him? heaven, hel, earth, sea, sun, moon, stars, al that you see, all that you possess, is sweetly replenished with the glory of this pure majesty: every thing receives from him, and gives up to him.

Ps. 19.1, 2, 3, 4.
If I descend into
Hell, thou art
there,

More might be said but I hope this is sufficient to inform any reasonable man, that I wholly adjure this conceit, or rather deceit of the world.

Now to the next.

Of the Divell.

The Divel is understood variously amongst men, either grosly, or corpulently by some, or more subtilly and mistically by others.

I am not now either to advance my own, or to fly in the face of any mans judgement. I am one under censure; it becomes not me to be over-busie in judging others, till I have cleared my self.

They say, I hold no Divel——

Truly if any thing ever was vented by me, that is infected with the least tang or tincture of such a principle; I shall heartily deplore my own weakness in it, and shall be ready to disown it, as the bastard brat of a vain and empty notion.

And on the contrary doe affirm.

That the Divel, *who was once an Angel of light, yet not keeping his first state, became a Denne, and receptacle of darkness; reserved in chains from the presence of the Lord til the great day.

*A true history
and pure mistery
Ep. Jude: v. 6,
Pet. 2.2; 4. 2.

He is that spirit or Mystery of Iniquity, which continually envies God in his pure ways and workings.

Thes, 2. v. 3. 4.
7. 8. Isa. ch. 19.

That dark Angel, or Messenger employed by the Almighty, to effect the purposes of his wrath and vengeance.

ve. 9. Job. I. 12.
2. cor. 1. 2. 7.
Ep. 2. 2.

The Prince of the powers of the air; an airy fashionist,[3] that can assume any form: That can form*, conform, reform, and deform at his pleasure: one that chiefly rules in the hearts of the children of disobedience.

2. Thes. 2[.] 9.

*Transform him
self into an Angel
of light.

Let the wise judge, and the righteous, gently smite me, if I deserve censure in what I have spoken.

I proceed——

Of Heaven.

Heaven is the center of the souls bliss and happiness.

Phil. 3. 20.

I can in no wise deny it, because my conversation is in it.

If there be no heaven, wheres ou[r] present enjoyment? Or what shal become of that future happiness which we all expect?

1. Cor. 15. 19.
Rev. 14. 13.

Heaven is the Christians rest, his divine Sabboth, where he keeps holy day to the Lord.

Did I ever insinuate a deniall of heaven? certainly it was because the darkness of hel covered my understanding.

John 17. 24.

To live with, and in God, to be raised up into the nature and life of Christ out of his somnolencie of flesh, is to live in the heavenly place;

Eph. 2. 6.

this we enjoy partly here, most fully hereafter.

Of Hell.

That there is no Hell, I in no wise can imagine, but contrary wise say,——

*The wicked shall be turned into hel, and all the Nations that forget God. Mat. 24, 51. Tophet is prepared.

That Hell is the appoynted portion of the * sinner, where in sinfull man is for ever to be tormented from the presence of the Lord: the inhabitants of whose dark mansions are ever weeping, wailing and gnashing of teeth.

Hell is a *Tophet of scorching displeasure; a fire kindled and maintained by the continued breath of the Almighty, whereby it becomes a dying life, or rather, a living death. The* breath or life of Eternity auguments and increases this death and misery, which death and hell hath a greedy Lake to receive it.

I hope malice it self will consent, that I am not guilty of this blasphemy.

I therefore proceed for my sweet invitations, to my silent feast, solemnize my devotions thitherward.

Of the Scripture.

Christ is the Eternall word of the Father, the saving, teaching, enlightening Oracle of heaven, to whom the Scriptures ascribe all honor and dignitie.

I do not remember that in any thing which I have written, or declared, I have given the captious world the least ground to render me guilty of denying the Scriptures.

Yet because I am charged with it through weakness and mistake in some, malice and impudence in others, *I* give this satisfactory hint.

I own the Scriptures as the inspirations of the Holy Ghost; to holy men of old: a history, or map of truth, wherein (if our learned Translators have not deceived us) is contained a true discovery of the dealings of God with his people in former times, and ages of the world: wherein the life of many a precious promise is lockt up. They are known to be the word of God to those in whom the spirit declares them; others do but call them, not knowing them to be so.

They bare Testimony to the great Oracle of Life and Salvation (Christ Jesus). They are the letter & sound of truth. The form (and but the form) of sound words where they are not corrupted with the false glosses of the learned. Joh. 5. 38. 39. 40
2 Tim. 1. 13.

I must embrace them, own them, honour them, yea, I cannot but delight in them because they bear the image and feature of that pure word which was from the beginning, and is so everlasting. Joh. 1. 1. 2.

Of sin, or God being the Author of sin.

The vulgar censure, is, a many headed ill favoured monster, it lookes many waies; it favourably entertains, and smoothly invites, and eagerly gapes after all reports whatsoever.

Some say I hold no sinn, and with the same mouth will be apt to conclude that I make God the author of sinn: Here must needs be a gross mistake on the one hand or other certainely.

I humbly acknowledg my over readiness to present some notions of this nature to a publique view: If any things that I have written, will claim relation to these, I here recede them, and leave them to the mercy, or rather judgement of those to whom their nakednesse and folly are palpably evident: and further say concerning sin, In Divinity anatomized.

That sin is that contagious leprosie, which hath Epidemically spread it self over the whole earth.

Neither the* righteous nor the wicked are free from it.

Sin is a transgression of the Law: unity was once the Law of man, he brake the Unity, run into the wilie intangles of devision and distance, and did plunge himself into the gulfe of sin, the abyss of misery. Ps. 14. 2, 3.
Rom. 3. 10.
Prov. 20. 9.
*The righteous sinneth seven times a day.

The Law or Command of Unity, was to knowe one, and only one (God.) Man will know more than one; know himself in a state of division; here creeps in sin, and brings down man from his uprightness, and a state of obliquity. Exod. 20 ver. 3.

Gen. 3, 5, 6.

Man, as man growing from the root of the first *Adam* (the Earthly fallen principle) is nothing else but a massie heap of sin, a cursed lump of foul impiety, and must certainly expect to receive the wages of iniquitie. 1 John, 1. 8. 10.

Sin makes every thing a curse and bitterness to us.

Were it not for this sin (or breach of the Law of Unity) all things would be sweetned with blessing, yea blest with a Divine sweetness.

1 Cor: 15, 56.

Death it self, the bitterest potion of sorrow, would be nectarized with a pleasant dulcitude, which (through sin) brings with it, (and bears in it) an unpleasing mordacity.

In fine, tis sin that corrups our judgements, stains our natures, burthens our spirits, and betrays our souls into the snares of endless, and easless Torment.

Again,

This being the lothsome nature of sin, who will dare to be so impudent as to affirm, That God is the Author of it? tis true, the Scripture in many places seem to countenance such a thing, if not wisely and soberly interpreted.

But it is not my work, as I said before, to condemn any, before I have cleared my selfe: it is enough for me to exonerat my spirit of that load which is laid upon me by a fair recession of the Error I stand charged with.

1 Ioh: I: 5. 6.
*He is of more
pure eyes than to
behold iniquitie.
Mat. 19: 17.

Let all therefore know, That I look upon God to be a single object of pure light, whose glorious nature cannot be touched with the least tincture of darkness; evill or sin may not, cannot* approach his perfectly pure presence.

He is good (and good it self) he doth good, nothing but good, al good: good is God, there's nothing good but himself.

Men, the best of men, things, the most excellent of things, they are all vanity & a lye; worse then vanity, vexation of spirit.

God, the Unity is good: all vertue, and true worth is bundled up in it. Contrary wise——The Divel, division, distance, sin, they are naught, start naught; evil, nothing but evil, continually evil.

The Divel is a lye, believe him not; sin is a lye; all that you see below besides God, it is a lie, froth, emptiness, winol and confusion.

Col. 3. II

God hath nothing to do with any thing that existeth not in himself, or is divided from himself: he is not the Author of division: he is all one is all variety: the divider is the Divel, God knows him not: the division is sin, God owns it not.

I say not then that God is the Author of sin.

Lastly, of the Tri-
nity

God is one simple, single, uncompounded glory: nothing lives in him or flows from him, but what is his pure individual self.

Unity is the Father, the Author and begetter of all things; or (if you will) the Grandmother in whose intrinsecal womb, variety lies occult, till time orderly brings it forth.

Ion. 14, 9.

Christ sayes of himself, I and the Father am one: and the Apostle saith, there are three that bare record in Heaven; the Father, the Word, and Spirit, and those three are one. Without controversie, great is the mystery. 1 Joh. 5. 7.

In the multiplicity or variety they are three, but in the unity or primary state, all one, but one.

The Father is not the Son, the Son is not the Spirit, as multiplied into form and distance; I may lawfully and must necessarily maintain three:——but then again trace them by their lineal discent into the womb of eternity, revolve to the center, and where is the difference?

The unity or Father in it self, is a massy heap of an undiscovered glory, which branches out it self into an orderly variety, and so admits of various names and titles: Father, Son, Spirit, three in name, but all one in nature.

Unity without variety, is like the * man in the Garden, solitarily slumbering in its owne profound retires; having nothing to delight in but it self. *Gen. 2. 21,

The Father will not therefore be without the Son, without the Spirit: It is not fit the Man should be alone. Gen. 2. 18.

But then again to contemplate variety without Unity, is to bee over-much expensive upon the weakness, and to set up the woman without the man, which are not indeed two, but one in Christ.

I love the Unity, as it orderly discovers it self in the Trinity: I prize the Trinity, as it beares correspondency with the Unity; Let the skilfull *Oedipus*[4] unfold this.

FINIS

Jacob Bauthumley

The Light and Dark sides of

GOD

Or a plain and brief

DISCOURSE,

OF

The light side { *God, Hea-ven and Angels* } The dark side { *Devill, Sin,* and *Hell.* }

As also of the Resurrection and Scripture.

All which are set forth in their Severall Natures and Beings, according to the spirituality of the Scripture.

Written by *Jacob Bauthumley.*

I thank thee O Father, Lord of Heaven and Earth, that thou hast hid these things from the wise and prudent, and hast revealed them to Babes, even so it is thy pleasure.

The spirituall man judgeth all things, and he himself is judged of none.

LONDON, Printed for *William Learner at the Black-more* in *Bishopsgate-streete.* 1650.

THE
EPISTLE
TO THE
READER.

I Have onely directed my discourse to thee, though I know the most unto whose hand it may come cannot read it; But that it will be a Barbarian to them, and they to It. However, if I be beside them; yet I am not beside my selfe. (If I be it is to God) The reason why I have not directed it to any particular man, or sort of men what ever: as is usuall in things of this nature, is, because I desire not any mans approbation of it, as knowing I am not subject to mans judgement: neither would I have any man to subject himself to mine: neither shall I be ashamed to own what I have writ for the present, or to cast it away for the future, if God shall lead me thereunto. I have cast up my accounts what all will amount unto, upon either of the former considerations, and so have sweet peace in my spirit, in my present thought; and apprehensions, leaving the issue of all to the wise disposing providence. All I desire is, that those to whom these few lines may come, would (if they can) be so charitable of me, as to conceive and judge, that I have not writ any thing with any spirit of opposition to any sort of men, under what forme of godlinesse soever, as knowing, that there is a sweet appearance of God in them All. And however my person, and parts be meane in the Worlds Eye, and so may cast an odium *upon the things that I hold forth; yet I shall runne the hazard in that kinde, and leave the Lord to gaine his own Honour and Glory in it; as seeing by sweet experience, it is one of his greatest designes in the World, to confound the high and mighty things thereof, by the most meane and contemptible; And so though men be not satisfied, yet herein I shall receive sweet content in my own spirit, that my worke shall either burne and consume, or else abide the fiery tryall of mens indignation; And as I shall wish no man to embrace it, or condemne me: So I shall neither thank them that do the one, or condemne them that do the other.*

For the subject matter of the Discourse, I must confesse they are things of that nature, that are not obvious to every capacity, and so lye obnoxious unto their censure; and when time was, I should have been as ready to have sat in Judgement against the Maintainer of such Principles; yet to me they are such as wherein the Mystery of godllynesse mainly consists, and so are not to be slighted.

And however, I do not looke that I, or any man else shall receive much by this, or any other Booke; which had almost perswaded me, to have been silent in this kind; yet was I inwardly enforced thereunto, to ease the burden that lay upon my spirit; which was one great motive to me, to act my part so publickly.

Besides, having converst with men under severall formes and administrations, not to speake of those of the inferiour sort, as Papists, Episcoparians[1] *and* Presbyterians; *But most that are got to the highest: as* Independents *and* Anabaptists, *commonly so called; and seriously viewing the carnall apprehention of things in themselves, and there mis-apprehention of the minde of God held forth by others, condemning them as Heriticall and Blasphemous, in whom the Mysteryes of the Kingdome are most clearly revealed, and they themselves placing Religion, and the Mystery of godlinesse in outward Ordinances, and administrations of which they are all but Shaddowes; Having a strong conceite of a Creature happynesse, and selfe injoyment; and so are acted to attaine to the End. In all these respects, I could not but gratifie them so farre, as to set forth what is held out by a certaine Generation of Men and Woemen in the World; That if it may be, there may be such a favourable opinion of us from them, that we neither deny there is a* GOD, Heaven or Hell, Resurrection *or* Scripture, *as the world is made to believe we do; And I thinke they are all as plainly, and briefly made out, as they themselves could desire.*

And further, I know by experience, that there are some with whom my spirit sweetly closed in the Unity thereof, and that travell with me in the same birth; yet are not able to bring forth their conceptions, for so much as many times, the Truth suffers by a weake delivery; and for their sakes have I held this Glasse before them, that so they may be the better able to describe themselves to others; and to help them to bring forth that out of their mouths, which perhaps may lye in the bottome of their hearts.

For these Reasons have I taken the boldnesse to set pen to Paper, though otherwise I was unwilling, desiring that, and no more of others then what I would do to them; which is, to let every man stand and fall to his own Master.

One thing I thought fit to premise, onely to satisfie any that shall be so weake, as to make it a matter of offence to them. In that I have not set downe the chapter and verse, of many places of Scripture, which I do hint upon all along the Discourse. To answer them, and so to salve up that pretended soare; I found things of such a Mysterious nature as they are, that while I was looking for them in the Letter of the Scripture, I was at a great losse, in the present delivery of my selfe, of those things which I found spiritually and secretly conveyed to me in the Spirit; and so rather than I would lose, or let passe what was spiritually discovered in me, I was willing to omit the outward viewing of them in a chapter or verse. Besides, there is nothing laide downe by me of Argument, or formall dispute, which might ingage me to an outward proofe of things, as men usually do in matters of controversie; and what is positively affirmed, there is punctually Scripture for. But my designe was mainly, to deliver my private Meditations, and apprehension of such things which are most carnally conceived of. I thought it not therefore necessary, to trouble my selfe or the Reader, with multiplicity of places of Scripture, to prove those things of which I had so reall and spirituall a Testimony of in my own spirit; and which I am confident, that the most spirituall man can set his seale unto. And yet I dare affirm to the most rigid spirit that workes in any man at this day against the things asserted, That there is not any thing positively affirmed; but I could with more ease prove the truth of them by divers Testimonies of Scripture and reason, then he could with any truth or Scripture oppose them; and any man that shall impartially weigh things, may see that there is nothing in the Treatise then the very Language, and correspondency of Scripture in the Letter of it: will easily speake, and sweetly comply with: in a spirituall sence. So much I thought good to premise by way of Preface to the Discourse: All that GOD aimes at in such things as are of this nature, is but to make out his owne Honour and Glory before men, and to gaine esteeme from them; And all I aime at, is, that we might resolve all the Comforts, Glory, and future felicity into GOD againe; and so to make GOD All, and the Creature nothing, and if in the Discourse, I shall detract or prevaricate from either of the Ends, I am much mistaken, and shall willingly confesse with that Prophet, O Lord thou hast deceived me, and I was deceived.

And so I leave the Discourse, and thee
together; and if you happyly agree, it
is all the fruite of my labour that I
expect to Reape; If not, I shall
willingly waite an opportunity, to make you
both Friends,

As I am to every man.

J.B.

THE
Light and dark sides
OF
GOD.

Concerning God.

God, what shall I say thou art, when thou canst not be named? what shall I speak of thee, when in speaking of thee, I speak nothing but contradiction? For if I say I see thee, it is nothing but thy seeing of thyselfe; for there is nothing in me capable of seeing thee but thyself: If I say I know thee, that is no other but the knowledge thy self; for I am rather known of thee, then know thee: If I say I love thee, it is nothing so, for there is nothing in me can love thee but thyself; and therefore thou dost but love thyself: My seeking of thee is no other but thy seeking of they selfe: My delighting enjoying thee, is no other but thy delighting in thy selfe, and enjoying of thy selfe after a most unconceivable manner.

If I say I prayse thee, blesse or magnifie thee; it is no other but thy praysing, blessing, and magnifying of thy self.

I say thou art infinite, but what that is I cannot tell, because I am finite. And therefore I am led to believe, that whatsoever thy Scripture or any man else speaks of thee, it is but thy meer condescention to speak to us in the language of men, and so we speak of thee to one another.

For this I know, that whatsoever the Scripture or any man else speakes what thou art, I know thou art not that, because no man can say what thou art. And therefore when the Scripture saith thou art a spirit: It is because a spirit is the highest thing or tearme that men can give or apprehend: For thou art beyond any expression, and therefore thou art pleased to cloathe thy self with such Titles and Expressions of spirit, love, mercy, power, strength, or whatsoever is amiable or high in esteeme among men, to honour thyself, and beget an high esteeme and lawfull respect of thyself from men.

And therefore whatsoever I speak or write of thee, it is from thy writing and speaking in me; for I really see, that thou dost not spe[a]k to men, but in men; because there is nothing in man capable of thy speaking or hearing, but thy self, onely this man declares outwardly what he hath heard and seen inwardly, and yet that outward Declaration is of God also; for thou being the life and substance of all Creatures, they speak and move, yea live in thee; and whatever any Creature is, it is that as it is in thee: And therefore thou art pleased to give thyself that Title, *I am*. This therefore I can say of thee, That thou onely art, and there is none beside thee: But what thou art I cannot tell. Onely this I see, that there is nothing hath a Being, but thy Being is in it, and it is thy Being in it that gives it a Being: and so I am ready to say with thy Servant: Lord whither shall I go from thy presence? For it is thy presence and Being, that is the subsistance and Being of all Creatures and things, and fills Heaven and Earth and all other places.

And therefore I cannot as I have carnally conceived, and as men generally do, that God hath his personall being, and presence in one place more then another, or that he hath a simple, pure, glorious, and intire being circumscribed or confined in a place above the Starres and Firmament, which the men of the World call Heaven: And that all Creatures here below, are the products of that Being, and had their Being of him, and yet distinct from him: But the spirit in me speakes otherwise, and saith, I must not ascend up to Heaven to fetch Christ thence, nor descend into the depth to fetch him from thence; for the Word is even in you, which Word is God, and God is the Word.

Nay, I see that God is in all Creatures, Man and Beast, Fish and Fowle, and every green thing, from the highest Cedar to the Ivey on the wall; and that God is the life and being of them all, and that God doth really dwell, and if you will personally; if he may admit so low an expression in them all, and hath his Being no where else out of the Creatures.

Further, I see that all the Beings in the World are but that our Being, and so he may well be said, to be every where as he is, and so I cannot exclude him from Man or Beast, or any other Creature: Every Creature and thing having that Being living in it, and there is no difference betwixt Man and Beast; but as Man carries a more lively Image of the divine Being then any other Creature: For I see the Power, Wisdom, and Glory of God in one, as well as another, onely in that Creature called Man, God appears more gloriously in then the rest.

And truly, I find by experience, the grand reason why I have, and many others do now use set times of prayer, and run to formall duties, and other outward and low services of God: the reason hath been, and is, because men look upon a God, as being without them and remote from them at a great distance, as if he were locally in Heaven, and sitting there onely, and would not let down any blessing or good things, but by such and such a way and meanes.

But Lord, how carnall was I thus to fancie thee? Nay I am confident, that there is never a man under the Sun that lookes upon God in such a forme; but must be a grosse Idolator, and fancie some corporall shape of him, though they may call it spiritual.

Did men see that that God was in them, and framing all their thoughts, and working all their works, and that he was with them in conditions: what carnall spirit would reach out to that by an outward way, which spiritually is in him, and which lie stands really possest of? and which divine wisdom sees the best, and that things can be no otherwise with him. I shall speak my own experience herein, that I have made God mutable as my self , and therefore as things and conditions have changed, I thought that God was angry or pleased, and to have faln a humbling my self; or otherwise in thankfulness, never looking or considering that God is one intire perfect and immutable Being, and that all things were according to the Councel of his own will, and did serve the designe of his own glory: but thought that my sins or holy walking did cause him to alter his purpose of good or evill to me.

But now I cannot looke upon any condition or action, but methinks there appears a sweet concurrance of the supreame will in it; nothing comes short of it, or goes beyond it, nor any man shall doe or be any thing, but what shall fall in a sweet compliance with it; It being the wombe wherein all things are conceived, and in which all creatures were formed and brought fourth.

Yea further, there is not the least Flower or Herbe in the Field but there is the Divine being by which it is, that which it is; and as that that departs out of it, so it comes to nothing, and so it is to day clothed by God, & to morow cast into the Oven: when God ceases to live in it then it comes to nothing, and so all the visible Creatures are lively resemblances of the Divine being. But if this be so, some may say: Then look how many Creatures there are in the world, there is so many Gods, and when they dye and perrish, then must God also die with them, which can be no lesse then blasphemy to affirm.

To which I answer, and it is apparent to me, that all the Creatures in the world; they are not so many distinct Beings, but they are but one intire Being, though they be distinguished in respect of their formes; yet their Being is but one and the same Being, made out in so many formes of flesh, as Men and Beast, Fish and Fowle, Trees and Herbes: For though these two last Trees and Herbes have not the life so sensibly or lively; yet it is certain there is a Life and Being in them, by which they grow to that maturity and perfection, that they become serviceable for the use of Man, as other Creatures are; and yet I must not exclude God from them; for as God is pleased to dwel in flesh, and to dwel with and in man, yet is he not flesh, nor doth the flesh partake of the divine Being. Onely this, God is pleased to live in flesh, and as the Scripture saith, he is made flesh; and he appeares in severall formes of flesh, in the forme of Man and Beast, and other Creatures, and when these have performed the designe and will of God, that then as the flesh of Man and other Creatures, came from the Earth, and are not capable of knowing God, or partaking of the divine nature, and God ceasing to live in them, and being gone out of them, that then they all shall return to their first principle of dust, and God shall as he did from all eternity, live in himself, before there was a World or Creatures: so he shall to all eternity live and enjoy himself in himself, in such a way as no man can utter: and so I see him yesterday, and to day, and the same for ever: The *Alpha* and the

Omega, the beginning and the end of all things.

Yea further, as God shall cease to live in flesh, and so all things shall come to nothing that are below him: Then shall he live in spirit, he will cease to live in the humane nature, and live in the divine, and so he is that eternall and everlasting life, in whom all the glory, beauty and excellency of Creatures are wrapt up; for as all things were let out of God: so shall they all give up their Being, life and happiness into God again; and so we may say truly, that God or the divine Being never dies; though the Clothing dissolve, and come to nothing, yet the inward man still lives; though the shadow dies, yet the soule or substance which is God, lives to all eternity. Further, to me it is cleare, that there is nothing that partakes of the divine nature, or is of God, but it is God. The reason is, because there are no distinctions in God, he Being one individed essence: however Man out of a simple ignorance, distinguish of his Will, and of his love, of his justice and mercy, of common guifts, and of spirituall, as they call them; yet I cannot see any such things in God, or that he is capable of any degrees of more or lesse, or that he loves one man more then another, or hates one man more then another. However the Scripture saith, *Jacob* have I loved, and *Esau* have I hated; it is but after the manner of men for I cannot see that there is love or hatred in God, or any such passions: that which admits of degrees is not perfect.

Indeed in respect of men, as they imagine God is angry and he is pleased, he threatens and he promises, he Commands and he punishes; but in God there is no such things, he being that *I Am*, which changes not; but all things are according to the Councel of his own will: And God loves the Being of all Creatures, yea, all men are alike to him, and have received lively impressions of the divine nature, though they be not so gloriously and purely manifested in some as in others, some live in the light side of God, and some in the dark side; But in respect of God, light and darkness are all one to him; for there is nothing contrary to God, but onely to our apprehension. And for the proud selfish Being which is the *Esau*, is contrary to the sincere and pure divine Being, which is the *Jacob*: But the being of both serve the designe of God as we shall in the sequell of the discourse shew. But to speak a little more of the present subject; I wonder how that Divinity came into the world, and which is still maintained and used by those that call them selves Divines; who doe still hould and teach others, that there are three persons in the God-head, and yet but one God.

Surely it is a mystery to mee; But I rather thinke it is a mystery of Iniquity, for I suppose a person cannot be without an essence, so that it plainly appeares there must be three essences in God, and yet these three must be but one; But I suppose the most of them have received so much new Light that they are ashamed of such a Tenent, there being nothing in Scripture or reason to countenance such a grosse and carnall conceit of God: But I shall not enter upon any thing controvertall: onely I shall give you what is made out in me, and I conceive no other what the Scripture holds out in the letter, and so it is true, that there are three that bear record in Heaven, and yet these three but one. He doth not speak three persons, but three, and that thus, as farre as I conceive: The Father is God from all eternity, who's Being was in himself, having all Beings wrapt up in himself; This God letting himself and his Being in severall formes of flesh is God the Son: For I do not apprehend that God was onely manifest in the flesh of Christ, or the man called Christ; but that he as really and substantially dwells in the flesh of other men and Creatures, as well as in the man Christ, though as the Scripture speaks, he was the most express Image, and that the fulnesse of the God-head dwelt bodily in him; that is, in respect of manifestation: but otherwise I conceive that God who cannot admit of degrees, can be said to dwell in him more than another, and I might shew that his Being in spirit, is much more glorious then his Being in flesh; the one being but a shadow and Type of the other.

But I forbear, because it may afford another discourse of it self, and returne to what we have in hand; and that is, that God the Sonne is God manifest in flesh. Now that we call Holy Ghost, is God living in Spirit, and all these are not three distinct Beings, onely one Being made out in three several tearmes. To make it a little plainer, the Scripture saith; *God is Love*; and yet it tells us of a threefold Love: The first is Gods Love to us, the second is our Love to God, the third is our Love to one another.

Now it is plaine, these are not three, but one: For by the same Love that God loves us, by the same Love we love him; we love him, because he loves us, and it is the same Love by which we love one another; and therefore the Apostle saith, '*He that loves not his brother, loves not God*: And so we have communion with God, when we have communion with one another: So that Gods Love to us, and our Love to him, and to one another; are not three loves but one: so in like manner: Love is the Father; this Love manifested in Flesh is the Sonne; this Love loving the loved, is the Holy Ghost, and these three are one.

The Father is God forming all things; the Son is God, who is formed and manifested in Flesh; the Holy Ghost is God, manifesting or revealing the manifested: thus the Father, Son and Holy Ghost, are not three persons, but one intire Being, made out in several expressions.

And thus I have done with this subject concerning God, being willing to loose my self in the thoughts of him, as knowing, that he cannot be known; and that all words, or expressions of Scripture or man come short of Him, and do but confound and darken the glory of that great Creator; who hath done all things according to reason, and is himself the reason and ground of all things; for in him they live, and move, and have their Being; and therefore to Him be the Glory for evermore.

Concerning Heaven.

Now for that which we call Heaven, I cannot conceive it any locall place, because God is not confined, or hath his Being or station in our setled compasse; and therefore I see that true which the Letter speakes, *The Kingdom of Heaven is within you*: and so I see Heaven to be there, where God displaies his own glory and excellency; For Heaven is nothing but God at large, or God making out himself in Spirit and Glory. And so I really see, that then men are in Heaven, or Heaven in men, when God appeares in his glorious and pure manifestations of himself, in Love and Grace, in Peace and rest in the Spirit; when God shews himself to be all the happiness, comfort and reward, and so this Heaven is not outward, or a place of any outward or carnall bodily happines as men dream of; but it consists in righteousness, joy & peace in the Holy Ghost; all which are spirituall and terminated in God alone. I do not, as I have carnally conceived, that when *Paul* was rapt up into the third Heaven, and heard and saw things unutterable, that he was bodily taken up, or heard God with an audible voice; No, but I rather conceive it some extraordinary appearance of God, filling the Spirit with glorious amazements and admirations of its own excellency. So that, when God doth gloriously appeare to the silencing of flesh, and overpowering the selfish Being in man, and fils the spirit with its own glory, then is God and his Heaven come in the spirit, and such an estate some may be & have bin sensible of, that they have so felt the over-powering of God in their spirits, that they could not tell whether they were in the body or out of the body: as was *Pauls* condition.

And this Heaven the Land of *Canaan* was a lively Type of, wherein God after he had by a strong hand, brought the Children of *Israel* from the bondage of *Egypt*, and through many dangers of the Wildernesse and red Sea, God at last brought them to a Land of rest, in which this is really made out to me; that it is the over-ruling power of God in us, that takes us from the *Egyptian* bondage of self and flesh, and through the Wildernesse and Sea; much toyling and tossing up and downe in selfe-Workes and hard duties, outward and carnall services; the Law still beating us to Workes of prayer, humiliation; making us to make Brick without Straw, and setting hard and cruell Task-masters over us.

But the truth is, as men fancy a high God though yet very carnally: so they fancy a high place for him above the Starrs, I know not where; & herein indeed God condescends to the weakenesse of men in the Scripture, to set himself and his glorious presence out to us, as if they were properly in one place more then another, when as we know, a Spirit is not any where confined, but the God of Spirits is in all and through you all. And so Heaven is his Throne & the Earth his Foot-stool; That is God is in low and dark appearances, as well as in the most glorious: God is the high and lofty one that inhabits eternity, and not any circumscribed place, and so he is in low Spirits.

And the truth is, where God is highest in the Spirit, he is so low in that Spirit, that they do not desire any glory out of himself; but are willing to be nothing that he may be all. It is very true that the Scripture saith, *We looke for new Heaven, and new Earth wherein dwells Righteousnesse*. And truly,

I find that where God dwells, and is come, and hath taken men up, and wrapt them up into the Spirit; there is a new Heaven and a new Earth, & all the Heaven I look ever to enjoy is to have my earthly and dark apprehensions of God to cease, and to live no other life then what Christ spiritually lives in me.

The Scripture speakes likewise of a Kingdom, and a City, and Mantions, and that Christ went to prepare a place for the Saints, all which are true in the Spirit; For when God raigns in the Spirit, he brings all into subjection under him, and so he is King and Kingdom himself; and Christ went to prepare and to make out himself in Spirit, and so he left the flesh to live in the Spirit, and his spirituall coming, was much more glorious then his carnall and visible presence with them. And the truth is, the one was but a pre[p]arative, and fore-runner of the other; so it is spiritually true, that he that was least in the kingdom of Heaven was greater then *John* the *Baptist*; where note that those carnall and outward observations of Baptisme, and other administrations that *John* was in, they were but the preparative & fore-runners of a more spirituall condition, the Kingdom of Heaven not consisting in them. And therefore it was reasoned, *Why do the Disciples of* John *Fast and Pray, Luke 9. and thy Disciples Fast not?* and Christ gives them the reason, so that we may say, through many tribulations we must enter into the Kingdom of Heaven: but when Gods power is destroying these enemies of our Peace, and bring us into that Land of rest, that spirituall *Canaan*, which we speak of, then do we cease from these labours. But truly, this I speake from experience, so long as men are under *Moses*, they cannot enjoy neither must they come into this Land.

And therefore, I do not wonder that the Scripture speaks, *Man shall seek to enter and not be able; and straight and narrow is the gate, and few there be that finde it* [Lu. 13. 23–4]. I would not speak to discourage any; but I really apprehend the greatest pretenders to Heaven scarce know what it is, or will ever enjoy it; but shall with *Moses* onely see it a farre off, God not being willing to do any great workes in their spirits: because of their unbelief; but what happyness and comfort they do enjoy, to whom God appeares thus spiritually in, none know but themselves. This is that heavenly *Jerusalem* spoken of in the *Hebrews*, into which the souls of just men made perfect are come into.

The text doth not say, we shall come to it hereafter; but that we are come unto it, and that we have full and actuall possession of it, and so saith the Apostle, *Our conversation is in Heaven*, which is nothing but the glorious appearance of God in our spirits, when of naturall we are made spirituall: we shall see the Scripture speaks of no other Heaven but what is spirituall, and not consisting of any corporall or bodily felicity, as men conceive God, being all the glory and happiness of the creature; and so he that believeth hath everlasting life within him, and abiding in him; because God there gloriously makes out himself to be the Life and happiness. To look for a carnall and sensible enjoyment of God, distinct from that pure and divine

Being of God, savours to me of a carnall spirit; because it sets up something beside God, when there is nothing that lives and is glorious to all eternity, but God. For as I said before, there is nothing in the creature capable of God; or to enjoy his glory, nor nothing is of God, but is God: because God cannot be devided, nor none can share with him in his Glory, he having not given any glory to any creature out of himself; but what ever the creature apprehends to be its own glory, it is truly and spiritually no other but Gods one Being and glory.

It was his presence, which is not to be understood of his carnall presence with them; but of his spirituall presence, which he promised to appear in them; and therefore the Baptisme of the Holy Ghost and fire, was the substance of which the water Baptisme was but a shadow; and so he that was least in the spiritual Kingdom, and had a spiritual enjoyment of him, was greater then he that was the greatest, and most strictest in the Observation of the outward Duties and Ordinances, that *John* was under, so that it is plain to me, that the spiritual presence of Christ, or God in the spirit, is the Kingdom of Heaven, into which whomsoever is entered, he ceases from the outward and formal use of outward Administrations and Ordinances, and so sits down spiritually in the Kingdom of the Father, and is as the Apostle saith, allready set down in the heavenly places; and when God thus spiritually appears in you, then you will be content with me, to sit down and enter with me into an eternall nothingness, and be willing to let God advance himself, glorifie himself unto all eternity, and so cast down your Crownes at his feet, in everlasting silence: Into which condition when you are brought, you shall not need to expect any other Heaven; for then shall you enter into that rest wherein you shall cease from that labour and toile of outward and formall duties: as seeing God to be that in you, which you expected in self.

If any shall say these things are true, but these conditions and this estate is reserved for another life: We cannot expect to be perfect here while we are in the flesh.

I answer, that it is true we shall not; that is, there is nothing of us that is capable of this spirituall enjoyment, and therefore we must know that our perfection lies not in any thing that the Creature is, but it lies in God, and in that respect, unless you will say God is not so perfect here as he will be; we are as perfect as ever we shall be, so that though this spirituall condition be not of us, yet it is in us, and what Heaven or Estate God will be in, when he ceases to live in the flesh, I think is as vain for us to imagine, as impossible to apprehend.

Yet if any man can tell me how he was before there was a World, I shall with as much ease tell him how he will be when the World ceases to be, and however men are so carnal, & women-like that they dream of a Heaven, wherein they shall sit one at the Right hand of God and another at the left, and hope to have much outward felicity and glory, when they have glorified bodies, as they imagine; yet for my part I look for no such condition, and I see nothing in the Scripture to strengthen me in such a conceit.

For however, it speakes of a City that hath twelve gates and streetes paved with Gold, and yet I suppose all do but point out the glorious condition that God will appear in upon Earth; and therefore I mind that there was a *Jerusalem*, that it is said came down from God out of Heaven: In which there was no Temple, nor needed any Sun or Moon; which as I apprehend, was but that there should be such glorious and spiritual dispensations and discoveries of God in the Saints; and that they should enjoy such a life as that they should not worship in any outward external way or forme. And should not need to be taught by men or meanes, or of any outward Administrations or Ordinances; But that the Lord God and the Lamb should be their light, and they should be immediately taught by him; and therefore it is said there was no Temple in it, the Lord and the Lamb, being the light, glory, Temple and all: which condition is glorious, and cannot but be Heaven to him that doth enjoy it, and into which I know some are brought, and have received the accomplishment of all those promises and Prophesies which are spoken of in Scripture, and have received that new name, which none know but they that have it.

And thus have I shewed you Heaven, as it appeares in my spirit, and for my part I see no otherwise of it, however men judge, I am willing to let fall any carnall apprehension of a visible or corporeal enjoyment of God, or any expectation of a happy condition out of God after this life and dayes are ended, being willing to resigne and give up to God what he is in me in flesh, that so God may be all, and advanced above all in the spirit. And for my part, I see the Lord so framing my spirit, that I am content to be nothing, that he may be all, though I must confess, when I think seriously of it, there is nothing so grievous to flesh and blood in me, as to think that all the glory and happiness that I expected to have had in a corporal and sensible enjoyment must be terminated in God onely.

This I am sure of, that if there be any such thing, I shall have my share among the rest, which for the present I think ridiculous to looke for; onely this, I wait what the Lord will do in my spirit for the present. And being sweetly refreshed in the spirituall Discovery of himself in me, which is to me *Heaven*.

Concerning the Angels.

For the Angels I see the world as much mistaken in them as in the former, for I really see that man lives in the Angelicall nature, and that Angels are also Spirituall and in man, and herein man is honoured in that God, tooke humane nature and not the Angelicall. For had he confined his own glory in himself, he had missed one of his opportunities of magnifying himself, and therefore he took the humane nature, and so was God manifest in flesh, as well as seen of Angels; and as the divine nature is in man, so is the Angelicall; and as the one acts, so doth the other; for may we not see the

Angels of God ascending and discending in man? Are not the motions of mans spirit here and there in a moment? cannot man ascend into the hights, and discend into the depths? Are not the motions of a mans spirit at one end of the World at one time, and at another end of it instantly again? Doth not God make his Angels spirits, and his Ministers a flame of fire. Is not every spirit of illumination? and spirituall discovery of God? an Angell of God to convey some light and influence to the Creature whence is it, that all those sweet and spiritual assistances and consolations are flowing in the spirit; but by the power and presence of these Angels? It is said the Devill left Christ, and Angels came and ministred to him, and comforted him. In which I really see every spirituall support and comfortable appearance of God, is an Angel of God. How do the Angels pitch their Tents about them that fear the Lord? which is no other, but that all providences and passages watch about them, and administer comfort unto them. I do not as I have conceived, that they are created spirituall substances distinct from God, and waiting upon God, as serving men about their Lord, to see what his pleasure is; and yet this I know, all accidents that are good or evill, crosse or pleasing, are of God, and are his Angels, and do his will. These are the Angels on which God rides in triumph, by which he plagues the World and doth great things in Heaven and Earth; and therefore I looke upon every glorious manifestation of the power and wisdom of God to be an Angell, when I read of Gods coming with thousands of his Angels. It refreshes my spirit to think that there will be times of more pure and spirituall glory manifested. Now there is here and there an Angel of spiritual discovery of God; then will the world be full of his glory, and all flesh shall see the salvation of God, I cannot conceive they have any fleshly forme or shape, though it is said, *Lot* received two Angels which is spiritually true, for there was something more then ordinary, of Gods mind discovered to him: And when I read of the Angel of the Lord smiting the Campe of the *Assyrians*, that there fell so many thousands in one night; I do not believe there was any visible appearance, but that there was an extraordinary appearance of Gods power which is called an Angell. And so whereever we read of Angels appearing to this or that Servant of God, I cannot look upon them otherwise then some more glorious appearance or manifestation of God, and his will and pleasure concerning things or persons. And whereas the Scripture speaks of good and bad Angels, I see onely this in them, that the one is pure discovery of God, the other the more impure & dark; for where as man had a glorious enjoyment of God, and lived in Gods light, when he left that & went to live in a self-being out of God; There were Angels, Hell, and his discoveries of God, became dark and confused, and so brought him into bondage; so that the dark and carnall knowing of God is the evill Angel, and the glorious and pure manifestation of God is the good Angel: So likewise the providences that fall out in the world, that tend to the comfort or well-being of Creatures, they are the good Angels, & the crosse providences & occurrences that do afflict and grieve a people or person, they are the evill Angells or Angels of wrath and displeasure, not that they are so indeed, but because the Creature doth misapprehend the mind of God in them; for all things, whether Angels good or evill, principalities, powers, life or death, things present, or to come, are for good to them that are called of God. When I read of *Michael* and his Angels, and the *Dragon* and his Angels fighting against one another; I see nothing there but the fleshly and dark apprehensions of God against the pure and spirituall: and as *Michael* overcame the *Dragon*; so the more pure and spiritual dispensations of God shall overpower the dark and carnall, and so those Angels of darkness shall be cast into their lake, and there be reserved to the great judgement day of the Lord within us, when he shall sit as a refiner in our spirits, then shall the chaffe be burnt up & consumed by the brightnes, and fire of these Angelicall appearances of God; & this was an Angel of God comforting me against all the aspersions of heresie & blasphemy, that the people of God lye under at this day; and so you see what I thinke of the Angels, and what they are.

And thus have I done with that which I call *The light side of God.* I come now to the dark, and shall begin with that first which is called Devill.

Concerning the Devill.

I see that which we call the Devill is also in man; and yet I cannot apprehend him to be a creature, as men generally do; For then I must give him a Being, and there is nothing hath a Being but God; (that is formally and properly) yet as men speake, though improperly, there is such a thing as we call Devill; which I conceive to be nothing but the fleshly Being; or, as men commonly speak, the corruption of nature; or, as the Scripture calls it, *the old Man*, and this also moves, and acts in all those things which we call sinfull. So that so far as a man lives in a sinfull being, so farre the Devill in him; and therefore when *Mary Magdelen* had 7 Devils cast out of her, it gives me to conceive, that every sin is a Devill and so far as a man is led aside of his own lusts, so far he is led by the Devill; and therefore he is called Satan, Tempter and Deceiver, with divers other expressions. And hence it is, that whatsoever is hatefull or hurtfull to man, we use to say, the Devill is in it: and so every thing that doth hinder or darken our spirituall comfort and peace, that is a Devill in us. God is Light, and in him there is no darkness; and it is as true, the Devill is darknesse, and in him there is no light at all: And so farre as [a]ny man is in that darknesse, so farre he is in the Devill, so much the nearer he comes to him: and therefore it is said, *You are of your Father the Devill, and his workes you do* [Joh. 8. 44]: God is the Way, Truth and Life, and the Devill is falsehood, his wayes tend to darknesse and end in death and destruction. This is the deciever that would perswade us of a happyness of our own, and a glory out of God; He is that Mystery of iniquity, that man of sinne whom the Lord is continually destroying, and for whose destruction God is man'd in our flesh; and as the Devill the deciever hath led us from God to live a life of our own: so God in us is reducing us againe to live in himself, and so the spirituall seed is breaking the head and power of the carnall; this Devill is the spirit of envy, malice, cruelty, ever seeking to devoure and rob us of that which is most precious to us. Men fear a Devill without them, and so fancy him to be terrible in their apprehensions, never considering that he is in them; and therefore it is said, *The Devil entered into Judas*, not but that he was in him before; but then was there a more then ordinary appearance of him, and so he is that *Judas* indeed, which is ever betraying the spirituall Christ into the hands of self and flesh, and is continually crucifying the Lord of life, and putting him to open shame, and vailing his glory under shadows, making men to take them for substances, and so is transforming himself into an Angell of light: and so makes men put light for darknesse, and darknesse for light: exalting himself, and perswading self and flesh to have high thoughts of himself: and seeking to put out all that spirituall light and glory, wherever it appeares in the spirits of men. So that, however men ascribe a Being and person, a Him to him; yet there is nothing so, neither would I call him any thing, but as it is the language of men to expresse ourselves to one another about that which wee call Devill.

And so I shall leave the Devill, and speak something of Sinne: because that is most like him, being of the nearest Kindred to him.

Concerning Sinne.

For Sin, I cannot tell how to call it any thing, because it is nothing; I cannot give it a name, because it is no substance or creature; It is rather Primitive then Positive, we call it and give it a Being, though indeed in it self it hath none. It is no act, for then it were visible; but Sin is inward and spirituall, as that is which we call Grace and Holinesse; it is therefore called spirituall wickednesse, it is rather the defect of Grace and a deficiency in the Creature, then any act as visible to the outward view.

Further, Sin as Sin admits of no degrees for that which we call a great sinne, is no more then that which we call the least; but because we would not be thought to lessen it while we speake of it, we shall give you our thoughts of it in the language of Scripture. And therefore we see, the Apostle describes it to our hands, where he saith, *We have all sinned, and are deprived of the Glory of God*. So hence I conclude, that Sinne is a coming short, or a deprivation of the Glory of God; and so farre as a man is short of that glory, or doth not live and act in that divine Being: so farre he sins, so farre as he is in darknesse, and hath his glory vailed in him: so far he is sinfull.

In brief, sin is a living out of the will of God; for God being the Supream will, and having ordered all things and persons to be in such and such a condition; this self and carnall Being wills something of its own below Gods

Will, and so prevaricates from that, and centers in his own will; and so sins. Hence it is, that Nations and perticular persons, are grieved and discontented with their condition, and set dayes & times a part, as if they could alter the Supreme Will; not considering, that the Supreme will must be subjected unto, and that they must receive evill from the hands of God as well as good; and not knowing, that all is in the ordering of the Supreme will, and so run to this and that outward and formall duty, and so are carnall and sinfull while they think they do God good service, and yet I do not condemn them in so doing; for to them it is their light, though they be truely and spiritually in darkness; and though men act in darknesse, yet God is there vailing his glory, and so they must needs sin; for sin is properly the dark side of God which is a meere privation of light.

Further, we must consider, that God gives not any Law or Rule out of himselfe, or beyond his own glory: And as himself and his own glory are the ultimate end of all actions, and the ground of them; and as they are spirituall & inward: so those spirituall and inward acts or motions that fall below, or tend to the crossing of this design of God, they are unlawfull: and yet, in some respect these also tend to the glory of God, and sin it self doth as well fall in compliance with the glory of God, as well as that which we call grace and goodnesse; for *sinne abounds that grace may abound much more.*

And however men speak of offending God by sin, and the Scripture speaks of provoking God to wrath by the sins of a people; yet indeed to me it is apparent, that God is no more provoked by sin to wrath, then he is allured to blessing by any holiness of a people or person: And therefore *Jeremiah* saith, *The Lords* hand is not shortned, that he cannot save, of his eares heavy that he cannot heare; but it is their sins that hide his face from them: In which I really see, that it is not as men generally take it, that sin causes God actually to withdraw himself, or to alter his purpose of good to the Creature; but the truth lies in this, that there is that people are as near and ready to be helpt and saved of God when they sin as when they do good. But onely this there is, that in the nature of sin, that guilt and condemnation to it, & that accusing power it is of in the Conscience, that men mis-apprehend and do misconceive the face or countenance of God to them, and sin it is, that is that vaile or covering over the face & glory of God, that hinders the shining of it in the spirit. For the Sun doth shine as clearly when the Cloudes interpose betwixt us and it, as when it is a clear day, onely it doth not so appear to us: and so it is with God, the sin is the Cloud that interposes betwixt God and us, though God be the same and all one to us when we sin, yet we do not so see it, so that it is not a peoples sinning or doing good that is any cause in God, of good or evill to the Creature; for what absurdity would follow if God should hide his face, and let out his love upon the Creatures sinning, or doing that which we call good: how mutable should we make God to be, whereas we know that all accidents and occurrences are the manifestations of that supream Will and Power which is immutable and unalterable, whether the Creature sin or do well:

And whereas some may say, then men may live as they list, because God is the same, and all tends to his glory, if we sin, or if we do well.

I answer them in the words of the Apostle: Men should not sin because grace abounds; but yet if they do sin, that shall turn to the prayse of God, as well as when they do wel. And so the wrath of man praises God as well as his love and meekness, and God glorified in the one as well as the other. And however this may seeme to countenance that God is the Authour of sin, and wills sin; yet to me it is plain, that there is nothing that hath a Being but God, and sin being a nullity, God cannot be the Author of it, and so falles not within the decree of God; for so far as God was in man, and made him, so far he is God; but it was the man, the self-being that found out many Inventions. And all things that God made were very good when he lookt upon them; But sinne God could not behold, because it was not.

Herein is God glorified in sinne, as contraries set together illustrate one another: and God is glorious and powerful in the destroying that fleshly Being, which is exalting itself against the divine. And therefore is God manifest in our flesh to destroy the workes of flesh in us; and he is plucking down those principalities and powers, and destroying that old man with his deceiveable lusts, and forming the new man which is himself, or the devine Being, and new man in us.

Further, I see that the reason why we cal some men wicked and some godly, is not any thing in the men; but as the divine Being appeares more gloriously in one then in another: so we say, the one is a Saint and godly, and the other is wicked and profane; and yet the one acts as he is carried forth by the Supreme power, and so doth the other: And if there be any difference it is not in respect of the creature, of what it is, or doth; for the same divine Being, is in the one as well as the other; but onely it doth not so manifest it self in the one as the other. And therefore, as I dare call no man good because there is none good but God: so I dare call no man wicked or ungodly, because it is God only that makes the difference, and who am I to judge another mans Servant?

And I see also that the same power that inables a man to do good, the same power prevents a man from evill. For neither the evill act or the good act are evill or good, as they are acts; and men can no more do evill then they can do good, as they call it: which may answer that common Objection that men make.

That if this be so, men may drink, swear, and be profane, and live as they list.

And I answer further, the sin lies not in these outward acts, for a man may do the self-same act, and yet not sin: that is, that a man drinks to excess, there is the sin, that a man drinks for necessity or delight, the same act and posture of body is put out in the one, as the other: And so I might instance in the rest, so that the sin is from within: The lust within, and an inward lusting after the Creature, beyond that end for which God hath designed it.

And further, this I affirm, that a man as man hath no more power or freedom of will to do evill then he hath to do good. I think *Joseph* had as many opportunities to commit folly as any man could have; and yet saith he; *How can I do this and sinne against God*? So that it was the power within which kept him, though questionlesse, he might have had a naturall inclination to have done the act as other men.

And I believe *Esau* had as much will and power as a man, to do his brother *Jacob* a mischief, and to take away his life; but when God once appeared to him, then instead of killing him he imbraces him & so might be instance in divers other examples. So that, hence I conclude, it is onely the powerfull presence of God in one man more then another, that one man acts not as vilely as another.

Again I apprehend further, that there is not two wills in God, as men generally teach and affirm; that is to say, an active will and a permissive will, and so a power to make a man to do good, and another kind of power to restraine a man from evill, and so men confound the power and will of God, when as indeed: they are not distinct in God; for Gods power and will are all one: his will is his power, and his power is his will: and by the self same act that he will things, by the selfe same act he doth things, and it is our weakenesse otherwise to apprehend; for God being one and intire, admitting of no distinction or division in himself, he admits of no variations, but all things are as that supreme will acts, and brings them forth; And I see according to the Councell of his will, they did no more that crucified Christ, then they that did imbrace him.

These things I write, not to countenance any unseemly act or evill in any man; And I know, God being purity it self, cannot behold uncleannesse, and his Spirit in me doth condemn it wherever I see it, and I cannot but reprove it where ever it is found; Neither can I so close in society or fellowship with those that are in darkness, or walk unbeseemingly not becoming the Gospel; and yet I know, that if the grace of God appeared in them, it would as well teach them, to deny ungodlinesse and worldly lusts: as to live righteously and soberly in the World: Onely, I desire to open the nature of that which we call sin, and to make it as spiritually vile as I can: For I see my self to have been mistaken, and I see others are in sin, as well as in that we call grace & goodnes; For as I have made the formall and outward performance of a Duty, the onely thing wherein grace and godliness did consist so: have I made the outward doing or not doing of an act to be the sin; But I really see, that neither the one or the other, as an act is either good or evill: But as godliness is a mystery and inward, and is within us: so is sin likewise a mystery and also within us; and therefore it is called, a mystery of iniquity, from whence proceeds murders, adulteries, and are they not from the lust within? The inward lust and acting, is the sin which is contrary or below God; the outward acting or putting forth of that inward lust, is the sin against man, and is below a man: and whether the thing or sinne be acted outwardly, or no, there is sin; And therefore, the spirituality of the Gospel is above the Letter, the Letter onely forbiding the outward act of adultery, but the spirituality forbids the very lust within; and therefore, he that looks on a woman with a secret and inward lust, hath committed the sin in the Spirit and heart: as if he had done the outward act, and is in Gods account an adulterer: And all the use I can make of the premises, duely considered, it rather aggravates the nature of sin, then extinuates or lessens it; for I can seriously reflect upon my own spirit, and see more sin within, then all the world can do without; I see that I have framed and fancied a God without me, and have given him an outward Worship while I have seem'd to be very spirituall, and so have been very far from that spirituall worship of him which is like himself, and consists onely in Spirit and Truth; for what a vaine thing is it to me for a man to put off his Hat, or kneele and show an outward reverence to an invisible God: and how carnall have I been, and men are in setting dayes and times a part to expresse an outward humiliation for an inward and spirituall sacrifice, whereas there is no humility but in the Spirit; and there is no spirituall exaltation of God; but when the Creature ceases from being, or doing any thing, and makes God All; whereas men think to get pardon and peace from God by a self-humiliation, prayers and duties and I know not what: and so give that to a duty and a prayer, which is the onely proper worke of God, who subdues our sinnes, and pardones them for his own Names sake.

And so I have done with that which we call sinne, which we call a privation of God, or the living below God; you see we have made it something and nothing, in respect of God it is nothing; for he knowes no defect, neither is he in darknesse: but is all glory and light.

Again, it is something in respect of the creature; because it is in darknesse and lives not in the light and glory of that God; and there is that in the Creature, which as a vaile covers and hides the glory of God, and so it is sinfull: and yet here is God in all this; for should the Creature share in the Deity, God would not be so glorious; and should the Deity partake of the Humanity, and be one with it, there would be no sin, and therefore is God manifest in flesh, but not to flesh; and therefore doth the Divine Nature and Being live in the Humane, but is not the Humane, nor is the Humane capable of any conjunction or union with the Divine; and therefore the Divine lives in it self, and the Humane or fleshly Being lives in it self; and as the fleshly Being is below the Divine: so men living in it are sinfull; and as that acts: so they act in, which is all at present I see of that we call Sinne.

Concerning Hell.

Having spoken of the Devill and Sin, Hell must needes follow; for no sooner did Man leave to live in the Divine Being, and so lived in himself; but he was turned out of *Paradise* to digg for his living, and to worke, labour and toyle, to maintaine a self-Being, and to procure a self-happinesse, and so presently he came to shame and misery; he eating of the forbidden fruite, which was his own holinesse, righteousnesse, all is cursed to him, and so the man is in Hell: so that our ceasing to live in God, and living in the self-Being, is the Hell; For that Angelicall life in us, being vailed and covered, we live in the Diabolicall; whence it is we are in Hell. As soone as man ceast to live in the light, but he would be knowing something, and doing something: so soone did he fall into a *Chaos*, and all was darknesse: and so that develish and self nature is in man, and he is reserved in chaines of darknesse till the judgement of the great day of Gods appearing in his Spirit, and till then he is in Hell, untill God Judge and burne up that flesh, and carnall knowing of him; and reduce him to his first Being, to live in God till then, he suffers the fire of Hel in himself so that the Hell in a mans selfe and the condemnation is, that a man is condemned of himself.

What adoe there is in the world to find Hell where it is, how many have puzled and beat their braines to find it out, as if it were a locall place? and therefore some because they would make it contrary to Heaven and as they fancie that the highest place, so they will be sure to make Hell the lowest, and therefore being as carnall in the one as the other, make it to be the lowest part of the Earth. Others, because they find a place speaking of the Devill, calling him the Prince of the Aire, they will make Hell in the Ayre I know not where. But as the Devill rules onely in Aierie and light spirits, so I look upon this to be a Aierie fancy: For as the Devill is, and hath his Throne and Seat in every man, so is his Hell; & truly for my part I think they cannot be separated, and therefore I conceive any man that is in bondage to his own lust; nay further he that is under the Law or in any formal or outward duty, & is so possessed with a spirit of bondage, that he must be so and so, do so and so, or else he must be damned, and in the doing of such and such things he shall be saved: this man is in Hell, and Hell in him, and needes no other Devill to torment him, but his own false and carnall apprehension of God; for as the spirituall appearance of God doth necessarily and formally make Heaven, and cause joy and peace in the spirit: So the dark and carnall conceit or knowledge of God must needes cause sorrow and lamentation, and makes Hell.

I do not much wonder at the carnall Papist, no more then at the carnall Protestant, the one fancying a carnall purgatory, the other a carnall Hell.

And I think the one gets as much money for frighting men with the one, and making them believe they can show them the way to avoid it, and bring them to Heaven, as the other doth in frighting them with purgatory, and making the poor people believe they can keep them from that. But I let that passe.

And however, the Scripture speaks of Hell, and expresses it by fire and brimstone, and the worme dying not, and many other expressions. It speakes as in other cases, after the manner of men, not that there is such visible and material formes of punishment: But that as fire and brimstone are the most fearful things to the nature of man; so doth the Scripture set out the miserable and fearfull Estate of a carnall condition, and what miseries and torments do accompany such an Estate. And what consequences have followed the outward man from being in such darkness, and what the absence of God hath caused in the spirit, the Scriptures and many daily examples do abundantly testifie: whose terrors and distractions in their spirits have been such as have been easeless and remediless, and made them willing to become their own Butchers, and all this hath been from a misapprehension and confused knowledge of God. The truth is, I shall speak from my own experience, so long as I was in bondage, to dayes, times, and set times, that I must pray so often, and do so much, frequent such Ordinances, so long I was in trouble and sorrow; for I really saw there was this and that failing, and miscarriage in every duty that I suffered torment in my spirit, for fear I should never attain my end, which was a carnall and sensible enjoyment of some happiness which I called Heaven, and when I was inlarged in this and that duty, I thought then all was well, and that I should go to Heaven: And so I was continually suffering the torment of Hell, and tossed up and down, being condemned of my self. And this is all the condemnation that I see is come into the World, that men love darkness rather then light, because their deeds are evill, That men live in love, the dark and fleshly Being, and not in the light, in the divine being; this is the condemnation not causally but formally: And this is that I found til God appeared spiritually, and shewed me that he was all the glory and happiness himself, and that flesh was nothing, and should enjoy nothing, and then I could not but cease from my former fleshly actings which caused nothing but fear and trouble, and saw God, or rather God made out himself in me joy and peace, and brought me into the glorious liberty of the Sons of God, whereas I was before in bondage to sin, law, an accusing Conscience which is Hell. And yet I cannot exclude God in all this, for if we descend into Hell he is there: He is in the dark, though we see it not as well as in the light that we see: He is in wrath and severity, and we are wisht to behold him in both; let there be never such confusions of spirit, never such terrors and Hell, let there be darkness and no light: yet there God is, there is some glimps of himself, in as much as there is a secret going out of the spirit towards God, and all the distractions the Creature lies under, is because it cannot enjoy the presence & love of God, & is there amidst all that darkness and raignes in the midst of his enemies, and so he descends into Hell, and returnes with a glorious tryumph, rising with abundance of joy and peace in the spirit: So that though the Earth be moved, and the great mountains which the Creature had made to it self, be tumbled up and down, and the Creature have no rest, but is easeless and restless, yet God is there as a Rock unshaken of any storme, but is sweetly refreshing and delighting himself with himself, and so enters into the strong mans house, and disarmes him, and bindes him hand and foote, and casts him into utter darkness.

And to summe up all, if there be any that think this is not Hell enough to be inwardly and spiritually tormented. Let them but consult with those that have been under spirituall desertions as they are called, and have cryed out as if their bones had been broken, and would have chosen death rather then life, and thought they could have indured many burnings to have been rid of such a condition.

And I think they will tell them there is no other or need be no other Hell, and all this comes from a dark and carnall knowledg, or rather ignorance of God, for certain it is, God demns none. But the condemnation is of a mans self, and in a mans self.

If any shall say, all this is nothing; I care not, if this be all the Hell, and that it lasts no longer then this life; But is there not a Hell hereafter, that is, the Hell to think of Eternity, and that the Creature shall be everlastingly tormented, and indure the wrath of God to all Eternity?

For answer hereunto, I must professe, I do not know of any such thing, nor do I conceive what should be thus tormented; for that which men call a soule, I had thought to have made it a particular of the present discourse; but I shall referr it to further consideration, onely to stay any mans appetite that desires my opinion of it, I shall onely give him this morsell to chew upon, and that is this.

I do wonder how any man can make it to be capable of any torment, when as it is well known, it came immediately from God, and is no other but of God, and if I may say further without offence, it is God; for that which is of God is God, because God cannot be divided. All men grant it is immortall, and came from God pure and undefiled: And how then it should be impure, I know not; for this I really see, that though it was infused into the body, yet I am sure it was not of the body, nor could the flesh be capable of such a thing as we call union with the spirit, and so the soule is in the body; but is not of the body or the body, but really distinct; and so it is in flesh but not flesh, and so it is God manifest in flesh: But not in union or conjunction with flesh, but hath a distinct and formall difference, both here and hereafter, the one returning to nothing, the other living to all Eternity.

And further, how this soule, as men speak of, should be impure and sinfull, I know not; for how flesh should defile a spirit I cannot Imagine, being that I am sure, and as every man will grant, That no effect can be produced beyond its cause; but every effect hath its rise and originall from its proper cause: And so hath God laid in nature the body proper to the seed, and to every seed its own body. And a man may as well gather Grapes of Thornes, and Figs of Thistles, as to conceive, it can be that a visible or fleshly substance can corrupt a spirituall and invisible substance: But then you will say, where is the sin all this while? you will say then, sin is nothing, or that there is no sin. To which I have partly answered in the foregoing Subject spoken of, which because it is so faln in my way, I shall speak a little further in answer to you.

First, I shall grant, and I think it is no lesse then blasphemy to affirm otherwise, that God is not the Authour of sin, or that any sin can be in him, he being light, and in him is no darkness at all, and so the soule being of him, it must needes be pure and holy, not admitting any mixture of flesh, or that which we call corrupted nature. And yet againe

Secondly, I cannot conceive there should be sin, untill God was pleased to let out himself in flesh: But for before he lived in himself, and so there could be no sin, there being nothing but God.

Thirdly, Inasmuch as this flesh is a vaile or covering, wherein this soule or divine Being lives: this God, soule, or divine nature, (call it what you will) the glory and beauty, the purity and excellency thereof being darkened and obscured, there is the sin: For whatever men conceive of things, this I really apprehend, That that which we call the soule, that is as men generally make it.

The understanding, reason, judgement, will, and affections are not positively or actually infected with sin; but onely are obscured, and cannot be so gloriously manifested, by reason of the flesh or fleshly Being: and so God tooke flesh upon him, and through the vaile that is the flesh, did destroy, and doth condemn sin in the flesh: So that whosoever prays or prophesies with a vaile or covering upon his head: Christ which is God in the Spirit, such a one dishonoureth his head, which is Christ, because he suffers something to come betwixt God and him. So that by this time, I suppose you see what I conceive of sin, and where it lies, and what I conceive of that we call soul, and of the body or fleshly part of man, wherein I have been forced to make a little digression, because things are mysterious.

And to come to the point in hand, concerning a Hell hereafter, what it should be, or what should be tormented in it, I do not as yet apprehend; for the soul came pure, and is of the essence of God, could not be corrupted, and the body not capable of any impressions of God, and returns to its first principle of earth: so that unlesse you will imagine a Hell in God, which you would account Blasphemy to speak: I cannot fancy or imagine any such Hell hereafter as men dreame off.

The truth is, there is nothing lives to all eternity but God: every thing below God perisheth and comes to nothing: and as all things had their subsistance and Being in God, before they were ever manifested in the world or Creatures: so in the end, whatsoever is of God, or God in the world at the end of it, they shall all be rapt up into God againe. And so as God from all eternity lived in himself and all things in him: so when he shall cease to live in flesh and creatures, he will then live in himself unto all eternity, and will gloriously triumph over Sin, Hell and death; and all Creatures shall give up their Power and Glory unto God backe againe, from whence it Originally came, and so God shall be All.

However, if any man can imagine, that there will be any dark appearance of God hereafter, or unto all eternity, then may he conclude a Hell; for as sin is the dark appearance of God: so is Hell an inseperable companion of it; but to imagine the one or the other hereafter, or to all eternity, would render me in my owne apprehension one of those whose property it is to believe every thing; but I know whom I have believed.

Thus have I done with that part of my discourse, which I call the dark side of God, which I divide into three parts which we call *Devill, Sin,* and *Hell*: In all which I have indeavoured to clear God, and to make the Devill and sin as vile as I can, but am far short of the one or the other, wanting words to express my self in either, onely what was upon my spirit thou hast in the Letter.

Concerning the Resurrection.

Now let us come to deliver our selves about that which we call Resurrection, and to express it as it is in me. I see it also to be spirituall and inward, and is also of that which is the inward man: For though I know the inward man which is God or the divine Being, admits of no degrees, either is more or lesse; but yet in as much as this God is more gloriously manifested at one time more then another in man.

Hence it is that we give this Title of resurrection of the Creature after this life is ended. But truly for my part, I am fully satisfied in my own spirit with those words of Christ, where he saith, *I am the Resurrection and the life*: and I see it fully made out in me, that Christ spiritually is that resurrection, which I thought should be of the creature. And I cannot tell what in the creature should rise or be capable of such glory and happinesse beside God, and so I see that which I did expect to enjoy hereafter onely proper and peculiar of God, for I really see that after God is manifest in flesh, and seen of Angels, preached in the world, and believed in, that then he shall after all this be received up into glory, and that flesh and bloud cannot inherit the Kingdome of God: and that nothing lives to all eternity, but pure Divine glory: I cannot conceive any other resurrection then of carnall to be made spirituall, and that is no other then the spirituall appearance of God: so that when I would find out what the resurrection is, I reflect upon my own spirit, and trace the goings of God there, and there I can find God rising from one degree of glory to another, and changing me into his image by his spirit: and so I see how he hath led me from one dispensation to another, and from one ordinance to another, till at last he appears so spiritually that he over-powers all flesh and formes which I admired in my carnall condition, and appears to be that temple, glory and light himselfe, which I had thought to have had in a sensible and carnall enjoyment hereafter, so that I am led to believe that there is no such outward felicity to be enjoyed in this resurrection: but that it is God arising in the spirit, and shining brighter and brighter, till the perfect day & making all the creature-apprehensions, and knowledge of God to cease, and this resurrection I clearly finde in my owne spirit, that the most glorious and inlarged parts and abilities in prayer, speaking, or otherwise, in which I have delighted, and no question but I did enjoy God in them, though in a darke and low estate: these I say, the glory and beauty of them are all withered and vanished before the bright and glorious appearances of God in the spirit; for the Son in me having delivered up his Kingdome, and those fleshly and formall manifestations, and outward bodily worships ceasing, God is all in all, so that I can neither in *Jerusalem*, or in the Mount, or in any outward form or duty worship God, knowing that he is only to be worshipped in spirit & truth, and that though God was with me in my former carnall and dark condition, and did lead me in it gently, yet all was but to raise up himselfe, and to be that spiritually in me in another way then that which I expected, and so of naturall he hath made me spirituall, which is the spirituall resurrection that we are speaking of.

And further I really see that the flesh of man, and of all other creatures differ not any thing in the nature of them indeed, in respect of the kind and manner, some flesh is of men, some of Beasts, and some of fishes: but as flesh none of them are capable of any more glory then one another, all being of the same mould, and comming to the same end, and though the spirit in them, or whatsoever is God in them, return to their originall, which is God, and so lives in him again, yet the fleshly part returns to dust from whence it came: and as the man dies, so dies the beast; as dies the wise man so dies the foole, one end is to them all as *Solomon* speaks: and whereas men imagine that there is a fleshly resurrection, and that the same body flesh and bones shall rise and remain a corporall and visible substance: how this should be I am sure they do not know themselves: for however men speak that the corporall body shall be made a spirituall, to me it is ridiculous, because the Scripture saith, *That which is borne of flesh is flesh* [John 3.6], and can remaine in no other capacity. And besides, I hope no man will deny, that a spirituall thing can be seen of a fleshly, or that an externall organ of the body can see an internall and invisible thing, the Apostle makes it plaine, that the things which are seen are temporall, and the things that are not seen are eternall. Now how it can stand or consist with reason or Scripture, Logick or Rhetorick, that men should hold and maintaine that men should visibly see one another in heaven as they call it, and know one another, and see their visible shape, as they lived in on the earth, & yet they maintaine on the other side this is a spirituall body: I cannot see if this be divinity, then I am not in the humanity; but indeed I am willing to give way to their weaknesse, because I have been as childish my selfe, only I cannot but take notice of the *Babell* and confusion that men are in, and yet thinke themselves the only Embassadours of peace, and as if all knowledge and spirituall learning were confined to them, but laying my hand gently on their fore, I let them passe, and go on to that in hand.

And whereas the Scripture speaks of a spirituall body, I conceived that there is a spirituall body, and that this body must be raised: which spirituall body I apprehend to be nothing but the divine Being, or God in spirit: termed a Body for these two reasons as I conceive: First, because God is the body and substance of all things, and so it is said, that this God dwelt bodily or substantially in the man Christ, he being that person in whose flesh God did more gloriously appear then in any other, so he was the most expresse Image of his Fathers person, and in this respect God may be termed a spirituall Body, though for my part I dare not imagine him to have either person or body. Secondly, God may be stiled a spirituall body; because this body or divine Being is, and hath its Being in many Members. And so God is stiled the head of the body, and Christ is the head of the Church, which is his body, wherein I really apprehend that all the apperances of God in the Saints as they are called, & all the manifestation of God in flesh, or in any fleshly or outward dispensation or form; they are but the Carkes and shadow of God who is the body or substance of them all, and all these dying and vanishing as they shall: God shall onely live and raise himself a spiritual body, and therein live to all eternity; so that it is spiritually true, that the body which is fleshly shall perish, and the spirituall body shall be raised, as we shall have occasion in the sequel of the discourse to make out; but because men are still poring upon a Scripture without them to prove a carnall Resurrection, and will believe nothing but what they think the Scripture speaks in the letter, though indeed they erre, not knowing it or the power of God: I shall a little condescend to their weakness in this kind: though for my part, if there were not a letter in all the Bible to strengthen me in my opinion of the Resurrection I should not much care, nor need I the testimony of it as to my self; for I have a surer word within, to which I take heed: yet I say for other mens sakes, I shall take the most principall places of Scripture that men look upon, which speak of the Resurrection, and in the spiritual discoveries of them, if there be any thing to strengthen them in their opinion, I shall and must give way.

And we shall begin with that which is the prime piller of their Faith, and that is the 1. of the *Corinths* 15. from the beginning to the end of it. It being the whole subject of the discourse therein to treat of the Resurrection: The drift of the Apostle is to prove the spirituall Resurrection of Christ to be as sure and certain as his fleshly; and by the same Argument that he proves the one, by the same he also proves the other, in a spiritual sense. And the comparison lies not betwixt the fleshly rising of Christ, and the fleshly rising of men, as most men imagine; but between the fleshly rising of Christ in the humanity, and his spiritual rising in the divinity, and so all along, you shall see the comparison holds betwixt the naturall and the spirituall, and not betwixt the naturall and the naturall. And that we may see plainly it appears in the 47. verse, *The first man is of the Earth earthly; the second man is from Heaven who is the Lord*: so that we see, he compares the outward earthly man, and the Lord from Heaven which is the spiritual, and shewes evidently, that it is not the earthly man that is raised, but the spirituall, and so Christ after the flesh was but of the earthly man, and so must be destroyed and subdued, as wel as other things and formes, which did accompany that earthly being, and as the one vanished out of sight before the Apostles; so must the other, and that this may not seeme strange to any man, that the flesh of Christ must be destroyed, as well as other things. It is plain in the 28. verse.

So that it is apparent, that the Sonne of man being of the first *Adam* after the flesh, must as well be subdued and perish with the fleshly forms and administrations that did accompany him: For certain I am, that as he was God or the divine being in him, he could not be subdued, so that it is very clear, that it was the fleshly appearance that must needes come to nothing as well as the fleshly forme in other Creatures; and so Christ did cease to live in the flesh, that he might more transcendently live in the spirit, and so he laid down his humanity to live in the Divinity: and so it is true what the Apostle saith in the 20. *v.* That as Christ is risen from the dead, and is become the first fruits of them that sleep and are dead in him, so such as are dead in him shall surely rise. That is, they shall as surely rise to a spirituall condition as they have been spiritually dead in him. And so he goes on in the 22. verse. As in *Adam* all dyed, so in Christ shall all be made alive: Here is still the comparison betwixt the natural and the spirituall: that is, as sure as the fleshly *Adam*, and outward visible forme dies, so it is as certain, they that are in Christ or the spiritual man, shall be made alive and quickened, and God shall rise and appear in more power and glory in that life of the spirit then ever he did in the fleshly forme or shape. But to go on, The first fruits is Christ, and then they that are Christs at his coming: which is thus, that as Christ herein was the first fruits of them that did live in the spirit; as he saith, a little while, and you shall see me, and a little while, and you shall not see me, because I go to the Father: that is, he was to lay down the flesh to live in the divine and spiritual life, in which he appeared after his ascension, and so was as good as his word, and did come in spirit; so it should be as spiritually true, that they should partake of the same spiritual life, and live in the same spiritual Resurrection as he, and live in the Father as he did; and therefore he comforted them, and told them, I ascend to my Father and your Father, to my God and your God: But yet in the mean time, till the Son of man and all fleshly formes were subdued to the Father, till men were brought to live in the Father, and to live in a spiritual life: till then Christ must raigne, till then there must be outward formes of Christs death, and there must be manifestations of God in flesh, and outward Ordinances. But when these are subdued, then men must rise, or rather God will appear to be that spiritually which they before enjoyed, onely in an outward manner as is argued by the Apostle in the 25. verse: And the last enemy is death: And certain it is, this death must be destroyed; and the dead must rise, or else death cannot be destroyed:

Now this must needes be a little opened, that so we may see what the Resurrection is; for certainly, the dead must arise, or else Christ cannot be risen.

For the opening of which death we shall take the same method as the Apostle doth here, to compare the natural with the spiritual. Then we say a man is dead, when a man is void of all visible sence and motion, when he ceases to act or move, when the life is departed, when the life is departed, when the being ceases to live in the flesh, that he cannot move to any outward or naturall act.

And so a man is spiritually dead, or dead in Christ, when a man ceases to be or act any thing in the things of God; but is moved and acted, as God is in him: when there is nothing of the self-being appearing; in a word, when to the world he appears to act nothing, do nothing in an outward and formall way, so that men think there is no spiritual life in him.

Then doth he die in the Lord, when he wholly resignes up all his grace, abilities, knowledge of God into God, and knowes not what he doth, or is or should know ceasing from his own reachings forth after God, living and being to any self-enjoyment, or expectation of any future felicity, life or comfort out of God: For it is certain so long as the Creature thinks that he must act or do something to attain salvation, or be any thing distinct from God, so long he is alive without Gods life, and so must needes be miserable, and therefore the Apostle saith, if in this life our hope was, we were most miserable: which life is not to be understood of the fleshly Being: But in this life that is, if our happinesse comforts did depend upon our owne self-actings, and on our own being any thing, were we most miserable.

But our hope is, that all our felicity and comfort is terminated and centred in God onely. And so Christ spiritually in us is the hope of glory, which is a mystery; and so being dead in Christ, when Christ rises, we shall be sure to rise with him: so that there is a sweet truth in that Scripture, where it is said, That the day of a mans death is better then the day that a man is borne: For better it is for a man to die spiritually, then to live naturally.

And so none of us liveth to himself, or dyes to himself; but whether we live or dye, all is in the Lord: and he is glorified in the death, as well as in the life: for our life is hid with God in Christ, as the Apostle saith to the *Collossians*: [3.3] though we be dead as he saith, and nothing appeares of life to our selves or others, yet we need not fear; for the life is hid with God in Christ: And when Christ our life shall appear: and so appear as to be our life and happinesse, then shall we appear glorious, but it is in him; when Christ rises so spiritually and gloriously, to subdue and destroy the fleshly being, which is the death and causes death; for no sooner did sin enter, but death entered with it, then doth Christ the spirituall being and life triumph. And then is death swallowed up of life, and mortality of immortality; That is, flesh is swallowed up of spirit, and death the fleshly being is swallowed up of life, the spirituall being. And then shall be brought to passe that saying, O Death where is thy sting! O grave where is thy victory! But thanks to God, for it is he that gets the victory: again as it is in the naturall, so it is in the spirituall.

This Resurrection is set forth by the resemblance of the graine of Corne, and it holds out a lively resemblance of the spirituall life and death, and of the spirituall Resurrection of the naturall; for as the graine of Corn dyes before it lives, and in this death there is life hid: so in this spirituall death there is spirituall life, though it be hid and lye buried in the grave of earthly and carnall apprehensions: as God gives the one a Body, and is himself the substance and Body, and the life: so doth the spirituall Body, the inward and spirituall life which is God, rise to more glory then ever he did appear in the earthly and outward forme; and as the fleshly appearance dyes and ceases, and as in the death there is life so God when he ceases to live in flesh, he lives and rises with much more glory in the Spirit: And yet it is true, till the fleshly and outward form or formall Being suffers the Divine cannot reigne; and therefore in the midst of death there is life, and God doth but dye in weaknesse to rise in power: Not that God is weak, but he is buried and hid in the carnall sense and life, to rise with more strong and glorious appearances of himself, which is the spirituall Resurrection; which is further illustrated, by the terrestriall Bodies, and the heavenly Bodies which doth but further confirm the spirituall rising of Christ; For though there be a glory in the terestriall and outward dispensations and manifestations of God in them, so when God is pleased to uncloath himself, and to let out himself in pure and heavenly dispensations, when these come and appear, and that God puts on the heavenly clothing, then is the corruptible swalled up of the incorruptible; For it is true, that flesh and blood cannot inherit the Kingdom of God, nor corruption put on incorruption: but when there shall be a change, and of naturall we become spirituall: and when the last Trumpe shall blow, that is, when God shall gloriously sound forth his one praise & nothing but spirituall power appears; Then shall the dead hear the voice of the Sonne of God and live, and the dark and carnall appearances of God shall give way to the more pure and spirituall; and then shall God gloriously triumph over Sin, Death and Hell, and live without any vaile, in his own pure and divine glory. The consideration of which is sufficient, to perswade me to be stedfast and to abound in the work of the Lord; knowing that though my labour be in vaine, as to self, or flesh, yet is is not in vaine in the Lord: he being the end and summe of all.

Thus have I as briefly and plainly as I could gone over the substance of the whole Chapter, though much more might be spoken; being conscious to my own spirit, that I have not hid or concealed any clause, which might serve to speak for a carnall Resurrection: or for a rising of the body after its dissolution here in any visible form or shape; But that as the light is in me so have I manifested it out to others; and do onely referre myself for tryall, to that light which manifests all things, leaving other men to their own darke and carnall apprehensions of a carnall Resurrection; and conclude, that the Resurrection is from the carnall to the fleshly Christ: from Christ living in the flesh, to his living in the Spirit, which is that I call the Resurrection; and if time and mens patience would suffer, I could easily prove, that whatsoever Christ as man was, or did from his Birth to his ascension, in his life and death in the flesh; they were but all Types and shadowes of what he would be, and work in his glorious coming in the Spirit, and so they are applyed all along, if men wil let the Scripture speak in the very Letter; but I let it passe at present.

And further, to gratifie mens weakness, I shall proceed to another Scripture, which is as carnally urged as the former, to prove a carnall Resurrection; and that is in *Matthew*, concerning Christs reasoning with the

Sadduces,[2] they denying the Resurrection: And Christ proving it to them, by saying, That he was the God of the living and not of the dead: and so, that though *Abraham, Isaack* and *Jacob* were dead long agoe; yet they lived; But to open this Scripture, we must know what Resurrection the *Sadduces* denyed, and what Resurrection Christ proved; I affirm, that it was the spiritual Resurrection which they denyed and that appeares plainly, by that in the 23 of *Acts* 8. where it is said, that the *Sadduces* deny the Resurrection or Angell or Spirit; but there is no mention of the Resurrection of the Body. And so it is clear, that Christs argument to them was to prove a spirituall Resurrection, and so it holds a full proof of what we affirme, and a full answer to the *Sadduces*; For God is not the God of the dead, but of the living: not of flesh, but of Spirit: And so *Abraham, Isaack* and *Jacob*, they did really and spiritually live in God, though they were dead in the flesh; So that I conceive, and it is clear to me, that a Spirituall and Angelical appearance of God, is that Resurrection which is held forth, and which should be; and they are the *Sadduces* that deny this spirituall Resurrection.

Another Scripture which is alledged to as little purpose, is that in *Iob.* 19. I know my Redeemer lives, and that I shall see him with these eyes; I do wonder, what a God men fancy to be seen with a fleshly eye: I alwayes took God to be a Spirit & invisible, and that no created fleshly things was able to see him. I cannot imagine then how *Jobs* eyes, which were and should be in a visible form and shape, should be capable of such a Divine invisible vision: But yet if *Job* was so carnall to conceive, that his fleshly eyes should see a spirituall God: yet I am not.

And if any man shall say, that Christ hath a Body in heaven which he lived in when he was upon the earth: and that may be seen being visible and corporall; for that when any man shall prove heaven a locall place, and that God the Fathour sits there, and receives petitions from his Son Christ, as men do visibly here on earth: then I shall give him an answer, neither have I so learned Christ to make him to consist of flesh and bloud, or bodily shape in heaven (as men call it) for though it be said, that *Steven* saw the heaven opened, and Christ sitting at the right hand of God, yet am I not so carnall to believe, That *Stevens* fleshly eyes might see up above the stars, and skies, and that the house top might be open where he was, and so he bodily saw Christ sitting in a bodily shape at the right hand of God in heaven. As a Divine of *Leicestershire* did affirm to me, in a private conference that he thought it might be so. But his divinity being as little as his person I leave him, as knowing that the man Christ left his fleshly being to live in the divine, which is void of all forme and shape, or to be seen visibly by any outward or corporeall substance, and that no light can see him, but his own, and when men live in this light, then they will agree with me, till then, I must leave men to their dark and carnall apprehensions, In the meane time I am content to be nothing that God may be all, and to let fall my thoughts of any glory or excellency hereafter, as a creature; as knowing that the fleshly man dies, that the spirituall may be raised, and that all creature or sensible enjoyment of God shall cease in eternall silence; and it is fruit and joy enough in my spirit, that God hath so discovered himself in me that I can willingly resolve all my comforts, joy and peace into God, who is that endlesse and infinite Ocean, and rather desire to be comprehended of it, then to comprehend it: so that by all that hath bin alleadged, I cannot see that there is any thing in that called Scripture to prove any fleshly living of the body after this life, but that all things and Creatures below God perish and die, and God onely lives, and rises in more power, and glorious appearance then ever he was in when he lived in the flesh: which is that resurrection which is spirituall, and which we have endeavoured to make out, and so I leave it, and come to the last Subject of my discourse, which is that we call *Scripture*: and because men are as carnall about that as any of the former, and because the ground of all the mistakes in the former is onely the mis-apprehension of the Scripture we shal insist upon that a little the more larger, and so conclude.

Concerning the Scripture.

If you take Scripture as it was written by the Prophets and Apostles: It is a forme of wholesome words, a perfect rule, for all outward actions, a true Guide for a mans outward conversation among men: The liveliest expression of the mind of God, of all other books; setting forth all conditions, estates and enjoyments of all men in the world, it is the word in flesh, *The word was made flesh*, it is the highest discovery of God in the truest testimony of God in the world: I do verily believe, that what pitch soever any man hath or can attain unto, but it is able to speak to him in it thus, it is in the letter, and the out-side of it.

But if you ask me what I make Scripture? I look upon it to be spiritual, and so it is the Law written in the heart, and so it is spirit and life, as Christ saith, *The words that I speak are spirit and life*: [John 6.63] so that what Christ speaks spiritually, that is Scripture, and so it is the power of God; for take Scripture as it is in the History, it hath no more power in the inward man, then any other writings of good men, nor is it in that sense a discerner of the secrets, as it is in the History, so it is to be believed above all other writings in the world; but as it is a mystery, and God being the substance of it, so I must believe it as God makes it out in me: I must not build my Faith upon it, or any saying of it, because such and such men writ or speak so and so, But from that divine manifestation in my own spirit; for the Scripture, as it is written outwardly, is but an outward witnesse of that which is within; and the spirituality of it wherein the life and being of it doth consist, is made out by a spiritual discovery. I do not go to the letter of Scripture, to know the mind of God; but I having the mind of God within, I am able to see it witnessed, and made out in the Letter; for if I do a thing lawfull from the Letter, yet if I be perswaded in my own spirit I should not do it, I sinne. Yea further, that power and authority which the Scripture hath, is not because hath and such men writ it; but from that divine manifestation in them: And so indeed, if I have the same discovery that they had; then I can say, it is the word of God, otherwise I lie; for it is one thing to believe the Scripture, because such and such write it, as most men do: and it is another thing to believe it because God saith so in me; and so it is the spirituall speaking of God that is the Scripture, and so that is true. They that are of God hear Gods Word. Now no man can hear God, but as God speaks. And it is as true, that as God speaks spiritually; so no man hears him but in a spirituall manner, and so we hear Gods word. And therefore it is said often in the 1. *Rev. He that hath an eare, let him hear what the spirit saith to the Churches*; Which cannot be understood of a carnall eare, because every man hath that; but as the Spirit speaks spiritually: so it is the spirituall eare that hears the Spirit: For all the outward speaking or hearing of men or Scripture, cannot reach the Spirit. Further, the Scripture I do apprehend, as it is written outwardly, is God clothed in fleshly tearmes and expressions, and speaks in the language of men, as when he speaks of himself; and he uses such expressions as are highest in mens esteem, and his commands, threatnings and promises admonitions, exhortations, they are all as men speak to one another; for I dare not believe God is this or that, or can be named by any title, or that he ever threatned any people or Nation; or promised any, that upon such and such terms they should have this or that, or upon neglect of him they should suffer this or that; for to me it plainly appears, that there is neither wrath or anger, love or hatred in God, or that God was any thing more or lesse to a people, upon their sinning or doing any good; For then a thousand absurdities would follow. But the truth is, because men apprehend anger when they sin, and God pleased when they do well; therefore men speak as one to another, and God so far condescends, as to speak to men in their own language; But that he is so in himselfe, I should think blasphemy to affirme; for I am confident there is never an error or tenent in the world as men maintaine; but if men take that for Scripture, which they call the Bible, it doth fully and literally countenance and uphold: and I know no other way in the world, to uphold the authority of Scripture, than to make it spirituall. And whereas men speak that we deny Scripture: I must confesse for my part, than I know no greater door opened to the denying it, then for men to presse, and urge men to do such and such things, because the outward word saith so and so: indeed, so far I shall deny it as the Letter is inferiour to the Spirit: so far I conceive the letter doth vaile and shadow the spirituality of it. And if men have the Law in their hearts, and be taught of God, they need not run so often to a great Bible, to relieve themselves in straights and doubts as men generally do, never reflecting upon their spirits, to see what God speaks there; I do not speak it to condemn the practise, neither is the fault in the Book, but in mens carnall conceits of it; and seeing men make an Idoll of it, and think the reading and perusing the outward word, is enough to cure all their wounds, and to resolve their doubts; so that as men look upon God outwardly and carnally: so do they have recourse to an outward word, to strengthen their carnall apprehensions. Truly, I must confesse ingeniously, that as to my own spiritual enjoyment, I see nothing of any concernment in it, or in looking upon it, but onely this I see, and so it is some comfort to me to read, that God hath discovered himself in others as well as in me, and that the spirit speaks the same in me, as it did in them. But for any thing of God that I look to attaine unto by reading or looking upon it, I do not care whether ever I look upon one again or no: And yet this is no detracting from the glory or authority of Scripture; because the Scripture is within and spirituall, and the Law being writ in my spirit, I care not much for beholding it in the Letter; but as to the ends aforesaid. And the truth is, it is the Law in the spirit that is the true Bible, the other is but a shadow or counterpart of it; and therefore I do not expect to be taught by Bibles, or Books, but by God: nay further, I do not do anything, or abstain from any thing, because the outward letter commands or forbids it: but by reason of that commanding power which is God in me, and his speaking is the power of God to salvation, and it is in that by which I live, and by which I act: and so the Apostle speaks of the law outward, that it was not made for the righteous, but for whoremongers, and such and such.

And so I see, that if men were acted & guided by that inward law of righteousnesse within, there need be no laws of men, to compel or restrain men, and I could wish that such a spirit of righteousnesse would appear, that men did not act or do things from externall rules, but from an internall law within: Again to speak a little further, concerning the Scripture, men generally speak, that we must do nothing but what we have a rule for, and are asking, what warrant have you to do such a thing? shew a rule from Scripture, and then we will believe you, or else it is but a whimsey, and I know not what; Truly, it is true, and I would those that talk most of a rule, did see that rule; for the safest and prime rule that I know for any man, is that pure spirituall law and rule of righteousnesse which is within, and so far as any man doth any thing beneath or beyond that, so far he doth that which he hath no warrant for: but who must judge of this rule, whether this or that be according to the mind of God or no? To this I answer, in the words of Scripture, because men will soonest believe me: That it is the spirit which searches all things, even the deep things of God: and there is no knowing the spirit but in its own light which is spiritual, & therefore I think it not so safe to go to the Bible to see what others have spoken and writ of the mind of God, as to see what God speaks within me, and to follow the ducture and leading of it in me, I shall sooner, and so others shall sooner, mis-apprehend the mind of God in other men, then in my self, and the same law and rule being in me which was in those that writ the Bible, and to which internall and spiritual rule within, I must take a measure and scantling of all my actions, I had rather measure them from or by a rule within, then by any outward rule or word whatsoever; for the one, that is to say, the Bible without, is but a shadow of that Bible which is within, which is the Law spiritual, the safest and onely rule.

If any man shall say, that I may be deceived, and take that for a discovery of God which is but a fancie of my own Brain: I answer, I may mis-interpret the outward Scripture, and so run as great a hazard that way, and as soon fall into errour, because it speakes of and to men in variety of Estates and conditions, and so if I take that part of it, which doth not speak to my condition, I shall then make a false construction of it, so that I conceive the safest and surest rule to walk by, is that law of the spirit, and as many as walk according to that spirituall rule, peace shall be upon them, and on the *Israel* which is of God; but as many as walk according to a rule without them and so look for a God and Scripture without, they shall be but at a losse, and live in continuall trouble and disquietment: and if I may speak my own experience without offence, so long as I lived and looked upon the outward scripture, outward commands and duties, set times of humiliation, prayer, & I know not what, I was always tost to and fro like the waves of the sea. But when God appeared and shewed me that there was no scripture God commands worships, but what were spirituall like himselfe, and within men, and what he was the author and end of, and that all things else were but shadowes; what sweet, peace and comfort, I then did, and do now enjoy, I might tell you if I could; for the truth is they are unspeakable: and so it is the spirituall discovery of God that is the Scripture I look upon: and if so, then I must needs inferre, that those in whom Christ is spiritually discovered, and that live in a spirituall enjoyment of him, they must needs be best able to speak the language of the Scripture, and to give the sense and meaning of it, and are best acquainted with the originall: for God being the Authour of it, they in whom he is most spiritually discovered must needs know the mind of it, and what Scripture is; which may exclude all outward parts of learning, arts, and other qualifications, which men boast of; for though they may serve to speak scripture outwardly, and help to expresse men to one another, and to read it in the severall translations of it, from one Nation to another; yet they all come short of the spirituall discovery of God, and so are not essential to the knowledge of him; he being onely known and seen in his own light. And which may likewise condemne the *Romane* Clergy, I think the *English* Divines may take their part herein; That having attain'd a little skil in the several languages of several countrys, and received ordination (as they call it) they think themselves so invested with power above their brethren, that none must be infallible or authentick in the interpretation of Scripture, but themselves and men of their order; and unlesse they will say themselves that private men (as they call them) cannot have the same, or more spirituall discovery of God then themselves, I do wonder that they should so advance themselves, and undervalue or despise others.

But we shall let them passe and return to what we have in hand, and we shall see both the Authority and end of Scripture, laid down by the Apostle in the 2 of *Tim*. 3. 16. where he saith all Scripture is given by inspiration of God, and is profitable to teach, &c. that the man of God may be made perfect; where we see plainly what I have spoken all along, That the inspiration which is spiritual and of God, is the true & proper ground why men are taught, and no man can be taught, but it must be by a spiritual inspiration, or else it is not of God: and so the Scripture is not of any private interpretation; but holy men speak as they were inspired: so that, that which gives the rise & ground of Scripture is Gods speaking in men, or inspiring men, and they best know what is Scripture, in whom God most powerfully speaks. And it is as true that God speaks spiritually in man, and not in any audible voice or forme of words; for I do not conceive he ever spoke so to any, he being void of all shape and form, or bodily Organs. And when God so speakes that from naturall, they are made spiritual, then is it indeed they are spiritually taught. And to this sweetly falls in that of *David*: thou hast taught me truth in the secret parts; then indeed men men come to be convinced of their former weak and carnall condition, when God spiritually discovers himself in them: So that it is not the reading or perusing of the Scripture in the letter of it: for so a man may read all his life-time, and be never the better that teaches men spiritually: But when the Scripture is spiritually made out, and interpreted in them, then they are taught: And then it is, that the man of God is made perfect; then doth the inward fleshly Being, or carnall man appear dark and carnall, and the spirituall or the man of God, comes to be perfect: and this spirituall man is able to judge all things as the Apostle saith, then can he spiritually discern the Scripture in him, and so can read it true in the outward letter; For I really see, that all the knowledge of the Scripture in the letter of it, reaches no further but to a historicall and fleshly knowledge of God, and indeed to this kind of knowledge, which many do boast of, the Scripture is very helpfull. But he that knows no further then the outward letter, knowes but Christ after the flesh. And though so I have known Christ, Scripture and God, yet henceforth know I them so no more; they being spirituall. Again, this I conceive, that all the whole story and letter of the Scripture, doth but set out and speak but of two estates and conditions of men or in men: that is the fleshly Being and the Divine; the naturall and the spirituall man: And all these are presented to us in their several degrees and actings in each state, and personated in severall persons from the beginning to the end of the Bible. And so *Cain* and *Abel, Isaac* and *Ishmael, Jacob* and *Esau, David* and *Saul*; and so the good Kings and the bad, the good Prophets and the wicked, the true Apostles and the false; they do but all expresse both Estates, and are not so much to be lookt upon in their severall persons; but are really fulfilled and appliable to every man in each Estate, Degree, and Condition whatsoever. As to instance, it tels us of the Man Christ, who lived and died at *Jerusalem*, and that he rose from the dead, and ascended and past through all conditions: But alas, how farre is this from reaching the spirit, a man may read it, and believe it, and yet be never the better, do him no more good then any other History which we call prophane. But the spirituality and Comfort, and that which is spirit and life, lies in this to see him found in the spirit, to die in him, and to rise with him, to ascend and sit down with him in the heavenly places, being made conformable to him in the spirit to have the everlasting Gospel preacht in the spirit. All which the History and Person of Christ and the outward Gospel, are but shadows: the other is the sealed Book which none can read, till God open himself to be the Scripture: Then indeed can we understand what Scripture is, and then are we guided by that inward life and spirit of truth, more then by the outward letter, and teachings in the World. So that is not the History of Scripture that is the Scripture, or that is the word of God, but it is the spiritual speaking of *God*, which is the word of *God*, and is spirit & life. But some may say, doth not the word say, Hear and your souls shall live; and faith comes by hearing, and hearing by the word of God? Is not the Scripture and outward letter a meanes to convey the knowledge of God, and meanes to get Faith? To which I answer, it is true; but what living is it to which hearing is annexed. If an outward and carnall living and knowing of God, then the outward Scripture contributes to it; but if it be a spiritual living, which is a living in God, then that life must be enjoyed by a spirituall hearing: for all the outward hearing in the world cannot reach to that, so that to me it is plain, that then men spiritually live, when God spiritually speakes, and so this spiritual life is attained by a spirituall speaking of God; and when men heare that spiritual speaking, then their soules live spiritually in that, and so the word of Christ is verefied; That man lives not by bread onely, but by every word which proceedes out of the mouth of God, that is, it is not any outward or external way or meanes that supports the Spirit, but it is the divine and spiritual food, that the divine and spirituall man lives upon, and on that he feedes spiritually with sweet content and satisfaction: it being suitable to him; and such are the onely blessed that eat bread in the Kingdom of Heaven: for they never hunger or thirst after any externall or outward teaching or speaking of men; and so it is true, that faith comes by hearing. But what do you make of Faith? If it be a spiritual thing, as it is, then it must needes come by a spiritual meanes, which is a spiritual hearing, and so the following words explain it, That hearing comes by the word of God: Now it is apparent, that God speakes spiritually, and so he is heard and believed spiritually; and men cannot heare God speak, but it must be by a spiritual hearing, suitable to the speaking. But men are still objecting and say, did not Christ and the Apostles convince men of the truth of things by the Scripture, shewing things must needs be so. I answer, it is true, but the reasons plain which was, that because men were not able to bear Christs spiritual speaking, it being mysticall: therefore he speaks to them in parables, and in such a way as they could apprehend, and so did condescend to their weaknesse, and so Christ speakes of himself, that he needed not Iohns Testimony, he had a sufficient proofe with himself, and needed not any mans Testimony of him. And besides, as men did hasten their belief of things upon an outward letter: therefore Christ and the Apostle brought Scripture to prove things, that he might beat them with their own weapons.

And so alleadged Scripture to the Devill, to answer him in his own way. And the Apostles brought Scripture to prove a Christ in the flesh which some went about to deny, And whereas some alleadge that to the Law and the Testimony, if any man speak not according to that, it is because there is no truth in him. It is also true, if any man speak not from that spirituall Law in himself, and hath not the inward Testimony of the spirit within: in such a man there is no truth, let him speak what he will, and this is the grand cause why men do dispute and jangle about things, because men speak not from the inward experience and spiritual teaching, but from tradition and the outward letter. Nay I verily believe most of the Religion in the world is borne up, because others have held and done so before them, and they think it sufficient to walk in an outward conformity, in duties and Ordinances, and never eye the goings of God in their own Spirits: But this by the way, and all I drive at in this, and I hope no body will be offended, that I would make Scripture as it is to be spiritual, and not subject to the gross and carnall apprehensions and interpretations of any sort of men whatever; neither do I lessen the Authority of it in so doing; For the reason of all the mistakes in and about the Scripture, is not in the Scripture, but in mens carnall apprehensions of it. For if men were spiritual, they might judge it also to be spiritual as God himself is. And I would have men settle it upon a sure foundation, which is God and that Divine within us, which is pure and Divine Scripture.

FINIS.

NOTES

Unless otherwise stated, works cited are published in London.

ABBREVIATIONS.

BDBRSC	*A Biographical Dictionary of British Radicals in the Seventeenth Century*, eds. R. Greaves and R.L. Zaller, Vol. 1, A–F (Brighton, 1982)
CSPD	*Calender of State Papers Domestic.*
DNB	*Dictionary of National Biography*, 22 vols. (Oxford, 1921–2)
HMC	Publications of the Historical Manuscripts Commission.
CJ	*Journal of the House of Commons*, 34 vols. (1742–92)
Lewis and Short	*A Latin Dictionary*, Revised, enlarged and rewritten by C.T. Lewis and C. Short (Oxford, 1980)
OED	*Oxford English Dictionary* 13 vols. (Oxford, 1933)
RES	*Review of English Studies*

Introduction

1 Crisp, *Christ Alone Exalted* (1643), p. 214.
2 Anon., *A Justyfycation of the Mad Crew* (1650), Sig. A3ʳ.
3 Edwards, *Gangraena* (1646), iii, pp. 169–70.
4 See Christopher Hill, *The World Turned Upside Down* (1972), pp. 182–3.
5 Richard Baxter, *Plain Scripture Proof* (1651), p. 148.
6 Osborn, *The World to Come* (1651), Sig. A2ʳ.
7 Baxter, *Plain Scripture Proof*, p. 151.
8 See the newspaper, *Mercurius Pragmaticus*, 5–12 Feb. 1650.
9 Salmon, *Anti-Christ in Man* (1647), p. 19.
10 Bulstrode Whitelock, *Memorials* (1680), p. 430.
11 Ibid., p. 446.
12 Edwards, *Gangraena*, i. pp. 86–7.
13 Whitelock, *Memorials*, p. 446.
14 Leybourne-Popham MS. (HMC), p. 59.
15 Gerrard Winstanley, *A Vindication of those, whose endeavors is only to make the earth a common treasury, called Diggers*, in *Works*, ed. G. Sabine, New York, 1941, pp. 399–403; and *Englands Spirit Unfoulding*, ed. G.E. Aylmer, in *Past and Present*, 40, (1968), pp. 3–15.
16 *Justyfycation of the Mad Crew*, pp. 3, 4, 10, 14.
17 *CJ*, vi, pp. 423, 427, 437, 440, 443.
18 Ibid., pp. 474–5.
19 Ibid., pp. 453–4.
20 *CSPD* (1650), p. 133.

21   See pp. 201–2.
22   *CJ*, vi, pp. 474–5.
23   Tickell, *The Bottomless Pit Smoking in Familism*, 2nd edn (1652), passim.
24   *The Routing of the Ranters* (1650), p. 3.
25   I am indebted here to Frank McGregor, 'The Ranters: A Study in the Free Spirit in English Sectarian Religion, 1648–60', Oxford B. Litt. thesis, 1968, p. 63.
26   See the newspaper *A Perfect Diurnall*, 11–18 March 1650.
27   Freeman, *Light Vanquishing Darkness* (1650), p. 4.
28   A.L. Morton, *The World of the Ranters* (1970), p. 97.
29   Anthony Wood, *Athenae Oxoniensis*, (Oxford, 1721), Vol. 2, Col. 500.
30   Watkins, *The Puritan Experience* (1972), p. 147
31   George Fox *Journal*, I, p. 212.
32   MacGregor, 'The Ranters', p. 109–110.
33   Morton, *World of the Ranters*, p. 142.
34   Samuel Fisher, *Christianismus Redivivus* (1655), pp. 307–9.
35   John Reading, *The Ranters Ranting* (1650), p. 5.
36   *The Ranters Last Sermon* (1654), p. 4.
37   *Strange News from Newgate* (1650), pp. 2–3.
38   Tickell, *The Bottomless Pit*, p. 12.
39   Edward Stokes, *The Wiltshire Rant*, (1652) p. 33.
40   Gilbert Roulston, *The Ranters Bible* (1650), and *The Ranters Ranting* (1650), passim.
41   'The Experience of Edward Wayman', in John Rogers, *Ohel, or Beth-shebeth: A Tabernacle for the Sun* (1653), p. 409.
42   Wood, *Athenae Oxoniensis*; Alexander Gordon on Coppe in *DNB*.
43   Lockier, 'The Character of a time-serving Saint' in *Cavalier and Puritan*, ed. H.E. Rollins, New York (1923), p. 320.
44   George Foster, *The Pouring Forth of the Seventh and Last Viall* (1650), p. 18.
45   Coppe (pp. 83, 99), where the reference is Matt. 12.20; and Richard Sibbes, *A Bruised Reed and Smoaking Flax*, (1632), Sig. A1^r, where the reference is Isaiah 42.3.
46   Tickell, *The Bottomless Pit*, Sig. A1^r.
47   Boehme, *Signatura Rerum*, trans. J. Ellistone (1651), p. 18.
48   Warr, *Administrations Civil and Spiritual* (1648).
49   'I.F.', *John the Divine's Divinity*, (1648), p. 18.
50   The most famous work in this debate in Milton's *Areopagitica* (1644), though important radical stances were taken by Henry Robinson, *Liberty of Conscience: or its Sole Means* (1643), and John Lilburne, *The Second Part of Englands New Chains Discovered* (1649).
51   Tickell, *The Bottomless Pit*, Sig. A6^v, pp. 39–40.
52   Thomas Tany, *Thereaujohn his Theous-Ori Apokaliptical* (1651), p. 9.
53   *Hermes Trismegistus his Divine Pymander*, trans. J. Everard (1650).
54   Boehme, *Signatura Rerum*, and Samuel Hartlib, *Clavis Apocalyptica* (1651), with preface by John Dury.
55   Robert Browne, *A Treatise for Reformation without anie tarrying* (1585).
56   Peter Sterry, *The Comings Forth of Christ* (1650), p. 17.
57   Leybourne-Popham MS., (HMC) p. 39.
58   Tickell, *The Bottomless Pit*, p. 39.
59   Maria di Grazia, 'Secularization of Language in the Seventeenth Century', *Journal of the History of Ideas*, XLI, 2 (1980), pp. 319–30.
60   For instance, see John Booker, *Uranoscopia, or an Almanack and Prognostication, Being a Prospective Glasse, for the yeare of Christ, 1649*.
61   John Everard, 'Some Rayes of Glory Appearing' in *The Gospel Treasury Opened* 2nd edn. (1659), p. 417.

62 For a full exploration of the rhetorical background, see Perry Miller, *The Seventeenth-Century Mind*, Camb. Mass. (1954); and W.S. Howell, *Logic and Rhetoric in England, 1500–1700*, Princeton (1956).

63 William Perkins, *The Art of Prophecying* (1592). The first English translation occurred in the 1631 Cambridge edition of Perkins's *Works*, p. 668.

64 Osborn, *The World to Come*, p. 61.

65 Henry Vaughan, 'Childe-hood'; Thomas Traherne, 'The Infant Eye' and 'Innocencie'.

66 These emblems are of a high quality, particularly that prefacing *The Glasse of Righteousness*. Familist emblems are described by J.H. Hessels in 'The Bookworm' (1869), pp. 81, 106, 116, 131.

67 John Bunyan, *Grace Abounding to the Chief of Sinners*, ed. R. Sharrock, Oxford (1966), pp. 5–6.

68 *A Justyfycation of the Mad Crew* contains the other famous Ranter slogan, 'Ram me, Dam me', where Ram was supposed to stand for God.

69 Sheppard, *The Joviall Crew*, p. 10.

70 See Ann Laurence, 'Two Ranter Poems', *RES*, n.s. 31 (1980), pp. 56–9.

71 *The Arraignement and Tryall of the Ranters* (1650), p. 6.

Preface to *John the Divine's Divinity*

1 From the *Book of Common Prayer*. In the 1559 version, the exact words occur in the ceremonies for Public and Private Baptism (pp. 273, 279 in the 1976 edition of the 1559 version, ed. John E. Booty, Virginia), though the same meaning occurs in the Creed, 'incarnate by the Holy Ghost, of the Virgin Mary' (p. 250).

2 Spet on – Matt. 8.23; 14.65; John 9.6; buffeted – Matt. 26.27; railed on – 1 Sam. 25.14; Matt. 15.29; Lu. 23.39; imprisoned – Acts 22.19. Intullianated – thrown in, from the Latin, *infero, inferre*.

3 Ps. 107.16.

4 Ps. 2.9; Rev. 2.27; 19.5.

5 Isa. 2.19, 21.

6 Ps. 97.5.

7 Isa. 35.6.

8 Ps. 14.9; 150.4.

9 Ezek. 1.7.

10 Ezek. 3.3.

11 Coppe's pun on God; see 1 Cor. 14.33; Heb. 5.9; 12.2.

12 1 Tim. 1.20.

13 Gen. 19.5.

14 Heb. 13.2.

15 The Church of Great St Ellens lies at one end of Bishopgate. Coppe implies that he will be preaching there.

Some Sweet Sips, of Some Spiritual Wine

1 A bundle or collection.

2 It is difficult to exactly identify Mrs T.P. The Hook Norton parish register alone mentions three possible candidates with the same initials.

3 The action or fact of desiring, commonly coupled, as here, with 'wishing'.

4 'With many others, which are now fully described.'

5 As in key, 'clavis'.

6 Coppe is referring to the separatist communities, probably Baptist, which he moved in. It is improbable that these groups would have been explicitly Familist.

7 Referring again to Mrs. T.P.
8 Occurs frequently at the end of verses in the Psalter. It was supposed to be a musical or liturgical direction, perhaps indicating a pause or rest.
9 From Hab. 3.1, 'Shigionoth'. Coppe is imitating the prophet Habakkuk, and in Hebrew, the word means a kind of psalm. 'Seulah' (see previous note) occurs in Hab. 3.2, so that the liturgical element is enforced.
10 'Experience teaches.'
11 Another pun, diminishing Cromwell and Fairfax in the sight of God.
12 University slang for friends or associates. Used very specifically by Coppe, it predates the first recorded use in OED by 21 years.
13 'Thus I wish, thus I command, the wish stands for the command.' In Juvenal, *Satires*, 6, 223, 'Hoc volo, sic jubeo, sit pro ratione voluntas.' In context, this seems to be another divine voice for Coppe, another 'leitmotif', which irritated John Tickell (*The Bottomless Pit*, p. 38), since Coppe was using classical Latin as a claim for revealed religion.
14 One who needlessly repeats the same thing. OED spelling is 'bathologist'.
15 Coppe cites the Hebrew from Ps. 19.1., 'The heavens declare the glory of God; and the firmament sheweth his handywork.'
16 'O Lord thou art my strength.' Ps. 89.26 reads 'He shall cry unto me, Thou art my father, my body, and the rock of my salvation.'
17 A declension of the particles of wishing.
18 Expressing wish or desire.
19 'And this happened, while it was of little worth.'
20 Privilegiis – of privilege.
21 1 Cor. 3.22. Coppe inverts the meaning of Paul's explication here.

An Additional and Preambular Hint

1 'By force and arms.'

A Fiery Flying Roll and A Second Fiery Flying Roule

1 'The help of the father, A.C.'
2 Ezek. 21.27.
3 'The word sufficeth.'
4 Proverbial, 'are wise behind the time', and alluding to the Trojan's refusal to deliver Helen of the Greeks. According to *Lewis and Short*, the phrase was recorded by the grammarian Festus, from a tragedy, *Equo Trojano*, by Livius Andronicus or Naevius. Sed nunquam sera etc., – 'but it is never too late to mend'. In Seneca *Agamemnon*, II, 242, 'nam sera numquam est ad bonos mores via'.
5 One who holds extravagant opinions.
6 Coppe refers to the Biblical Covenants, which he views as superior to the Solemn League and Covenant of 1642.
7 Bray was the only senior officer to side with the Levellers at the Ware mutiny in 1647. He was subsequently imprisoned and discharged, due to the personal enmity of Col. Henry Lilburne. Coppe refers to Bray's imprisonment in 1649, along with the other Leveller leaders. See also Bray's entry in BDBRSC.
8 This is more obscure. Possibly 'the pattern of things according to God'. Fifth Monarchists were accused of setting up their own 'mule'.
9 Dan. 5.26–7.
10 Deddington parish register records the burial of Roger Maule on 25 April 1648.
11 Gamesome, playful, merry. Coppe is also suggesting wantonness. The Biblical story here is from 2 Tim. 4.10–14.
12 See p. 32.

13 Here, a light horseman.
14 Acts 5.1.
15 Michal was David's wife – 2 Sam. 6.16–23; 1 Chr. 15.29.
16 One who rigidly observes rules and forms. In the seventeenth century the word was synonymous with Puritanism.
17 Sedgewick was a Seeker, whom Clarkson was influenced by (p. 177). He seems to have had some concern for the poor, and believed enough in 'experience' to have faith in a Cambridgeshire village woman, who prophesied the Last Judgement. He was ridiculed, receiving the nickname 'Doomsday', but Coppe speaks here in defence of his altruistic inspiration.
18 To knock forcefully, beat or strike.
19 Matt. 21.31–2.

Letter from Coppe to Salmon and Wyke

1 Sleeveless coat or jacket of mail or scale armour.
2 Perhaps a mistranscription for 'the halter'. *OED* does not contain this word.
3 Infantry.
4 The gaoler at Coventry.

A Remonstrance of the Sincere and Zealous Protestation

1 Throughout Coppe refers to the 1650 edition of the Blasphemy Act, *An Act against Several Atheistical, Blasphemous and Execrable Opinions*, printed by Edward Husband and John Field, 'Printers to the Parliament, at London'.
2 A roaring, pulpit-thumping priest.
3 Coppe is referring to *The Ranters Declaration* (1650) and *The Routing of the Ranters* (1650).

Copp's Return to the Ways of Truth

1 'From the soul.'
2 Coppe simply refers back to the first part of this pamphlet, p. 133.
3 Implying a parental relationship with the spirit.

A Single Eye all Light, no Darkness

1 Like Coppe, Clarkson refers to the printed edition of the Adultery Act (p. 118). In this way, the language of the Act tends to permeate that of the pamphlets.

The Lost Sheep Found

1 When Clarkson was in prison for dipping, he had met Sedgewick and Erbury (p. 18 in the original edition of *The Lost Sheep Found*), and they had clearly influenced his defection from the Baptists.
2 William Kiffin was a prominent member of the Baptist community in London and was later to become a successful merchant. In the early 1640s he had been apprenticed to John Lilburne, but he led a successful pamphlet campaign in the late 1640s which aimed to dissociate the Baptists from the Levellers. See especially *The humble Petition and Representation of several Churches of God in London, commonly, though falsely, called Anabaptists* (1649).
3 This was Clarkson's first publication, in 1646, and, naturally it adopted a Seeker stance.
4 Giles Randall was responsible for the publication of many texts expounding the doctrine of the Spirit within, including the *Theologia Germanica*, and Nicholas de Cusa's *De Visione Dei* (see p. 25).

5   Thomas Gunne was another significant Baptist. He appears as representative of the fourth London Baptist Church in the 1644 *Confession* of the London Particular Baptists. For an interesting account of the Baptists, see Murray Tolmie, *The Triumph of the Saints* (Cambridge, 1977).

6   See p. 12.

7   There is no evidence that this was either Peter Sterry, the Puritan Platonist, or Thomas Sterry, another Puritan divine and author.

8   George Twisleton's regiment was quartered in Lincoln, Rutland, Leicestershire and Nottinghamshire in September 1649, which corresponds with Clarkson's record. See C. Firth and G. Davies, *Cromwell's Army*, 2 Vols. (Oxford, 1940).

9   Rom. 14.14.

10   John Saltmarsh took refuge at Wallis's house in Ilford during his last days. It is possible that the Mrs Wallis who accompanied Wyke to Coventry (p. 11) was Wallis's wife.

11   Mary Middleton also appears in *The Routing of the Ranters* (1650), pp. 4–5. Her husband's house was used for meetings of My One Flesh.

12   Barkstead's regiment kept order in London from January 1648, though it also served in the siege of Colchester in the summer months of that year. The troops were billeted in Whitehall, and showed no signs of Leveller agitation, unlike other parts of the New Model Army. They were responsible for the quelling of a number of mobs, so that it is doubtful if they were popular in the city. See Firth and Davies pp. 338–47.

13   Lilburne often refers to finance in connection with his persecution. See, for instance, *The trial of Lieut. Collonell John Lilburne*, by Clement Walker (1649), p. 13, and Lilburne, *The Prisoners Mournfull Cry* (1648), pp. 21–2.

14   Possibly Clarkson is referring to Samuel Ward of Cambridge, who wrote *Magnetis Reductorum Tropologium* (1637), which was translated in 1640. Woolerd remains unidentified.

15   Again possibly, this was Gilbert Clark, who was a student of Ward.

16   Here, the difference between Ranterism and Muggletonianism is seen in the re-appearance of an elect few in the latter.

A Rout, A Rout

1   Salmon is referring to the Engagement oath where all adult males were required to swear allegiance to the Commonwealth.

2   Christopher Hill, (*The World Turned Upside Down*, p. 218) makes the point that this is one of the only two places in seventeenth-century literature where he can find a reference to the death of God.

Letter from Salmon to Thomas Webbe

1   Ps. 45.14, 'raiment' in the authorized version.

Heights in Depths

1   Full of lead.

2   Undone, ruined, brought to nought.

3   One who flamboyantly follows popular (religious) modes.

4   Oedipus, of course, solved the riddle of the sphinx.

The Light and Dark Sides of God

1   Episcopalians, who preferred church government by bishops.

2   The Sadducees denied the resurrection of the dead, and of the existence of angels and spirits. They were not so much a sect or school as a political party, formed essentially of the nobility.

Index

Major topics (Antinomianism, millenarianism, etc.) refer to principal examples or discussions. Page references for entire tracts are printed in bold.

INDEX OF BIBLICAL REFERENCES

References in the text appear as in the original editions. Where allusions to chapters or books can be made more specific, I have done so in this index. Where a reference in the text appears to be incorrect, I have added the correct one in brackets here.